D0171268

The Jury &
the Defense
of Insanity

Rita James Simon

The Jury & the Defense of Insanity

with a new introduction by the author

Transaction Publishers
New Brunswick (U.S.A.) and London (U.K.)

New material this edition copyright © 1999 by Transaction Publishers, New Brunswick, New Jersey.
Originally published in 1967 by Little, Brown and Company.

This book is printed on acid-free paper that meets the American National Standard for Permanence of Paper for Printed Library Materials.

Library of Congress Catalog Number: 98–17014
ISBN: 0–7658–0447–6
Printed in the United States of America

Library of Congress Cataloging-in-Publication Data

Simon, Rita James.
   The jury and the defense of insanity / Rita James Simon.
      p.   cm.
   Originally published : Boston : Little, Brown, 1967.
   Includes bibliographical references and index.
   ISBN 0-7658-0447-6 (pbk. : alk. paper)
   1. Insanity—Jurisprudence—United States. 2. Jury—United States.
I. Title.
KF9242.S5   1998
345.73'04—dc21
                                          98-17014
                                               CIP

for
 Julian

CONTENTS

PREFACE

Rita James Simon's book on the jury and the defense of insanity in criminal cases is a result of the large-scale study of the American jury system undertaken at the University of Chicago Law School pursuant to a grant from the Ford Foundation and a special grant from the National Institute of Mental Health. We are pleased to add the book to that special shelf containing *Delay in the Court* (1959) and the *American Jury* (1966).

The study reports in depth on a series of jury *experiments*. It occupies a key place in the over-all Jury Project and demonstrates the richness of the Project's methods. If we may quote ourselves from the preface to *The American Jury:*

"One strength of the project was that it permitted multiple lines of inquiry. Aside from studying judge-jury differences by surveying the totality of the jury's business, we conducted experiments on sharply defined issues, such as the jury's handling of the defense of insanity, the impact of insurance, the response to the contributory negligence rule; conducted post-trial interviews, both in extended free-flowing conversations and with structured questionnaires; and examined jury selection procedures and voir dire strategies. We also conducted opinion polls on the jury among judges, lawyers, and the community at large. And we made the investigation of the costs of the jury system which led to *Delay in the Court.*"

The chance to use a variety of approaches enables us to corroborate findings and thus escape the unavoidable limitations of a single research method. Experiments on human institutions are rare, and, as a rule, highly artificial. The jury experiments are distinguished by an exceptional degree of realism involving real jurors in a real court, allowing us to have confidence in the validity of their results.

For the study of the jury, the experimental method has some major consequences. First, it makes it possible literally to try the same case over and over again to different juries and thus gives content to the notion that the outcome of a trial is but one in a series of possible outcomes and that it remains to some extent a matter of chance, depending on which jury hears the case. Second, it makes it possible to experiment in the precise sense of the sciences by injecting deliberate variations into the trial record to test what effect, if any, they have on the verdict. Mrs. Simon thus was able to learn how verdicts change if the testimony of expert psychiatric witnesses is varied in quality or, more centrally, if the traditional *M'Naghten* instructions on insanity are replaced by the instructions developed in the controversial *Durham* case.

The experimental method also gives the student of the jury access to important new aspects of his topic. We can, this time with propriety, record jury deliberations and thus place under scientific scrutiny the small group dynamics of the deliberation process — how the jury talks and thinks. We can also trace the relationships between the backgrounds of individual jurors and the ways they vote, thus testing the trial lawyer's hunches as to who makes "a good juror" for given purposes. And, finally, access to jury deliberations discloses a good deal about the popular sense of justice with respect to insanity and crime.

The two books, the Simon study and the Kalven-Zeisel study, intersect in a striking way. The broad survey, which was the foundation for *The American Jury,* rests on 3576 different cases. This experimental study rests essentially on two cases. Behind this contrast in numbers lies a fundamental point of method. The weakness of the survey is that it never tells us enough about the individual case; the weakness of the experiment is that it never tells us enough about other cases, and thus limits the possibility of generalization. This difference is particularly acute in the social sciences, where the multitude of relevant factors is so complex.

A special word should be said about the contribution of Fred S. Strodtbeck to this book. He developed, as a workable method, the experimental jury technique on which the book relies so heavily; he guided the design, the data collection, and the early stages of the analysis. Under his supervision the Project has done other experimental sequences; it is hoped to report these out at some future date.

Given the vagaries of Project organization and career plans, it has been Mrs. Simon's task to write up her study away from the University of Chicago, with only occasional advice and counsel. To a distinctive degree, the book represents her own personal effort and achievement.

The book adds to our knowledge about the jury, and is the first systematic study of how the jury behaves behind the closed doors of the jury room. But for us the fascination is that it permits us to be spectators at close range as the common man struggles with the perennial perplexities of personal responsibility.

HARRY KALVEN, JR.   HANS ZEISEL
The University of Chicago Law School

March 1967

ACKNOWLEDGMENTS

Many individuals and organizations helped make this study possible. The Ford Foundation and the National Institute of Mental Health provided the funds.* Members of the Jury Project staff at the Law School of the University of Chicago worked with me in preparing the transcript, recording the trials, and collecting the data. Those on the staff to whom I owe special debts of gratitude are Lee Hook for his statistical advice, Kathleen Beaufait for her help in supervising the field teams and for reading and discussing with me earlier drafts of the manuscript, and Charles Hawkins and Ellen Kolegar for their help in collecting and processing the data. Lauren Hickman and Margaret Parkman also helped collect data.

In his capacity as director of the Experimental Section of the Jury Project, Fred L. Strodtbeck provided immeasurable assistance and valuable advice. The idea of using real jurors and exposing them to recorded trials was his. He first employed this technique in a study of civil juries. Both Fred Strodtbeck and Harry Kalven, director of the Jury Project, reviewed earlier drafts of the manuscript. Especially after I began working on the final draft, Harry Kalven's advice and suggestions contributed a good deal toward making this a more readable manuscript. Hans Zeisel also read the manuscript and made many useful suggestions.

Members of the Sociology Departments at Washington University and the University of Minnesota were helpful in recommending graduate students who assisted me and others on the jury project when we were working in the courts in St. Louis and Minneapolis.

* National Institute of Mental Health research grant M2202(C2).

Other individuals to whom I owe debts of gratitude are Dr. Winfred Overholser, who helped select the incest trial as a vehicle for experimentation; Dr. Manfred Guttmacher, who assisted in the preparation of the model testimony; Judge David L. Bazelon and Justice Abe Fortas, who helped me better understand the legal context in which to place the Durham decision; and Judge John Biggs, Jr., for the information I received in conversations with him and from reading his book, *The Guilty Mind*. Much of the discussion in Chapter 1 (the legal history) is based on *The Guilty Mind*.

I especially want to thank Mike McGarry for being the most capable and efficient typist any author could wish for.

Finally, I owe two special debts of gratitude. One is to my husband for reading the manuscript innumerable times, for offering criticism and advice that were extremely valuable, and, most of all, for being patient and understanding during difficult periods. He showed an extraordinary willingness to continue to suggest ways for improving the text even after he saw many of his ideas brushed aside or ignored. I have no doubt that had I incorporated all of his suggestions the manuscript would have been much improved.

The other debt is to the subjects who participated in this study — the jurors. Without their cooperation and their willingness to participate fully in the task, this study would not have been possible. Much of the book is dedicated to showing the nature and quality of their participation, and in large measure the validity of this work is a reflection of the quality of their performance.

R. S.

April, 1967

The Jury and
The Defense of Insanity

Introduction to the
Transaction Edition

When I read the introduction I wrote over thirty years ago to *The Jury and the Defense of Insanity* I was struck by how many of the issues raised then about the jury system are relevant and pertinent today. Issues about how motivated and competent juries are to do their job, about how well jurors understand and follow judges' instructions, their understanding of expert testimony, and the extent to which their own backgrounds and experiences bias them in favor of or against certain defendants or plaintiffs are issues that are still being debated today. And still, after a jury renders its verdict in a highly publicized trial, such as the trial of John Hinckley when the jury found him not guilty by reason of insanity in his attempted assassination of then President Ronald Reagan, and the not guilty verdict reported by the jury in the O.J. Simpson criminal trial, there are demands for doing away with the jury system. Over the years more countries have followed the British (India, Australia, Canada) in reducing or discarding the jury in civil and most criminal cases.

The Jury and the Defense of Insanity provides a rare opportunity to observe how jurors go about the process of deliberating and reaching a verdict by following them into the jury room and recording their deliberations. The introduction that follows, with minor editorial changes, is the one that appeared in the 1967 publication.

This book provides a legal and social psychological perspective on the American jury system. More particularly, it is a study of the jury's reactions to criminal cases involving the defense of insanity. It is a legal study in that it is concerned with important legal questions: namely, rules of law, expert testimony, commitment procedures, and juror selection. It is a social psychological study because it focuses primarily on the factors that influence the opinions and decisions of individual jurors and juries as collective units. It examines (1) the relationship between the social psychology and economic background that jurors bring with them to the trial and the opinions they have about the case; (2) the information presented during the trial, especially the testimony of experts and the rules of law and verdicts; and (3) the relative influence of different persons on the jury in persuading others to accept their view of the case.

The study also examines the jury as an institution by noting how responsive it is to the expectations of the judiciary and of the larger community. The most basic of these expectations is that the jury will do its job and reach a decision. Hung juries are expensive and time consuming. In reaching its decision, the jury is expected to adhere to some generally prescribed rules of law about burden of proof, extent of proof, and weighing of testimony. The jury is also expected to use the substantive instructions applicable to the particular case and charge. The jury is expected to spend its time discussing the case, not listening to a baseball game, reading a newspaper, or talking about a coming political campaign. In our analysis of the jury as an institution, we report how the participants in the system respond to these various types of demands.

Most of us are impressed with the role that the criminal jury has played historically in the development of Anglo-Saxon democracy. But few of us know very much about how a jury actually goes about deciding to acquit or convict a person accused of a crime. A unique quality of this research is that it describes how the jury determines its verdicts by following the jurors from the courtroom into the jury room. Inside the jury room, it listens to the jury consider the evidence, the experts' opinions, the circumstances surrounding the crime, and the rules of law. It compares the opinions that an individual juror has about the trial with the juror's social background, his personality, and his participation in the deliberation. It also tries to evaluate the importance of the institutional setting, namely, the courtroom, and the assumption of the role of juror on the individual opinions and on the collective decision.

Criticism of the jury[1]

The jury system is important in our society for symbolic as well as for practical reasons. It is important symbolically because it represents a basic democratic belief in the intelligence of its citizenry to decide and to rule. It is important realistically because it makes decisions that affect major institutions and that may affect you and me.

The roots of the American jury system are traceable to ninth-century France and later to England when it was imported by William the Conqueror. In its earliest form in England and in France, a jury was a group of the defendant's neighbors who were expected to answer questions as both witnesses and triers of fact.

In its earliest days on American soil, especially prior to Independence, the jury was the champion of the popular cause. In the words of Jerome Frank, a critic of the modern jury system,[2] "the jury was considered . . . as a bulwark against oppressive government, acclaimed as essential to individual liberty and democracy." After the Revolution, the right to trial by jury was guaranteed by our federal Constitution and by the constitutions of the separate states. So it remains today.

But over the past century, particularly in the last three decades, the jury has been used less and less frequently. In En-

---

[1] For a summary of the debate over the strengths and weaknesses of the jury system see Kalven, The Dignity of the Civil Jury, 50 Va. L. Rev. 1055 (1964), and Kalven and Zeisel, The American Jury (1966); also see Broeder, The Functions of the Jury, 21, U. Of Chi. L. Rev. 390 (1954).

[2] Frank, Courts on Trial 108 (1963).

gland it has been virtually abandoned in civil actions and is used only in major criminal cases. In the United States it is used much more widely but is subject to ever-increasing criticism. Since the results of our study are generally favorable to the jury, we think it appropriate to highlight some of the major criticisms that have been offered against the jury.

At the core of the criticism is the belief that the jury does not determine its verdict on the basis of the evidence and that the members of the jury do not have the special skills and training that are needed to make a rational decision about the kinds of disputes with which they are confronted. Some critics of the jury urge its replacement by a body of persons selected on the basis of their expert knowledge of the particular issues raised by a given case, or by a bench trial in which the judge would be free to seek the advice and guidance of experts.

Some critics would replace the jury only when the complexities of a contract dispute, an antitrust action, or the medical questions involved in a plea of insanity case are to their minds beyond the purview of the general public. But those who would abolish all jury trials argue that the application of law is too difficult for laymen. They believe that the court's instructions to the jury concerning the rule of law, the testimony of expert witnesses, and the distinction between evidence and opinion are beyond the comprehension of a jury, and that the jurors come into the courtroom too burdened with the weight of their own business to listen to evidence.

In 1954, Carl Becker, a noted historian and student of American institutions, had this to say about the jury system:

> Trial by jury as a method of determining facts is antiquated and inherently absurd—so much so that no lawyer, judge, scholar, prescription-clerk, cook, or mechanic in a garage would ever think of a moment of employing that method for determining the facts in any situation that concerned him.[3]

[3] Id. At 124.

In 1937, Osborn, a noted legal scholar and observer of many jury trials, wrote:

> When a groups of twelve men, on seats a little higher then than the spectators, but not quite so high as the judge, are casually observed it may appear from their attitude that they are thinking only about the case going on before them. The truth is that for much of the time there are twelve wandering minds in that silent group, bodily present but mentally far away. Some of them are thinking of sadly neglected business affairs, others of happy or unhappy family matters, and after the second or third day and especially after the second or third week, there is the garden, the house-painting, the new automobile, the prospective vacation, the girl who is soon to be married and the hundred and one other things that come to the mind of one who is only partly interested in the tedious proceeding going on before him. There is probably more wool-gathering in jury boxes than in any other place on earth. . . . It is plainly said by those whose opinions command the utmost respect that the administration of the law in this land is on a lower plane than other phases of government and is unworthy of the civilization it poorly serves.[4]

Another group of critics do not focus their objections on the institution per se or on the formal procedure by which it is expected to reach its decision but on the method of selecting persons for jury service and on the personnel that composes the typical jury. They observe that in many localities persons who are officially exempt from jury service or who are most easily excused to perform effectively. For example, professional men and women are exempted from jury duty in almost every jurisdiction.

One critic noted that:

> The democratic process itself seems designed to ensure the legislative exemption of persons most capable of resolving factual disputes. Jury service often involves bearing economic

[4] Ibid.

sacrifices, especially for those persons whose daily incomes are in excess of the per diem pittance meted out to jurors. It is only natural to expect that groups possessing substantial influence will utilize it for the purpose of securing legislative exemption. As the groups which can exert such pressure must posses a relatively small membership, the usual result is the exemption of doctors, lawyers, dentists, and educators of every grade and description.[5]

Other critics of the method of jury selection point to the practice prevalent in some communities of excluding persons on the basis of racial or ethnic characteristics. The result is, they argue, that in some communities certain groups are so heavily under-represented on jury panels that the phrase "a jury of one's peers" has lost all practical meaning. The almost total absence of blacks on southern juries is an extreme example of the deliberate exclusion of an important group.[6]

The book is not to be taken as an effort to resolve the debate. Our decision to study how the jury functions in response to a plea of insanity was governed by specific substantive interests which we discuss below. We do not analyze the jury with an eye toward evaluating the *correctness* of its decisions—only the *intelligence of the process* by which the decisions are arrived at.

The jury and the rule of law

The type of case we are talking about, involving the defense of insanity, represents a very small proportion of crimi-

---

[5] Broeder, The Functions of the Jury, 21 U. of Chi. L. Rev. 390 (1954).

[6] On this matter Mr. Justice Murphy spoke for the Supreme Court in Glasser v. United States, 315 U.S. 60, 85, 86 (1942), when he said: "The exercise of the duty of selection must always accord with the fact that the proper functioning of the jury system requires that the jury be a body truly representative of the community and not the organ of any special group or class. The deliberate selection of jurors from the membership of particular private organizations definitely does not conform to the traditional requirements of jury trial."

nal trials.[7] Yet the use of an insanity defense has caused a great deal of discussion and controversy, among judges, lawyers, psychiatrists, newspapermen, and behavioral scientists, especially in recent years. The stimulus for much of the interest and discussion about the defense of insanity has been the adoption by one of the federal district courts of a legal doctrine which sets up a new criterion for determining criminal irresponsibility. The new formula, known as the *Durham* rule, was adopted in the District of Columbia in 1954.[8] In brief, it states that a defendant is excused *if his act was the product of a mental disease or defect.*

The *Durham* rule displaced in the District of Columbia the century-old *M'Naghten* rule,[9] a doctrine that is still used in almost all states and federal jurisdictions in the United States, and throughout most of the British Commonwealth. Under the *M'Naghten* rule the defendant is excused only if he did not know what he was doing or did not know that what he was doing was wrong.

Many psychiatrists and some lawyers welcomed the adoption of the *Durham* rule in the District of Columbia[10] as the beginning of a new era in the relationship between the disciplines of law and psychiatry, and as a major step forward in the public's willingness to understand and treat persons who are insane.

Others who were skeptical of the intrinsic merits of the *Durham* rule questioned its practicability for a jury, which, under existing court procedures, has the final say. Indeed, one of the main arguments in support of the *M'Naghten* rule is that the *M'Naghten* standard is understandable and usable

[7] The figure is generally estimated at about 2 percent for criminal jury trials.

[8] Durham v. United States, 214 F.2d 862, 45 A.L.R.2d 1430 (D.C. Cir. 1954). Note the bibliography at the end of the book for a detailed listing of articles about the Durham decision and the Durham rule.

[9] M'Naghten's Case, 10 Cl. & Fin. 200, 8 Eng. Rep. 718 (H.L. 1843).

[10] For a good early discussion of the impact of the Durham decision, see Insanity and the Criminal Law, 22 U. of Chi. L. Rev. 317 et seq. (1955).

by a jury of laymen, because juries should, and in fact do, consider mental illness (when it is offered as the defense to a criminal charge) a moral problem, in which the ability to distinguish right from wrong is a crucial determination.[11]

Thus, the first major issues that we examine in this study are the jury's reactions to alternative legal criteria for determining criminal responsibility. Specifically, we compare the jury's preference between the *M'Naghten* rule and the *Durham* rule, and in addition consider a version of a trial that omits any reference to a formal legal criterion in order to determine the jurors' native sense of justice or equity. In that version the jury is instructed as follows: "If you believe the defendant was insane at the time he committed the act of which he is accused then you must find the defendant not guilty by reason of insanity."

The jury and expert psychiatric testimony

A second important inquiry in our study of the jury is related to the controversy over rules of law. It concerns how, and how well, the jury understands and evaluates expert psychiatric testimony.

Many supported the *Durham* rule because they expected it to bring about improvements in the quality and candor of the psychiatrist's testimony.[12] They believed that *Durham* (a) would free the psychiatrist from the moral trappings of the *M'Naghten* criterion and permit him to testify on matters about

---

[11] For the strongest contemporary arguments in support of the M'Naghten rule, see the writings of Jerome Hall, especially Psychiatry and Criminal Responsibility, 65 Yale L.J. 761 (1957), reprinted in Hall, Studies in Jurisprudence and Criminal Theory (1958); Responsibility and Law, 42 A.B.A.J. 917 (1956); Psychiatry and the Law, 38 Iowa L. Rev. 687 (1953); and Mental Disease and Criminal Responsibility—M'Naghten v. Durham and the American Law Institute's Tentative Draft, 33 Ind. L.J. 212 (1958).

[12] See, for example, Wechsler, The Criteria of Criminal Responsibility, 22 U. Of Chi. L. Rev. 367, 367–376 (1955).

which he had expert knowledge; (b) would permit and encourage the psychiatrist to present a clinical analysis of the defendant which would include all aspects of his personality, not only his cognitive ability to distinguish right from wrong; and (c) would allow him to trace the origins of the defendant's condition and its relationship to his criminal acts.

On the other side, supporters of *M'Naghten* warned that under the *Durham* formula, the psychiatrists' definitions and explanations for deviant and criminal behavior are so different from those applicable in a court of law that any increase in the prominence of their testimony would threaten the traditional beliefs of criminal law.[13]

But in the final analysis, it is the jury's decision that determines the defendant's fate. This study brings to bear fresh empirical evidence on a major point of contemporary controversy in the legal community. The question that we hope to answer is: How much sympathy and understanding does the jury have for the psychiatrist's role in the proceedings and for his testimony under each of the rules of law?

What does the jury believe about the disposition of "insane" defendants?

A third area of inquiry goes to the jury's understanding about what will happen to the defendant if it should find him not guilty by reason of insanity. Does the jury understand the consequences of its verdicts on the court's disposition of the defendant? Most lawyers agree that a jury understands the consequences of its verdict in the typical criminal trial. But they do not agree about what the jury understands will happen to a defendant who is acquitted on grounds of insanity, and almost how the jury's belief affects its verdict.

[13] For a good review of the role of the psychiatrist in a criminal trial, see Overholser, The Psychiatrist and the Law (1951); Guttmacher, The Psychiatrist as an Expert Witness, 22 U. of Chi. L. Rev. 325–331 (1955); Guttmacher and Weihofen, Psychiatry and the Law (1952); Roche, The Criminal Mind (1960).

These topics—jurors' reactions to rules of law, to expert psychiatric testimony, and to disposition of "insane" defendants—are the major topics of the study and are represented formally in the experimental design. But the book is concerned also with several other topics, which are mentioned below.

Jurors' backgrounds and their verdicts

A question of great practical significance to the trial lawyer, whether defense counselor or prosecutor, is: Which jurors are likely to be sympathetic to his side? We did not conduct actual voir dire of pretrial examination of prospective jurors. But we have a remarkable amount of information about the jurors' backgrounds and verdicts. We compared reactions to the rules of law and the expert psychiatric testimony of jurors in different social categories. We also inquired about jurors' attitudes toward mental illness, psychiatry, and other related topics and compared those responses with verdicts. Opinions and attitudes on these topics are generally solicited in community surveys and public opinion polls. In this case the jurors' responses represent public opinion after the opinions have been mobilized around the issues in question.

Social process in the deliberations

Although the social process of the deliberations is not a major theme in this study, it is considered at various places throughout the book.[14] We look at the jury as a small problem-solving group engaged in face-to-face interaction, and we compare the performance of men and women and of persons in different occupational categories. Under social process we also compare satisfaction scores, willingness to be tried before a jury as opposed to a judge, and the relative lengths of discussion under the different legal doctrines.

[14] See especially Chapters 3, 6, and 9.

Method of study

A comment about method. By using real jurors (that is, persons serving their regular period of jury duty), and exposing them to recorded trials, we gained legitimate access to the inner sanctum of the jury room and in that way were able to record jury deliberations. This technique (which is described in detail in Chapter 2) has the additional advantage of allowing us to expose many different juries to the same trial and to compare their verdicts and deliberations without disrupting the realism of the experience. Thus, we believe that the way in which we collected the information increases the importance of the findings and places them in a different category from the conclusions that have been drawn about the jury from theoretical inquires from selected interviews with jurors following a sensational trial and from ex post facto analyses by lawyers who had either just won or just lost a case at the hands of a jury.

The over-all organization of the book

The book is divided into five major parts. The first part covers the background of the study and the method. Chapter 1 reviews briefly the origins and history of the defense of insanity in English and American courts. It traces the criteria of criminal responsibility from the pre-*M'Naghten* era to the adoption of the Durham formula. Chapter 2 describes the method and presents the research design.

The second part of the book describes the impact of the major experimental variables on the jurors' verdicts. Chapter 3 reports juries' reactions to the alternative rules of law. Chapter 4 discusses the juries' understanding and evaluation of expert psychiatric testimony. Chapter 5 reports the juries' reactions to information about commitment.

Part three describes the influence of social status and attitudes on the jurors' decisions. Chapter 6 compares the reactions of different types of jurors. Chapter 7 also focuses on the jurors rather than the jury; jurors' attitudes towards mental illness, psychiatry, and other related topics are compared with verdicts.

The fourth part focuses on the juries' deliberations and discusses the major issues that determine a jury's decision. Chapter 8 presents numerous quotations direct from the jury room about reactions to the crime, the defendant, the rules of law, the expert testimony, and the testimony of other witnesses. More than any other, Chapter 8 describes concretely how a jury behaves.

The fifth and final part presents a look to the future from two perspectives: from the vantage point of the jury and from the court. Chapter 9 describes the jurors' recommendations as to the criteria of criminal responsibility which the law should adopt in future cases. It also offers some general indicators of the jury's preference for the *M'Naghten* or *Durham* rules.

In Chapter 10 we leave the experimental jury room and review, briefly, some of the courts' recent decisions in criminal trials involving the defense of insanity. With the few data that are available we compare the juries' preferences for *M'Naghten* and *Durham* with the willingness that the courts have shown to adopt the *Durham* rule. Chapter 11 provides a brief summary of conclusions.

Finally, in Appendix A, we reproduce a full deliberation, and so, appropriately, the final word about the jury comes from the jury itself.

PART I

History and Method

The Defense of Insanity in English and American Courts: A Brief Review

In order to fully appreciate the significance of the *Durham* decision, we need to place it in historical perspective.

We offer this far from comprehensive review of the courts' experiences with the insanity defense and with different criteria of criminal responsibility in the hope that it will accomplish three objectives: (1) provide a historical context for the *Durham* decision, (2) increase the reader's appreciation for the historical and practical significance of our findings, and (3) increase the reader's appreciation for the difficulty and complexity of the jury's task.

Judge John Biggs traces the origins of the defense of insanity in English law to the reign of Henry III (1216-1272).[1] In the historical summary that follows we borrow heavily from Judge Biggs' scholarship. He finds that persons who committed homicide were pardoned if they were believed to be of unsound mind, and that such occurrences were not unusual. By the reign of Edward I (1272-1307), complete madness became acceptable as a defense to a criminal charge. Until then, the life of an insane criminal could be saved only by a pardon from the king.

By 1581, the relationship between the lack of a guilty mind

[1] Biggs, The Guilty Mind (1955). The Guilty Mind is based on lectures that Judge Biggs gave as recipient of the Isaac Ray Award, given each year by the American Psychiatric Association to an individual who "has made a laudable contribution to the improvement of the relationship of law and psychiatry."

or a felonious intent and the lack of criminal responsibility was well established. In that year William Lambard, a noted legal authority, published a handbook, *Eirenarcha,* for justices of the peace that served as a standard reference. In it the author stated:

> If a madman or a naturall foole, or a lunatike in the time of his lunacie, or a childe y apparantly hath no knowledge of good nor euil do ki a mā, this is no felonious acte, nor any thing forfeited by it . . . for they cānot be said to haue any understanding wil. But if upō examinatiō it fal out, y they knew what they did, & y it was ill, thē seemeth it be otherwise.

According to Judge Biggs, "knowledge of good and evil" as a test of criminal responsibility originated with this reference by Lambard.

About a century later, Sir Matthew Hale, Lord Chief Justice of the King's Bench, wrote his influential *History of the Pleas of the Crown* and in it distinguished two forms of insanity: total insanity and partial insanity. Hale defined total insanity as "absolute madness," a condition which leaves the victim "totally deprived of memory and reason." Hale claimed that such a condition excused a criminal act because the offender could not be deemed to have a felonious spirit or intent. In theory, partial insanity could also excuse an offender; but, in the words of Lord Hale, "it would be a matter of great difficulty." In practice, the courts behaved as if the defense of insanity was unavailable to any accused who retained even a vestige of sanity.

Mr. Justice Tracy's instruction in the trial of Edward Arnold [2] in 1723 characterized the court's practice. Mr. Justice Tracy said: "In order to avail himself of the defense of insanity a man must be totally deprived of his understanding and memory, so as not to know what he is doing, no more than in infant, a brute, or a wild beast." [3] The defendant was

[2] The Trial of Edward Arnold, 16 State Trials 695 (1723).
[3] Id. at 764-765 (1724).

found guilty and sentenced to death.[4]   Mr. Justice Tracy's phrase "no more than an infant, a brute, or a wild beast" marked the origin of the so-called "wild beast test."

For the next seventy-five years, or until the end of the eighteenth century, English courts grafted the test of knowledge of good and evil and the concept of insanity with ever increasing firmness.   With the dawning of the nineteenth century, however, a case arose that challenged, at least temporarily, the relationship between insanity and knowledge of good and evil.[5]   In the opinion of many contemporary jurists, it exemplified the operation of the criminal law of England at its best.

James Hadfield, a soldier noted for bravery in battle, attempted to assassinate George III and was indicted for high treason.   During the trial, testimony revealed that Hadfield's desire to kill the king was motivated by a delusion that he, the defendant, was the savior of all mankind.   He thought that in order to gain worldly recognition it was necessary that he sacrifice himself as had Jesus Christ.   The defendant concluded that an assault on the life of the king would attain his end of execution and, through it, martyrdom.

From all accounts, Hadfield's appearance at the trial was grotesque.   He had sustained terrible head wounds during battle, and Thomas Erskine, his counsel, stated that "his head hung down as though it has been almost dissevered" and that he had "been cut across all the nerves which give sensibility and animation to the body."   The prosecution argued that the defendant's behavior (in the purchase of gun and powder and slugs for a pistol and in his concealment of the pistol) indicated that he was neither an idiot nor a madman "afflicted by the absolute privation of reason."

In his opening statement Lord Erskine, anticipating the *Durham* rule one hundred and fifty years early, argued that a man could know right from wrong, could understand the na-

---

[4] Arnold was "respited" by Lord Onslow, the man he shot, and remained in jail for over thirty years.

[5] Hadfield's Case, 27 State Trials 1281 (1800).

ture of the act that he was about to commit, could manifest a clear design, foresight, and cunning in the planning and executing of it, but that if his mental condition produced or was the cause of the criminal act, he should not be held legally responsible for it.

Lord Kenyon, the Chief Justice, recommended to the jury that Hadfield's trial be terminated. The jury accepted the court's suggestion and acquitted the defendant, because "he was under the influence of insanity at the time the act was committed."

The decision in the *Hadfield* case was considered a landmark because it rejected two concepts previously accepted by the court. It denied that the defendant must be totally deprived of *all* mental faculty before he could be acquitted; and it severed the tie between insanity and the ability to distinguish good from evil, or right from wrong.[6]

In the next dozen years, three cases were heard in which the defendants were charged with murder and pleaded insanity.[7] In each case, the English courts returned to the law of criminal responsibility formulated by Mr. Justice Tracy in the *Arnold* case of 1723. All three of the defendants were found guilty and executed. In one of the trials, Lord Chief Justice Mansfield charged the jury as follows:

> . . . it must in fact, be proved beyond all doubt, that at the time he committed the atrocious act with which he stood charged, he did not consider that murder was a crime against the laws of God and nature. There was no proof of insanity which could excuse murder or any other crime.[8]

[6] Without wishing to mitigate the importance of this decision in foreshadowing later developments in criminal law, we think that the fact that the defendant *looked* as if he was "totally deranged" could not have failed to influence not only the minds and feelings of the jury, but those of the bench as well.

[7] The Trial of John Bellingham, reported in 1 Collinson, Idiots, Lunatics etc. 636 (1812); Rex v. Offord, 172 Eng. Rep. 924 (1831); Regina v. Oxford, 9 Car. & P. 525, 545 et seq. (1840).

[8] Collinson, *supra* note 7, at 636.

By 1840, in the opinion of Judge Biggs, ". . . the English common law was rapidly developing a procrustean theory of criminal responsibility for the mentally ill and only the meet occasion was required to bring forth full-blown a complete and disastrous rule of laws." [9]   With these remarks, Judge Biggs introduced the case of *The Queen Against Daniel M'-Naghten*,[10] one of the most thoroughly discussed and controversial cases in English and American law.

Daniel M'Naghten was a Scottish woodcutter who assassinated Edward Drummond, secretary to the Prime Minister, Sir Robert Peel, in the mistaken belief that the secretary was the Prime Minister. M'Naghten, "an extreme paranoiac entangled in an elaborate system of delusions," [11] believed that the Prime Minister was responsible for the financial and personal misfortunes that were continually plaguing him. During the trial nine medical witnesses all testified that the defendant was insane.[12]   Although the form of the insanity was not officially designated by the medical witnesses, psychiatrists today who have read reports of the trial believe that M'Naghten was "under the influence of a form of mental disorder symptomized by delusions of persecution in which Peel appeared as one of the persecutors." [13]   So convincing was the defense's plea that at the end of the testimony Lord Chief Justice Tindal, sitting with two other judges, came close to directing the jury's verdict. He told the jury: "I cannot help remarking in common with my learned brethren that the whole of medical evidence is on one side — that it seems almost unnecessary that I should go through the evidence.

[9] Biggs, The Guilty Mind 95 (1955).

[10] 4 Reports of State Trials, New Series 1839-1843, 847 (1843).

[11] Glueck, Law and Psychiatry 44 (1964).

[12] Dr. Isaac Ray, the father of forensic psychiatry in the United States, participated indirectly in the proceedings. Ray's book, Medical Jurisprudence of Insanity (1838), was quoted at some length during the trial, especially the section which attacked Lord Hale's definition of insanity.

[13] Guttmacher and Weihofen, Psychiatry and the Law 403 (1952).

I am, however, in your hands." [14] He then instructed the jury:

> The point I shall have to submit to you is, whether on the whole of the evidence you have heard, you are satisfied that at the time the act was committed . . . the prisoner had that competent use of his understanding as that he knew that he was doing, by the very act itself, a wicked and a wrong thing? If the prisoner was not sensible at the time he committed the act, that it was a violation of the law of God or of man, undoubtedly he was not responsible for that act or liable to any punishment flowing from that act . . . If on balancing the evidence in your minds, you think the prisoner capable of distinguishing between right and wrong, then he was a responsible agent and liable to all the penalties the law imposes. If not . . . then you will probably not take upon yourselves to find the prisoner guilty. If this is your opinion, then you will acquit the prisoner. [15]

The jury found the defendant "not guilty on the grounds of insanity." Daniel M'Naghten was committed to Broadmoor mental institution, where he remained until his death in May, 1865, about twenty years later.

Queen Victoria, the House of Lords, and the newspapers of the day disapproved of the verdict in openly angry and bitter tones. [16] M'Naghten's attempted assassination of the Prime Minister marked the fifth attack on English sovereigns and their ministers since the turn of the century. In 1800 Hadfield had attempted to kill King George III. In 1813 Bellingham had assassinated Spencer Perceval, Chancellor of the Exchequer and Lord of the Treasury. Between 1840 and 1842 two attempts had been made on Queen Victoria's life. Now Daniel M'Naghten, a defendant who admitted that he attempted to

---

[14] The Queen v. Daniel M'Naghten, 4 Reports of State Trials, New Series 1839-1843, 847, 925 (1843).

[15] Ibid.

[16] In Glueck, Law and Psychiatry 44 (1964), the author reports that Queen Victoria, in a delightful blend of wit, wisdom, and royal concern, said that she "did not believe that anyone could be insane who wanted to murder a Conservative Prime Minister."

assassinate the Prime Minister, was declared not guilty on the grounds of insanity and was sent to Broadmoor, a place described by the press as a retreat for idlers. The government and newspapers interpreted the court's action to be a direct disregard of the dangerous and threatening state of affairs.

The case of Daniel M'Naghten probably would have had a place of distinction in English criminal law even if the uproar had ended on this note of public indignation. But more was still to come. The House of Lords called upon the fifteen judges of the common law courts to respond to a series of questions on the law that the Lords would ask them. In effect, the judges were being asked to account for a miscarriage of justice. Their actions had been severely criticized by the Crown, the House of Lords, and the press, and now they were being confronted directly with their misdeeds.

Lord Chief Justice Tindal answered for all the fifteen common law judges save Mr. Justice Maule, who gave a separate set of answers. Tindal said:

> The first question proposed by your Lordships is this: "What is the law respecting alleged crimes committed by persons afflicted with insane delusion in respect of one or more particular subjects or persons; as, for instance, where at the time of the commission of the alleged crime the accused knew he was acting contrary to law, but did the act complained of with a view, under the influence of insane delusion, of redressing or revenging some supposed grievance or injury or of producing some supposed public benefit?"
>
> In answer to which question, assuming that your Lordships' inquiries are confined to those persons who labour under such partial *delusions* only, and are not in other respects insane, we are of the opinion that, notwithstanding the party accused did the act complained of with a view, under the influence of insane delusion, of redressing or revenging some supposed grievance or injury, or of producing some public benefit, he is nevertheless punishable according to the nature of the crime committed, *if he knew at the time of committing such crime that he was acting contrary to law;* by which expression we understand your Lordships to mean *the law of the land.*
>
> Your Lordships are pleased to inquire of us, secondly, "What

are the proper questions to be submitted to the jury, where a person alleged to be afflicted with insane delusion respecting one or more particular subjects or persons, is charged with the commission of a crime (murder, for example), and insanity is set up as a defence?" And, thirdly, "In what terms ought the question to be left to the jury as to the prisoner's state of mind at the time when the act was committed?" And as these two questions appear to us to be more conveniently answered together, we have to submit our opinion to be, that the jurors ought to be told in all cases that every man *is to be presumed to be sane,* and to possess a sufficient degree of reason to be responsible for his crimes, *until the contrary be proved* to their satisfaction; and that to establish a defence on the ground of insanity, it must be clearly proved that, at the time of the committing of the act, the party accused was labouring *under such a defect of reason, from disease of the mind, as not to know the nature and quality* of the act he was doing; or if he did know it, that *he did not know that he was doing what was wrong.* The mode of putting the latter part of the question to the jury on these occasions has generally been, whether the accused at the time of doing the act knew *the differences between right and wrong;* which mode, though rarely, if ever, leading to any mistake with the jury, is not, as we conceive, so accurate when put generally and in the abstract, as when put with reference to the party's knowledge of right and wrong in respect to the very act with which he is charged. *If the question were to be put as to the knowledge of the accused solely and exclusively with reference to the law of the land, it might tend to confound the jury,* by inducing them to believe that *an actual knowledge of the law of the land was essential in order to lead to a conviction;* whereas the law is administered upon the principle that every one must be taken conclusively to know it, without proof that he does know it. *If the accused was conscious that the act was one which he ought not to do, and if that act was at the same time contrary to the law of the land, he is punishable;* and the usual course therefore has been to leave the question to the jury, whether the party accused had a sufficient degree of reason to know that he was doing an act that was wrong; and this course we think is correct, accompanied with such observations and explanations as the circumstances of each particular case may require.

The fourth question which your Lordships have proposed

to us is this: "If a person under an insane delusion as to existing facts, commits an offence in consequence thereof, is he thereby excused?" *To which question the answer must of course depend on the nature of the delusion;* but, making the same assumption as we did before, namely, that he labours under such partial delusion only, and is not in other respects insane, we think he must be considered in the same situation as to responsibility as if the facts with respect to which the delusion exists were real. For example, if under the influence of his delusion he supposes another man to be in the act of attempting to take away his life, and he kills that man, as he supposes, in self-defence, he would be exempt from punishment. If his delusion was that the deceased had inflicted injury to his character and fortune, and he killed him in revenge for such supposed injury, he would be liable to punishment.

The question lastly proposed by your Lordships is: "Can a medical man conversant with the disease of insanity, who never saw the prisoner previously to the trial, but who was present during the whole trial and the examination of all the witnesses, be asked his opinion as to the state of the prisoner's mind at the time of the commission of the alleged crime, or his opinion whether the prisoner was conscious at the time of doing the act that he was acting contrary to law, or whether he was labouring under any and what delusion at the time?" In answer thereto, we state to your Lordships, that we think the medical man, under the circumstances supposed, cannot in strictness be asked his opinion in the terms above stated, because each of those questions involves the determination of the truth of the facts deposed to, which it is for the jury to decide, and the questions are not mere questions upon a matter of science, in which case such evidence is admissible. But where the facts are admitted or not disputed, and the question becomes substantially one of science only, it may be convenient to allow the question to be put in that general form, though the same cannot be insisted on as a matter of right.[17]

Most legal historians believe that the court had not intended to establish a precedent by its actions in the *M'Naghten* case. It had not intended to formulate general rules concerning the assessment of criminal responsibility of the insane that would

[17] 10 Cl. & Fin. at 211-212, 8 Eng. Rep. at 723. (Emphasis supplied.)

be applicable without regard to the facts and circumstances of a particular case. But the judges were under pressure, and their responses to the questions put to them by the House of Lords reflected their political discomfort. The responses that the judges gave to the Lords established a criterion of criminal responsibility of the insane. From that time until the present, every case heard in English courts was, and is still, decided along the principles established by the judges' responses to the House of Lords interrogation.

Less than a decade later, the *M'Naghten* rules were adopted in the federal and most of the state courts of the United States.[18] In later years only one state, New Hampshire, adopted a rule that was not in line with the *M'Naghten* formula.[19] In 1868, Joseph L. Pike killed Thomas Brown with an ax in the course of a robbery. Pike's defense was insanity. When the case came to trial, Chief Justice Perley instructed the New Hampshire jurors along the following lines:

If . . . [the jury] found that the defendant killed Brown in a manner that would be criminal and unlawful if the defendant were sane — the verdict should be "not guilty by reason of insanity" if the killing was the offspring or product of mental disease in the defendant; that neither delusion nor knowledge of right and wrong nor design nor cunning in planning and executing the killing and escaping or avoiding detection, nor ability to recognize acquaintances, or to labor or transact business or manage affairs, is, as a matter of law, a test of mental disease; but that all symptoms and all tests of mental disease are purely matters of fact to be determined by the jury.[20]

[18] At the present time some seventeen states supplement the M'Naghten rule with another and still older formula: the doctrine of "irresistible impulse." That is, if the criminal is compelled to act by a force or impulse beyond his control, he may be exempted from responsibility. This rule has an American origin, dating back to 1834. See State v. Thompson, Wright 617, 622 (Ohio, 1834). Irresistible impulse is not used in any of the state courts as the sole criterion of responsibility.

[19] State v. Pike, 49 N.H. 399 (1870).

[20] Id. at 402.

Under such instructions, the issue of the accused's mental condition, whether he had the capacity for criminal intent, became a question of fact, not of law. It became a matter for the jury to determine, not for the court to define. Dr. Isaac Ray, the noted medical authority, was a strong influence in the court's formulation of the new instruction.

Chief Justice Perley's charge to the jury in *State v. Pike* was confirmed in a later decision. In *State v. Jones*[21] the key words in Judge Charles Doe's charge to the jury were: "If the killing was the offspring or product of mental disease, the defendant should be acquitted." [22]

The court went on to say:

> Whether the defendant had a mental disease seems as much a question of fact as whether he had a bodily disease; and whether the killing of his wife was the product of that disease was also as clearly a matter of fact as whether thirst and a quickened pulse are the product of a fever. That it is a difficult question does not change the matter at all. The difficulty is intrinsic, and symptoms, phases, or manifestations of the disease as legal tests of capacity to entertain a criminal intent — are all clearly matters of evidence, to be weighed by the jury upon the question of insanity; if it was, a criminal intent did not produce it; if it was not, a criminal intent did produce it, and it was a crime.[23]

The decisions in *State v. Pike* and *State v. Jones* are today the law in New Hampshire. But the New Hampshire rule has had little impact outside the borders of that state, and has failed to gain adoption in any other jurisdiction for almost a century.[24]

Other jurisdictions continued to adhere to the *M'Naghten*

---

[21] 50 N.H. 369 (1871).

[22] Ibid.

[23] Id. at 322.

[24] According to Professor Weihofen, only a few reported cases have been found in which counsel urged adoption of the New Hampshire rule, and in these it was definitely rejected. Weihofen, The Urge to Punish 7 (1956); People v. Hubert, 119 Cal. 216, 51 Pac. 329 (1897); State v. Craig, 52 Wash. 66, 100 Pac. 167 (1909); Eckert v. State, 114 Wis. 160, 89 N.W. 826 (1902).

"right from wrong" formula. For example, in *State v. Palmer*[25] the Supreme Court of Missouri upheld a finding of guilty and the subsequent execution of a twenty-year-old feeble-minded defendant. The trial court instructed the jury: "If the defendant knows the difference between right and wrong, he is criminally responsible. . . . Weakness of reason should not shield one who has committed a crime."[26]

In 1907, the Supreme Court of California upheld the first degree murder conviction of Frank Willard, a defendant who twice before had been committed by a judge of the Superior Court of California to a state hospital for the insane.[27] Willard was convinced that he had been appointed by President Theodore Roosevelt to arrest evil doers. A Georgia court of appeals upheld the lower court's conviction in *Bridges v. State*,[28] saying:

> The evidence amply authorized a finding that [the accused] was an idiot (and a dangerous one at that); but under all the facts of the case as disclosed by the record, this court cannot say the jury were not authorized to determine from certain parts of the evidence, and the legal inferences arising therefrom, that the accused had sufficient reason to know that the act he was about to commit . . . was wrong; and, the finding of the jury having been approved by the trial judge, and no error of law upon the trial being complained of, this court is without authority to interfere.[29]

The growing tension between the cognitive-moral emphasis of the *M'Naghten* formula and the emotional-clinical concerns of modern psychiatry were shown most dramatically in the cases of *Smith v. Baldi*[30] and *Fisher v. United States*.[31] At the end of his first trial in 1948, James Colbert Smith was found guilty of first degree murder; his sentence was death by

[25] 161 Mo. 152, 61 S.W. 651 (1901).
[26] 161 Mo. at 168, 61 S.W. at 655.
[27] State v. Willard, 150 Cal. 543, 89 Pac. 124 (1907).
[28] 43 Ga. App. 214, 158 S.E. 358-359 (1931).
[29] 43 Ga. App. at 214, 158 S.E. at 359.
[30] 192 F.2d 540 (3d Cir. 1951).
[31] 328 U.S. 463 (1946).

execution. From that time until his eventual commitment to a Pennsylvania state institution for the criminally insane, Smith or Smith's case was before the courts about a dozen times.[32]

The defendant had been committed repeatedly to reformatories or mental institutions from the time he was nine years old. At sixteen he joined the Army. Four years after his discharge from the service he confessed to the killing of a taxi driver. Between his discharge from the Army in June, 1944, and his killing of the taxi driver in 1948, Smith had been hospitalized or imprisoned on four separate occasions for a total time of more than two years. The first time he was hospitalized his disorder was diagnosed as a catatonic type of schizophrenia. Altogether he had never been solely on his own responsibility for longer than nine months from the time he was sixteen years old.

When the defendant's execution appeared inevitable, and after the Supreme Court had taken the view that he had not been denied due process, Smith was given a final examination by a commission set up under the new Pennsylvania Mental Health Act. The doctors declared that the defendant was chronically insane. Under such condition, according to the law he could not be executed.[33]

Fisher v. United States[34] also involved a defense of insanity to a murder charge. In this case, the defendant was found guilty and executed. Julius Fisher had worked as a janitor at the Cathedral of St. Peter and St. Paul in Washington, D.C. He had attended school until he was fourteen, but was unable to complete the third grade. He was an alcoholic; he had

[32] "At least thirty-five justices and judges of the federal and state courts and fifteen attorneys never extricated themselves from a 'footless' question: the cost to New York, Pennsylvania, and the United States was at least $250,000." Roche, Insanity and the Criminal Law, 22 U. of Chi. L. Rev. 322 (1955).

[33] The defendant kept insisting that he was entirely sane and that all of his difficulties and his criminal conduct were caused by a "heardo" machine run from the City Hall in Philadelphia. This belief Smith maintained even though he was informed repeatedly that his only chance of escaping the electric chair would be proof of his insanity.

[34] 328 U.S. 463 (1946).

syphilis; and there was evidence of consequential organic damage to the brain. His work at the cathedral, however, was
satisfactory. He appeared to have no difficulty in his personal contacts and was liked by his employers.

In a quarrel with the Cathedral's librarian, after she had
called him a disparaging name, Fisher choked and stabbed her
to death. The psychiatrist who testified described him as an
impulsive and aggressive psychopath with low emotional response. At the trial, Fisher was found guilty and sentenced
to death. This verdict was upheld by the United States
Court of Appeals for the District of Columbia and later by
the Supreme Court, in a five-to-four decision.[35]

Mr. Justice Frankfurter wrote in his dissent:

> . . . the justification for finding first degree murder premedi-
> tation was so tenuous that the jury ought not to have been left
> to founder and flounder within the dark emptiness of legal jar-
> gon. The instructions to the jury on the vital issue of pre-
> meditation consisted of threadbare generalities, a jumble of
> empty abstractions equally suitable for any other charge of
> murder with none of the elements that are distinctive about
> this case, mingled with talk about mental disease.[36]

In a separate dissent, Mr. Justice Murphy said:

> . . . there are persons who, while not totally insane, possess
> such low mental powers as to be incapable of the deliberation
> and premeditation requisite to statutory first degree murder.
> Yet under the rule adopted by the court below, the jury must
> either condemn such persons to death on the false premise
> that they possess the mental requirements of a first degree
> murder or free them completely from criminal responsibility
> and turn them loose among society. The jury is forbidden to
> find them guilty of a lesser degree of murder by reason of

[35] In its appeal, the defense claimed that Fisher's disorder should be
considered as showing partial responsibility and a lack of the deliberation and premeditation necessary to constitute first degree murder.
But the conviction for first degree murder was affirmed. The court
said that Fisher's capability should be judged as if he were a normal
person. Id. at 487.

[36] Id. at 486.

their generally weakened or disordered intellect. Common sense and logic recoil at such a rule.[37]

In 1954, the United States Court of Appeals for the District of Columbia handed down its decision discarding the *M'Naghten* rule and introducing a different legal basis for determining criminal responsibility in *Durham v. United States*.[38]

Unlike most trials involving a defense of insanity, Monte Durham's crime was housebreaking rather than murder. The defendant, a twenty-six-year-old resident of the District of Columbia, had a long history of mental disorder and petty thievery. He had been committed on several occasions to mental hospitals and had served time in prison for passing bad checks. He received a medical discharge from the Navy. On at least two occasions, he attempted suicide. Two psychiatrists testified that he was suffering from a psychopathic personality with psychosis. But when the psychiatrists were asked if, in their opinion, the defendant could distinguish right from wrong, each answered in a manner similar to the psychiatrist in the *Fisher* case:

> I can only answer this way: I can't tell how much the abnormal thinking and the abnormal experience in the form of hallucinations and delusions, delusions of persecution — had to do with his anti-social behavior. I don't know how anyone can answer that question categorically, except as one's experience leads him to know that most mental cases can give you a categorical answer of right and wrong but what influence these symptoms have on abnormal or anti-social behavior —

The court interrupted to say: "Well your answer is that you are unable to form an opinion, is that it?" The doctor answered: "I would say that it is essentially true for the reasons I have given." [39] The judge in the district court instructed the jury along the lines of the *M'Naghten* rule, and the defendant was found guilty.

[37] Id. at 492.
[38] 214 F.2d 862, 45 A.L.R.2d 1430 (D.C. Cir. 1954).
[39] 214 F.2d at 874-875, 45 A.L.R.2d at 1445-1446.

An appeal was granted, and the case was heard before a three-man bench of the appellate court.[40]   Having decided to grant the defendant a new trial on other grounds, the court went on to announce its new rule for insanity.   Speaking for the court, Judge David L. Bazelon stated the new formula:

> The rule we now hold must be applied on the retrial of this case and in future cases is not unlike that followed by the New Hampshire court since 1870.   It is simply that an accused is not criminally responsible if his unlawful act was the product of mental disease or mental defect.
>
> We use "disease" in the sense of a condition which is considered capable of either improving or deteriorating.   We use "defect" in the sense of a condition which is not considered capable of either improving or deteriorating and which may be either congenital, or the result of injury, or the residual effect of a physical or mental disease.
>
> Whenever there is "some evidence" that the accused suffered from a diseased or defective mental condition at the time the unlawful act was committed, the trial court must provide the jury with guides for determining whether the accused can be held criminally responsible.   We do not, and indeed could not, formulate an instruction which would be either appropriate or binding in all cases.   But under the rule now announced, any instructions should in some way convey to the jury the sense and substance of the following: if you the jury believe beyond a reasonable doubt that the accused was not suffering from a diseased or defective mental condition at the time he committed the criminal act charged, you may find him guilty.   If you believe he was suffering from a diseased or defective mental condition when he committed the act, but believe beyond a reasonable doubt that the act was not the product of such mental abnormality, you may find him guilty.   Unless you believe beyond a reasonable doubt either that he was not suffering from a diseased or defective mental condition, or that the act was not the product of such abnormality, you must find the accused not guilty by

---

[40] The court of appeals concluded that the trial judge had not properly applied the prevailing evidential rule that "as soon as 'some evidence' of mental disorder is introduced, sanity, like any other fact, must be proved as part of the prosecution's case beyond a reasonable doubt."   See Tatum v. United States, 190 F.2d 612, 615 (D.C. Cir. 1951).

reason of insanity. Thus your task would not be completed upon finding, if you did find, that the accused suffered from a mental disease or defect. He would still be responsible for his unlawful act if there was no causal connection between such mental abnormality and the act. These questions must be determined by you from the facts which you find to be fairly deducible from the testimony and the evidence in this case.[41]

Concerning the *M'Naghten* rule, Judge Bazelon said:

By its misleading emphasis on the cognitive, the right-wrong test requires court and jury to rely upon what is, scientifically speaking, inadequate, and most often, invalid and irrelevant testimony in determining criminal responsibility.

The fundamental objection to the right-wrong test, however, is not that criminal irresponsibility is made to rest upon an inadequate, invalid or indeterminable symptom or manifestation, but that it is made to rest upon *any* particular symptom. In attempting to define insanity in terms of a symptom, the courts have assumed an impossible role, not merely one for which they have no special competence. . . . [It] is dangerous "to abstract particular mental faculties, and to lay it down that unless these particular faculties are destroyed or gravely impaired, an accused person, whatever the nature of his mental disease, must be held to be criminally responsible . . ." In this field of law as in others, the fact finder should be free to consider all information advanced by relevant scientific disciplines.[42]

Quoting from the report of the Royal Commission, he continued:

The sufferer from [melancholia, for example] experiences a change of mood which alters the whole of his existence. He may believe, for instance, that a future of such degradation and misery awaits both him and his family that death for all is a less dreadful alternative. Even the thought that the acts he contemplates are murder and suicide pales into insignificance in contrast with what he otherwise expects. The crimi-

[41] 214 F.2d 862, 871-872, 45 A.L.R.2d 1430, 1442-1443 (D.C. Cir. 1954). (Court's footnotes omitted.)

[42] 214 F.2d at 871-872, 45 A.L.R.2d at 1442-1443. (Court's footnotes omitted.)

nal act, in such circumstances, may be the reverse of impulsive. It may be coolly and carefully prepared; yet it is still the act of a madman. This is merely an illustration; similar states of mind are likely to lie behind the criminal act when murders are committed by persons suffering from schizophrenia or paranoid psychoses due to disease of the brain.[43]

Certiorari was denied by the Supreme Court, and the *Durham* rule remains law for the District of Columbia.[44] In its adoption of the *Durham* formula, the court emphasized its similarity to the New Hampshire rule of 1870. But the principles adopted under the *Durham* rule have their origins in cases that go back much further. In *Hadfield's Case* in 1800, Sir Thomas Erskine suggested that a man could know right from wrong, but, if his mental condition produced or was the cause of the criminal act, he should not be held legally responsible for it.[45]

The adoption of the *Durham* rule in the District of Columbia was widely hailed in most psychiatric and some legal circles as the beginning of a new era. It was regarded as a sign that the law would recognize the growing prestige and knowledge of psychiatry, and would work with it in the disposition of criminal cases, especially those in which the issue of insanity was introduced. Others who were more skeptical, both of the intrinsic merits of the rule and of its practicability, asked: How will it fare in the hands of a jury? The results of our research offer a partial answer to that question.

[43] 214 F.2d at 873-874, 45 A.L.R.2d at 1444.

[44] When Monte Durham was retried in the district court under the *Durham* or product formula, he was found sane and guilty. United States v. Durham, 130 F. Supp. 445 (1955), *rev'd,* Durham v. United States, 237 F.2d 760 (D.C. Cir. 1956).

[45] Hadfield's Case, 27 State Trials 1281 (1800).

CHAPTER 2

Experimental Juries—
Method and Research Design

The purpose of this chapter is to familiarize the reader with the technique that was used for obtaining information about juries' behavior. Our discussion is largely descriptive and it focuses on the jury in criminal cases involving a defense of insanity. Professor Fred L. Strodtbeck originated the idea of conducting jury experiments within the institutional context of the court.[1] He first introduced the technique in his study of civil juries. In his article Social Process, the Law, and Jury Functioning, Dr. Strodtbeck wrote:

> Since trials are ordinarily never repeated without change, a regular jury deliberation is always a response to a unique stimulus. This provides no guide for separating idiosyncratic from recurrent elements, and no determination can be made of the relation between any segment of the trial and the eventual verdict. . . . The radical contribution of the experimental perspective arises when any trial is considered to be a potentially reproducible event.[2]

The basic idea underlying the use of experimental juries is that it permits the same stimulus, namely a recorded trial, to be played over and over again before many different juries. It also permits the intrusion of systematic changes in the trial,

[1] Fred L. Strodtbeck is Associate Professor of Social Psychology in the Sociology Department of the University of Chicago. From 1953 to 1960 he was director of the Experimental Jury Section of the Jury Project.

[2] Strodtbeck, Social Process, the Law, and Jury Functioning, in Law and Sociology 149 (Evan ed. 1962).

either in the form of the inclusion or exclusion of pieces of evidence, and allows testing the importance of that information on the jury's decision. By reproducing the same event before different juries, we were able to obtain a distribution of verdicts for each trial. This distribution provides the same kind of information that could be obtained if the same case were tried over and over again before different juries within a given jurisdiction.

One of the main advantages of experimentation is that it permits a good deal of control over the phenomena under study. But the delicate choice which confronts each experimenter as he sets up his research design concerns the amount of control and precision of measurement which is he willing to relinquish for the sake of increasing the cognitive realism of the situation. The decision to conduct the jury experiments within the institutional context in which the behavior usually occurs, namely, the courtroom as opposed to the laboratory, added to the realism of the experience. It did, however, reduce the amount of control which the experimenters could exercise over the situation. The decision to use real jurors as subjects, that is, persons serving their regular terms of jury duty, rather than, for example, college students, was another decision which the experimenters made in favor of realism at the expense of control. But it was felt that both factors, conducting the research in the courtroom and using real jurors as subjects, added much more to the realism of the situation than was sacrificed in precision and control. Nevertheless, was anything crucial lost? We discuss this in later sections.

On the other hand, a disadvantage of experimentation is that all too often the researcher has to sacrifice breadth and scope for a narrow but precise examination of a specific aspect of a specific problem. Given a choice between a more superficial but extensive examination of juries' reactions to a great variety of defense of insanity trials in many jurisdictions throughout the country and an intensive, vigorous study of juries' reactions to two cases, we opted for the latter.

Specifically the experimental procedure consisted of the following steps.[3]   This procedure was used in both the civil and the criminal jury studies.

1. A transcript of an actual case that had been decided by the court was obtained. The transcript was edited and condensed from a trial that lasted, generally, two or three days to one that could be heard in about 60 to 90 minutes. The experimental transcript contained the lawyers' opening and closing statements and the judge's instructions to the jury, as well as the testimony of all the witnesses.

2. The "experimental" trial was then recorded, with the parts of the attorneys, witnesses, principals in the case, and the judge performed by persons associated with the University of Chicago, largely members of the law school faculty.[4]

3. With the cooperation of local bar associations and presiding judges in three jurisdictions, Chicago, St. Louis, and Minneapolis, subjects for the experiment were drawn by lot from the local jury pools. The jurors were assigned to these recorded trials by the court. A judge instructed them as to their duties by explaining the court's interest in this comprehensive study of the judicial process. He also told them that while their verdicts in the case could have no immediate practical consequences, the judges of this court were very much interested in the results of the study. A juror's service was not voluntary; it was part of his regular period of jury duty.

4. Before listening to the trial, each juror filled out a questionnaire. The questionnaire asked for much the same kinds of information that the trial lawyer seeks, during an extensive voir dire or pretrial examination of prospective jurors, in order

[3] In the over-all study of the American jury system, conducted at the Law School of the University of Chicago, a variety of methods were employed. They included interviewing jurors in their homes after the verdicts were announced and asking each juror to recreate the discussion as he perceived it; soliciting the reactions of judges to juries' verdicts over many cases and in many jurisdictions; and inspecting historical documents on the origins and development of the present jury system.

[4] On several occasions we tried using professional actors, but we abandoned the tapes because they sounded more like a Perry Mason show than an actual day in court.

to decide which jurors to challenge and which to accept. Questions as to the juror's age, occupation, marital status, ethnicity, religion, education, income, and other characteristics were included along with a series of general attitude items.

5. The jurors then listened to the recorded trial. The trial was interrupted once for lunch. Before leaving the court the jurors were instructed not to discuss the case among themselves.[5] After lunch the jurors reported back to the jury room and the trial was resumed.

6. After the trial, but before the deliberation, each juror was asked to fill out a brief questionnaire in which he was asked to state how he would decide the case at this time.

7. The jury was then ready to deliberate. It had been told before the trial began that its deliberations would be recorded. Everyone (the bailiff, the experimenters, etc.) left the jury room except the twelve jurors, who had been instructed to select one of their members as foreman.

8. When the jury reached a verdict, the foreman reported it to the experimenter. The jurors were given a final questionnaire in which they were asked about their reactions to the trial and to the deliberation. They were also asked if, sitting as a one-man jury, each of them would have found as the group did.

9. The jury was then taken in front of the judge to report its verdict. The judge thanked the jurors for their service and either dismissed them or sent them back to the jury pool for further duty.

One of the major advantages of the technique described is that it legitimately opens the doors to the inner sanctum of the jury room, and permits systematic observations of the jury's deliberations. But that there are weaknesses and difficulties in the procedure is apparent not only to critics of the approach but to its authors as well. The first and most obvious weakness is that the verdicts have no practical signifi-

---

[5] The lunch break is supposed to simulate, in microcosm, the more extensive opportunities that jurors have to get to know one another during a real trial before they begin to deliberate.

cance. The jurors are told at the outset of the experiment that their verdicts will not affect the defendant's fate. What evidence do we have that the verdicts from the experimental juries are comparable to the verdicts that real juries would have reached in similar situations?

Our strongest evidence is indirect. It comes from the deliberations themselves.[6] In the opening minutes of their discussion many of the experimental juries sound as if they, too, were doubtful about the meaningfulness of the whole experience; but then something quite dramatic occurred. The jurors became so involved in defending their own interpretation of the case and in convincing others of the correctness of their views that they forgot that their verdicts would have no practical significance. In several deliberations, one juror was heard to ask another something like the following: "Do you want to see that man turned loose on society again? Suppose this time he attacks your daughter, or mine?" Or jurors were heard to warn the group: "If we can't reach a decision in this case, they will have to call in another jury to decide it, and hung juries cost the county money."

The length of the deliberations is another indirect measure of the realism of the experience. The discussions lasted for many hours, usually long past the time when the court would normally recess for the day. On several occasions the jurors continued through the dinner hour until late in the evening, and once a jury was "locked up" and continued its discussion the next day before it finally reported that it was hopelessly hung. We found that the average experimental jury's deliberation lasted as long as the average deliberation for a trial that takes two to three days.

The recorded deliberations also proved to be very similar to those provided by interviews with individual jurors who sat on real cases, when each juror was asked to re-create the deliberation as he perceived it. Finally, the shifts in verdicts

[6] Chapter 8, The Sound of the Jury, is an anthology of jury observations based solely on the deliberations. Appendix A contains a slightly edited version of an entire deliberation.

that occurred in response to changes in the transcript were in the direction that we would have predicted from common sense experiences.

In the last analysis, we think that the results are real because all of the conditions in the situations were real, except for the trial:

1. The participants were selected by lot from the jury pool.

2. They received their instructions from a judge, who explained that their activities were to be considered as part of their regular period of jury duty.

3. The usual restraints that are part of the institutional atmosphere of the court prevailed during the experiment. There was no newspaper reading, whispering, or dozing by the jurors as the trial was going on.

4. At the end of the day, when the jurors had completed their deliberations, they were returned to the courtroom where the foreman reported their verdict to the judge.

5. If during the deliberations the foreman reported that they could not reach consensus, the experimenter's instructions to the jury were similar to those which they would have received from the judge.

A major source of controversy about the design was the use of recorded trials. We think that the advantages gained from using a recorded trial outweighed the disadvantages. Let us review a few of the details about the technique. The recordings were based on actual cases. The editing of the original transcripts consisted primarily of deleting repetitious testimony. For example, instead of having three policemen testify to the circumstances surrounding the arrest of the defendant, the edited versions would have only one. The recordings were not artistic, dramatic presentations. They contained much of the tedium, dullness, and repetition of a day in court. Many of the witnesses spoke in slow, monotonous tones. Others, suffering from nervousness or embarrassment (as do many persons testifying in a real trial), spoke softly and hurriedly and, at times, slurred their words. The attorneys supported their own witnesses more than they did those called by the opposition, but in all instances they sounded as if they were disciplined both by their own professional training and by a real courtroom situation. On the whole, we think that the recorded trials simulated successfully the tempo and the atmosphere of the live courtroom.

The decision to use recorded trials rather than live presentations was based on several factors. A recorded trial has the advantage over a live presentation of exposing different juries to exactly the same stimulus again and again. It also permits the introduction of systematic changes in different parts of the trial, as for example in the expert's testimony, and thereby allows comparison of the importance of that information to the jury. Differences in verdicts can then be traced to the juries' exposure to the systematic variations in the transcript. Finally, a recorded trial is much less expensive to produce than a live presentation and, once produced, the costs of running it are negligible.

The advantages of a recording over a film lie primarily in the relative costs of producing each, with a film being much more expensive. Also, exposing subjects to a film could induce an "audience" reaction in them. They are likely to become passive and less interested. The factors of costs and maintaining interest had to be weighed against the advantage that might be gained by having the jurors see the participants. All things considered, we think that using recorded trials added more to the rigor of the experiment than they detracted from the realism of the experience.

A brief comment about the subjects in the experimental juries. The jurors who sat on the experimental juries differed from jurors who listen to most real trials in one respect. They were not subjected to a voir dire or pretrial examination. The first twelve names that the clerk pulled out of the hat were called up from the jury pool and given their assignment. On the pretrial questionnaires, we obtained the background and demographic information that lawyers generally inquire about in deciding whether to accept or challenge a prospective juror. But we used the information for different purposes. We compared verdicts and background characteristics with the aims of: (1) predicting the relationship between social status and verdicts, and (2) checking the accuracy of the lawyers' rule of thumb beliefs about the relationships between status characteristics and verdicts. We did not use the background information for controlling the composition of the jury.

But the jurors who served on the experimental juries came from the same universe as jurors who are selected for real trials. In the three communities in which the jury experiments were conducted, persons are selected for jury duty from the voter registration lists.[7] All jurors wait in the jury pool for their assignments to a trial. Some jurors spend all or most of their two weeks in the jury pool waiting for an assignment. These are persons who have either never been assigned to a case because their names were never called or because they were challenged by an attorney or prosecutor each time they were called from the jury pool. The experimental jurors too were selected by lot from the jury pool, but unlike jurors in real cases, once their names were called they were assured of assignment to a trial.

For these reasons, we are satisfied that the jury experiments yield more than a science of mock-jury behavior. We are satisfied that they enable us to infer how, under these conditions, real jurors will behave in real trials.

A final comment about generalizing from our results. We ran the experimental juries in three large Midwestern communities: Chicago, St. Louis, and Minneapolis. We cannot say, for certain, therefore, that geographical region or size of community does or does not significantly influence juries' verdicts.[8] We know that geography and size of community affects people's choice of political candidates, their attitudes

---

[7] This practice is followed in almost all large cities and in many smaller communities. In some small communities, persons are selected for jury duty from the lists of community organizations.

[8] Hans Zeisel discusses this problem particularly as it applies to civil juries and devises an indirect measure of regional and community differences. See Zeisel, Social Research on the Law, Law and Sociology 124 (Evan ed. 1962). Also, see Kalven and Zeisel, discussion of regional variations in jury verdicts, Chapters 33 and 37 of The American Jury (1966).

toward minority groups, their beliefs about the dangers of fall-out, and other social and political issues. While we recognize the importance of regional variation on some issues, we do not believe that the reactions of jurors to a criminal case involving a defense of insanity will differ significantly in the East, South, or Far West. If we were observing jurors' reactions to civil actions or to trials in which race was an issue, we would be less willing to generalize our findings beyond the area and the type of community in which we conducted the research.

In conclusion, we wish to emphasize that one of the most important gains from the experimental jury technique is that it permits outsiders, lawyers, judges, behavioral scientists, and the interested public to hear the sound of the jury for the first time.

Experiment I: A housebreaking trial

The first step was to transform a real trial transcript into an abbreviated recorded version of the trial. The transcript was based on the 1954 test case, *United States v. Durham*. The charge was housebreaking and the defendant's plea was insanity. Most trials in which the defense enters a plea of insanity involve acts of violence against another human being. In deciding to experiment with the *Durham* case, we had to consider the advantages of a more typical insanity case, one in which the defendant was charged with murder or rape, or some other sex crime, and the test case that had served as the impetus for a new rule of law. In light of all the interest that had been aroused by the *Durham* decision, we decided to use the trial of Monte Durham as the basis for our first experiment.

The basic facts of the case

The case was renamed *People v. Martin Graham*. The transcript was edited and the trial was recorded. The facts of the case are summarized in the following paragraphs:

At approximately three in the morning, the defendant, Martin Graham, was caught by the local police in the act of rummaging through the upstairs apartment of a house he had entered illegally. The police found him kneeling in the corner of the room holding a T-shirt over his face and with about $50.00 worth of merchandise in his pockets. He offered no resistance to arrest.

The defense called two psychiatrists to testify concerning Graham's mental condition. One of the psychiatrists was familiar with Graham's mental history over a seven-year period; the other, since his indictment. Both doctors testified that in their opinion the defendant was of unsound mind at the time of the crime. They explained that the defendant had a long history of mental illness and hospitalization. He was discharged from the Navy when he was seventeen years old after a psychiatric examination showed that he suffered "from a profound personality disorder which rendered him unfit for naval service." A few years later he attempted suicide and was taken to a hospital for observation, where he was diagnosed as suffering from "psychosis with psychopathic personality." His last internment in a mental hospital occurred four months before he committed the crime for which he was standing trial. At the time of his last internment the diagnosis was "without mental disorder, psychopathic personality." He was discharged two months later.

When asked to describe for the court the specific nature of the patient's mental state, Dr. Barton described Graham's condition in this manner:

"The patient's condition has been diagnosed as a reactive psychoneurosis, emotional immaturity and a general psychopathic personality. The symptoms ordinarily associated with psychopathic personalities are irrational thinking, general unreliability, untruthfulness, insincerity, and lack of shame. Such patients usually exhibit poor judgment, although they have a superficial charm and good intelligence. They tend to engage in fantastic and uninviting behavior which may or may not be induced by alcohol. Their interpersonal relations are poor. They do things to get their own ends and show little concern for the effect it may have on others. These people are frequently liars and their demands on others are usually excessive."

Except for brief periods of lucidity, the defendant's testimony was incoherent. He was unable to account for his activities during the periods when he was not in a mental hospital; he did not remember where he lived; and he answered one question by saying: "People get all mixed up in machines."

The defendant's parents testified that their son was a model child until the age of thirteen, when he suddenly became ill with rheumatic fever. From that time on he had difficulty in school, paid no attention to his parents' attempts at discipline, and would wander off, sometimes for days, without informing them of his whereabouts.

Throughout the trial, the prosecutor directed his arguments toward two points: One, the case was a simple criminal action. The defendant broke into the Harris home on Aspen Street and was arrested in the act of burglary. Two, the defendant was feigning mental illness in order to escape responsibility for his crime. He had learned to depend on mental illness to extricate himself from difficult situations: at home, in the service, and, now, when he was facing criminal charges. The defense attorney maintained that the question of fact as to whether the defendant committed the act was not in dispute. The sole issue was the defendant's mental state at the time of the offense.[9]

Design of the housebreaking experiment

Changes in the experimental trial were introduced as a function of two variables: rules of law and information about commitment.

[9] The recorded trial did not duplicate exactly the fact situation of the original Durham trial. The differences between the two trials pertained primarily to omissions in the experimental version. By and large, corroborative, factual testimony was not included in the experimental transcript. In the original trial, two policemen testified to the defendant's behavior at the time of his arrest. In addition to the defendant's parents, the defendant's two older brothers testified about Durham's childhood. Also, in the original trial, the defendant had two associates both of whom pleaded guilty and were sentenced to one year in prison. The experimental and original transcripts were almost identical in the testimony of the medical experts and in the defendant's testimony. In general, anyone who is familiar with the original Durham trial would have no difficulty recognizing the relationship between it and the Graham case. In all important respects, People v. Martin Graham does not differ significantly from the test case, United States v. Durham.

Rules of law

One third of the jurors heard the trial under the traditional *M'Naghten* "right from wrong" instructions. In that version, the judge instructed them as follows:

> The law in this jurisdiction states that those who have, of their own free will and with evil intent, committed acts which violate the law, shall be criminally responsible for those acts; but where such acts are committed by a person who is incapable of understanding the nature, quality and consequences of his acts, or of distinguishing between right and wrong, there is no legal responsibility on the part of the defendant.
>
> The law does not say that every person who suffers from a morbid propensity or inclination to commit prohibited acts is excused from the legal consequences of any unlawful act he may commit. Only a morbid propensity or inclination to commit prohibited acts existing in the mind of a person incapable of knowing the wrongfulness of such acts can be grounds for finding not guilty by reason of insanity.
>
> It is the jury's function to determine from all the evidence, including the expert testimony, not only whether the defendant suffered from an abnormal mental condition at the time the crime was committed, but whether the condition was such that the defendant was unable to distinguish right from wrong behavior.

Another third were given the *Durham* "product of mental disease" instruction:

> The law in this jurisdiction states that those who have of their own free will and with evil intent committed acts which violate the law, shall be criminally responsible for those acts; but, where such acts stem from, and are the product of, a mental disease or defect, there is no legal responsibility on the part of the defendant.
>
> The law does not say that every person who suffers from a diseased or defective mental condition is excused from the legal consequences of any unlawful act he may commit. Only if the act was the product of a mental disease or defect can the accused be found not guilty on the grounds of insanity.
>
> It is the jury's function to determine from all the evidence,

including the expert testimony, not only whether the defendant suffered from an abnormal mental condition at the time the crime was committed, but also whether the criminal act was the product of mental abnormality.

The court instructed the last third of the jurors in a manner similar in each respect to those provided in the *M'Naghten* and *Durham* versions except that it omitted any reference to a criterion of responsibility. In that version, the jurors deliberated with full knowledge of the facts of the case and of the nature of the defendant's plea, but with no guidance as to the criterion they were to apply for deciding whether or not the defendant should be held responsible for his behavior. Those jurors were told only:

> If you believe the defendant was insane at the time he committed the act of which he is accused, then you must find the defendant not guilty by reason of insanity.

This instruction, of course, has no legal counterpart anywhere. But our purpose was to obtain information on the community's sense of equity and justice in the absence of formal, external legal criteria.

Commitment information

The second variable pertained to information that the jurors received about the procedure for committing or releasing the defendant should they find him not guilty by reason of insanity.

Half of the juries were told about an automatic commitment procedure before they began to deliberate. The judge said:

> I should like to add for your information that when a defendant is found not guilty by reason of insanity, he is presumed by law to be insane, and under the law of this jurisdiction the court must order him confined in a hospital for the mentally ill, where he will remain unless and until it is determined by the authorities of that hospital that he is of sound mind, at which time he will be released.

The other half of the juries were given no information about what would happen to the defendant if they found him not guilty by reason of insanity.

Table 1 summarizes the experimental design for the housebreaking case. Thirty juries were exposed to six versions of the trial. Each version of the trial was played before approximately equal numbers of juries in Chicago, St. Louis, and Minneapolis.[10]

TABLE 1. THE EXPERIMENTAL DESIGN: PEOPLE V. MARTIN GRAHAM

	M'Naghten	*RULES OF LAW* *Uninstructed on* *responsibility*	*Durham*
Informed about automatic commitment procedure	5*	5	5
Not informed	5	5	5

* The frequencies in the cells represent the number of replications in each version.

Concomitant changes in the script

We have spoken of the difference between the *M'Naghten* and *Durham* treatments as if it were confined entirely to the formal instructions. While this is the main difference, a dilemma between realism and precision in the experiment arises because it is not the sole experimental difference. A trial under the *Durham* rule will normally generate questions to the psychiatric expert and answers from him that would not arise in a *M'Naghten* trial, and vice versa. Thus, in order to reproduce the difference between the two rules of law realistically, concomitant changes had to be made in the testimony of the psychiatric experts in the two versions. As a result, whatever we shall say later on about the difference between

[10] The individual and group verdicts for each city were examined separately. When we were satisfied that the verdict patterns for all the cities were similar, we dropped the separations by city.

Durham and *M'Naghten* will not only refer to the different instructions on the law but will include the differences in the concomitant testimony as well.   There is no way of saying anything about the effects of the instructions separately from that of the concomitant testimony.   This might seem, at first, regrettable.   But had we changed *only* the instruction, we would have tested a situation that cannot arise in reality; hence we would have in fact tested nothing.

The following describes the psychiatric testimony under *M'Naghten:*

> Defense Attorney: Now, Doctor, one final question: From your knowledge of the defendant's medical history, would you say that Martin Graham was capable of distinguishing right from wrong conduct at the time of the crime?
> Witness: Concerning the defendant's acts on July 13, I just can't say.

Later, on cross examination of the same witness:

> Prosecuting Attorney: Doctor, did I understand you correctly, did you say that you have not formed an opinion as to whether the defendant could tell right from wrong on July 13?
> Witness: Yes, I have no opinion on that.

The second doctor, on cross examination:

> Prosecuting Attorney: One final question, Doctor: Would you say that Martin Graham could tell right from wrong on July 13?
> Witness: Well, he might answer questions correctly.
> Judge: No, I don't think that is the question, Doctor — not whether he could give a right answer to a question, but whether he, himself, knew the difference between right and wrong in connection with governing his own actions.   If you are unable to answer, why you can say so; I mean, if you are unable to form an opinion.
> Witness: I can only answer this way: I can't tell how much the abnormal thinking and abnormal experiences in the form of hallucinations and delusion — delusions of persecution — had to do with his anti-social behavior.   I don't know how anyone can answer that question categorically

except that one's experience leads him to know that most mental cases can give you a categorical answer of right or wrong. But what influence these symptoms have on abnormal behavior or anti-social behavior, well, I just don't know.

In the *Durham* version of the same housebreaking trial, the first doctor testified as follows:

Defense Attorney: Well, Doctor, would you say he was suffering from a diseased mental condition on July 13, at the time he was found housebreaking?

Witness: It would be my opinion that Graham was suffering from a diseased mental condition at that time.

Defense Attorney: And now, Doctor, would you say the crime was the product of such diseased mental condition?

Witness: Well, I can definitely say this. The diseased mental condition did lower somewhat Graham's capacity to control his conduct.

Later, on cross examination, the same witness:

Prosecuting Attorney: Doctor, would you say the defendant would not have committed the crime in question if he had not been mentally ill?

Witness: Well, that's not easy to say, put that way. All I can say is that his mental condition did affect his capacity to control his conduct.

The second doctor, on cross examination:

Prosecuting Attorney: Can you definitely say that the crime would not have occurred if it had not been for the defendant's mental condition?

Witness: Of course not. Burglaries happen every night; a mentally healthy man *could* commit a burglary. What I said before [interrupted]

Judge: Doctor, would you say that the defendant's criminal action on the night of July 13, was a product, that is, a direct consequence of his mental condition?

Witness: Your Honor, concerning the defendant's behavior on a particular night, well I'm afraid I just couldn't testify to that. As I said before, however, from what I've observed of the symptoms of the defendant's illness I would say that his actions were certainly influenced by his mental disease.

In the *uninstructed* version, neither doctor was asked to give his opinion as to whether the defendant could distinguish right from wrong, or as to whether the defendant's acts were a product of mental disease.

Experiment II: An incest trial

An exactly parallel process was followed in the development of the incest case.

In most cases in which a defense of insanity is introduced, the insanity issue is complicated by the issue of capital punishment, since the crime involved is usually murder, kidnapping, or rape. A charge of incest offers an interesting opportunity to examine jurors' reactions to a heinous offense without having to take into account public attitudes toward capital punishment. We also wanted to find out if the topic of incest could be adequately discussed by a group of men and women who were meeting for the first time. Our guess was that the institutional context of the court would provide enough structured impersonality so as to allow the jurors to participate in a discussion that under most conditions would be extremely threatening and anxiety provoking.

The basic facts of the case

In the original District of Columbia trial of *United States v. King*,[11] the jury deliberated eight hours before it reported that it was hopelessly hung six to six. In a subsequent bench trial (the defendant waived his right to a jury trial), Judge Edward A. Tamm found the defendant not guilty by reason of insanity and ordered him committed to St. Elizabeth's Hospital.[12] The facts of the renamed case are summarized below.

Jason Lunt, a lieutenant in the Fire Department, lived with his wife, two sons, and two daughters, in a metropolitan city on the East Coast. The series of events leading to his

[11] United States v. King, Dkt. No. 655-5 (D.C. Cir. 1956).
[12] The Durham rule was used in both the jury trial and bench trial.

arrest were initiated by his younger daughter who went to the police after she had been approached for sexual intercourse two days in succession. His wife had been aware of the incestuous relationships for some time and never reported the situation, nor did she testify during the trial. The defendant had no history of criminal indictments or mental illness.

A series of lay witnesses were called by the prosecution. They included the defendant's two daughters, who testified that they had had sexual intercourse with their father for fourteen years. The Deputy Fire Chief and an old family friend and associate at the Fire Department both testified that until the incidents reported in this trial were made public it was their belief that the defendant was living a normal life with the members of his family. In defense cross-examination, it came to light that the defendant had been erratic in his work and at the time of his arrest had been home on sick leave ordered by the physician attached to the Fire Department. The defendant did not take the stand; but the statement he gave to the police officers at the time of his arrest was offered in evidence by the prosecution. In his statement, the defendant acknowledged further that these acts had been committed over a period of fourteen years and that during this time he sought to avoid pregnancy of his daughters by instructing them in the use of contraceptive devices.

The two psychiatrists, the only witnesses called by the defense, testified that the defendant was suffering from paraphiliac neurosis, which they claimed could be traced to unresolved oedipal tensions. In addition they believed that the defendant's total lack of affect of involvement with his present situation was an indication of mental disorder. They also reported that for ten to fifteen years the defendant had been drinking heavily. But the doctors never indicated that the defendant was suffering from a psychosis, and on cross-examination they explicitly stated that he was not.

The final witness for the prosecution, called in rebuttal, was a psychiatrist who had neither examined nor seen the patient before his appearance in the courtroom. He testified that "paraphiliac neurosis" was not a "mental" but an "emotional" disturbance.

The recorded trial and the original trial were practically identical. We wish to stress that we did not "clean up" the experimental version by deleting accounts of violent or perverted sexual behavior. The facts heard in the courtroom of the original trial were the same facts listened to by jurors who heard the recorded trial.[13]

Design of the incest experiment

As in the housebreaking experiment, six versions of the incest trial were prepared. In this experiment the changes were a function of variations in the rules of law and in the testimonies of the medical experts.

Approximately one third of the juries heard the trial under the *M'Naghten* instructions, one third under the *Durham* instructions, and one third under the *uninstructed on responsibility* version. The instructions that appear above for the housebreaking trial are essentially the same as those used by the court in the incest case.

In the incest case, the defense called only two witnesses; both were psychiatrists who examined the defendant between the time he was arrested and the time the trial began. Two versions of psychiatric testimony were prepared.

Half of the juries heard expert psychiatric testimony that followed closely the testimony actually heard in the real trial and that we think is typical of the kind of testimony usually heard in the courtroom. The typical testimony described the defendant's current symptoms and gave them psychiatric la-

[13] We might mention, primarily because the jurors make so much of this point in their deliberations, that although the defendant's wife is alluded to on several occasions, by both the daughters and in the defendant's own statement, she does not appear as a witness, nor is there any indication that she is even present in the courtroom. The defendant's statement also mentioned rearing two sons "in the strictest moral sense, neither of whom smokes, drinks, or curses," but neither of the sons was called as witness; nor was any further mention made of them during the trial. There was a brief reference to the older daughter's marriage but neither side called the husband as a witness; nor did they make any attempt to probe his position in the family. These "mysteries" contributed to the drama of the original trial. We tried to retain this lack of closure and sense of incompleteness in the recorded version.

bels but offered almost no historical or developmental account of the origins of the defendant's behavior.

The other half of the juries heard testimony that we optimistically describe as model testimony. In the model version the psychiatrists offered a longer and more detailed clinical history of the defendant's illness from his infancy until his indictment. When medical labels were applied, they were defined in language that should have been understandable to the average layman. In the model version, the psychiatrists made more of an effort to tie together the defendant's clinical history and symptoms with his current behavior. The model testimony lasted almost twice as long as the typical testimony.

Excerpts from each version of the psychiatrists' testimonies that illustrate the differences between model and typical responses appear below. The first excerpt is from the model version. It begins at a time when Dr. Weinstein, a psychiatrist called by the defense, is being questioned on direct examination.

Question: Doctor, could you re-create for us, perhaps in some detail, a picture of the defendant's illness as you see it?

Answer: As is the usual practice in psychiatric examinations, in the initial interviews I sought to obtain an intensive case history of the patient's life, placing special emphasis on his very early childhood experiences. In this case, I would say that the defendant's earliest childhood experiences have resulted in a situation in which he still carries around with him deep conflicts and anxieties concerning his relationship with his mother. Now, of course, these conflicts and anxieties are deeply repressed, that is, the defendant is not aware of them; he does not by any means understand that his infantile experiences are causing problems for him today. To be more specific, let me tell you a little of the defendant's childhood experience. Would that be all right?

Mr. Houston: Yes, Doctor, go right ahead.

Witness: Jason Lunt's father either died or deserted his family, we are not sure of which, when the patient was six months old, and from then on until the time his mother remarried (the defendant was then six years old), the patient slept in the same bed with his mother. Until the patient's sixth year there were no other adult males in the home with whom the patient could establish a father-son relationship. At the time of the mother's proposed remarriage the defendant was extremely upset and protested bitterly to his mother against the marriage. Now it is generally believed that the oedipus complex, which in boys is represented as love for the mother and both identification and hate for the father figure, starts in the third year of life and reaches its climax in about the fifth year. Thus, at the height of the patient's oedipal attachment to his mother he was forced for the first time to share his mother's attentions with a man with whom he had no previous contact. The stepfather, as it turned out, was a stern quiet man who exhibited no love or interest in his stepson. The patient was unable to identify with this man as a father figure. Two years later, when the defendant was eight years old, a half brother was born, of whom he was extremely jealous.

The patient's history indicates that he practiced masturbation from the time he was three years old. Young boys, employed by his mother in her confectionery business, I believe it was, first introduced him to this practice, by so engaging themselves in his presence. Also, when the patient was between the ages of three and six, his mother, as part of her confectionery business, ran a dance hall; and it was there that the patient had an opportunity to observe patrons of the establishment engage in perverse sexual acts.

Question: Now, Doctor, would you say that these experiences which occurred in the early years of the defendant's life can account for the defendant's behavior when he is a grown man?

Answer: I would say that they can and do. Let me explain it in this way.

Experiences that occur in early childhood constitute the groundwork from which the sexuality of the adult subsequently develops. Any adult who is blocked in his adult sexuality falls back to infantile sexuality as a substitute, because the child experiences his sexuality with the same emotions the adult feels toward his.

An overcoming of oedipal strivings, and replacement by adult sexuality, is the prerequisite for normality, where as an unconscious clinging to oedipal tendencies characterizes the neurotic mind. Anything that increases fears and thus increases sexual repressions causes disturbances in the subsequent overcoming of the oedipus complex. Furthermore, the oedipus complex is most outspoken in only children, and special complications may be present when there is less than a three-person family group: this is, when one of the parents is not present.

Now, if I could just go on a little longer to fill in some more details from the patient's history.

Mr. Houston: Yes, Doctor, please do.

Witness: The patient met his wife soon after he entered high school, and they began dating steadily. A few months after they graduated from high school they were married. The patient had dated no other girl during this period. About two or three months after the couple were married, their first child was born. Since then they have had three other children, so that their family consists of two boys and two girls. There appears to be no indication of any abnormality in the patient's relationship with his sons, or in the sons' behavior generally. The patient claims that his wife has always been frigid, and that intercourse with her was no source of release for him. He also insists that he is over-sexed. He continued masturbation, though with considerable guilt, until he was past forty years of age.

Question: Now, Doctor, from all the information that you have acquired, what are your conclusions?

Answer: I would say that Mr. Lunt is what in psychiatric terms we call a psychoneurotic. Now, by the term psychoneurosis, I mean to describe someone who, on the whole, manages to conform to the demands of ordinary living, but who is the victim of his own inner conflicts. The conflicts usually show themselves in a variety of ways, for example, the person may become overanxious, he may have compulsions. But essentially such a person appears to be all right even in the eyes of people with whom he may have daily contact, in the sense that he appears to be in touch with reality.

Question: Doctor, given the patient's personal background and experiences, would it be your opinion that behavior such as the type described in this case is a likely outcome?

Answer: Well, it's always an extremely difficult task to predict or foresee from a person's childhood just what particular behavioral patterns will result when he is an adult, but I would say that for this patient an incestuous relationship is not an unexpected result.

The following section, occurring at approximately the same point in the defense's examination of Dr. Weinstein, characterizes the typical version:

> Question: Would you kindly tell us what you have learned on the basis of the examination?
>
> Answer: It is my opinion that Mr. Lunt is a psychoneurotic patient of long standing. I cannot state specifically the exact date that it started but a total review of his history leads me to conclude that it is of some years' standing. The patient's early developmental history indicates that because of the death or desertion of his father, a very strong emotional dependence developed between mother and son. This undoubtedly is an important factor in the development of the patient's neurosis which led to his abnormal sexual behavior. The unhealthy state of affairs may be characterized as an oedipus complex.
>
> Along with this, we have the appearance, when the patient was six years old, of a cold rejecting stepfather, thus causing the patient's fears to reach the force of castration anxiety; and thus was a further crippling influence insofar as his sexual development was concerned. I might add that one often finds such a background in paraphiliac neurosis.
>
> And I believe that this condition existed during the period of the alleged offense.

Table 2 summarizes the experimental design for the incest case. Sixty-eight juries were exposed to six versions of the trial. As in the housebreaking experiment, each version of the trial was played before approximately equal numbers of juries in Chicago, St. Louis, and Minneapolis. The verdicts for each city were examined separately. We found no differences in the verdict patterns of juries in the three cities and collapsed those categories.

TABLE 2.   THE EXPERIMENTAL DESIGN:
PEOPLE V. JASON LUNT

Expert psychiatric testimony	RULES OF LAW		
	M'Naghten	Uninstructed on responsibility	Durham
Model	9	11	13
Typical	11	11	13

Concomitant changes in the script

The changes in psychiatric testimony necessitated by the variations in the rules of law are described below.

Under the *M'Naghten* rule, on cross examination the first doctor testified as follows:

> Prosecuting Attorney: Doctor, from all your examinations of the defendant, would you say that he was able to distinguish right from wrong?
>
> Witness: In the sense that he was probably aware of the fact that incest was socially and morally wrong, I would say that he could distinguish right from wrong.

The second doctor testified on cross examination:

> Prosecuting Attorney: Let me ask you this, sir: From the examination that you made of him and the conclusion that you reached that he is a paraphiliac, would you say that this individual is able to distinguish between right and wrong?
>
> Witness: In my opinion, he is.

In the *Durham* version on direct examination the first doctor testified as follows:

> Defense Attorney: Doctor, I direct your attention to the fact that there is filed in this case a report which is signed by Dr. Hawley, who is the Director of Billington State Hospital, dated as of March 15, 1956, and that report is made in response to a direction of this court. In the report made to this court, Dr. Hawley states: We conclude that Jason Lunt is suffering from a mental illness of long standing, and that the crimes with which he is charged were the products of this mental disease. Now, Doctor, did you come to the conclusion that the offenses which are complained of here were the products of the defendant's disease?
>
> Witness: It seems to me that the term "product" of a disease as the term is conventionally used, is not quite applicable here; in the sense that the defendant's behavior is really almost a symptom of an underlying illness; in other words, the behavior is so closely connected with the illness that one cannot think of it as being a result of the illness, but as a manifestation of hidden anxieties or fears, all of which have their roots in very early childhood.

The second doctor, on direct examination, said:

Defense Attorney: Doctor, one final question. Would you
say that the offense with which the defendant is charged is
a product of this mental illness?

Witness: I would say that the defendant's behavior and his
illness are part and parcel of the same over-all picture; his
behavior in this situation is an overt manifestation of his
psychic problems.

In the *uninstructed* version neither doctor was asked
whether the defendant could distinguish right from wrong or
whether the act was a product of mental disease.

Combined design: Housebreaking and incest experiments

The six versions of the housebreaking trial were played before 30 juries and the six versions of the incest trial before
68 juries. In the housebreaking case, the changes in the testimonies of the witnesses were a function of the variations in the
rules of law. The commitment variable did not alter the testimony of any of the witnesses; it altered only the instructions
that the judge gave to the jury at the end of the trial. There
was no attempt to introduce model psychiatric testimony in
the housebreaking experiment. The *M'Naghten* version of
the trial offered essentially the same testimony that the jury
heard in the first district court trial. The *Durham* version
was based on the testimony given in the second district court
trial.

In the incest experiment, both variables, rules of law and
psychiatric testimony, necessitated modifications in the testimonies of the expert witnesses. In addition to differences in
the psychiatrists' responses on questions pertaining to criminal
responsibility, the model and typical versions made changes
necessary in the length and detail of the experts' testimonies.
All the juries in the incest experiment were told about the
automatic commitment procedure if the defendant was found
not guilty by reason of insanity.

The combined design for both experiments looked like this:

TABLE 3. COMBINED EXPERIMENTAL DESIGN: HOUSEBREAKING AND INCEST TRIALS

SECOND VARIABLES: COMMITMENT OR PSYCHIATRIC TESTIMONY	FIRST VARIABLE: RULES OF LAW			
	M'Naghten	Uninstructed on responsibility	Durham	Total
	Housebreaking Trial (with typical testimony)			
Commitment information				
Given	5	5	5	15
Not given	5	5	5	15
Total	10	10	10	30
	Incest Trial (with commitment information)			
Expert psychiatric testimony				
Model	9	11	13	33
Typical	11	11	13	35
Total	20	22	26	68

A note on the limitations of the design

Unfortunately, it is not possible to compare the juries' verdicts between the two trials with the aim of explaining whether a defense of insanity is more likely to be successful against a charge of incest as opposed to a charge of housebreaking. Had we constructed two trials which were alike in all respects except that defendant A was charged with incest and defendant B with housebreaking then it would have made sense to compare juries' verdicts between trials. But it is difficult to imagine Martin Graham committing incest. If he had, the psychiatrists would have diagnosed his condition quite differently than they did that of Jason Lunt.

The chart below describes graphically the additional experiments that would have to be run before any comparative statements could be made about the relative effectiveness of an insanity plea to a charge of incest or housebreaking.

DEFENDANT'S MENTAL CONDITION

Nature of the crime	Psychotic (patently insane)	Not psychotic (observably not insane)
Mild (housebreaking)	A	Data missing
Heinous (incest)	Data missing	D

Our data apply only to cells A and D. We do not know how the jurors would have responded if Martin Graham had been charged with incest and Jason Lunt with housebreaking. Because of the limitations in our design, we view each trial as an independent event.

Verdicts in the housebreaking and incest trials

Before describing the juries' verdicts in the two trials, we wish to emphasize that the law, either under *M'Naghten* or under *Durham,* does not prescribe a specific set of symptoms for insanity. Medical experts may give opinions as to whether the defendant was suffering from a mental disease, and they may describe the symptoms and etiology of the disease. But the jury alone must decide whether the defendant's illness should excuse him from responsibility.

Remember that in the *housebreaking* trial, both psychiatrists called by the defense testified that, at the time of the crime, the defendant was suffering from a "psychopathic personality *with* psychosis." The experts then reviewed the defendant's record of intermittent confinement to mental hospitals, discharge from the service on medical grounds, attempted suicides, reports of hallucinations, incoherent speech, and an unstable work record. When the defendant took the stand his testimony sounded dazed and incoherent.

In the *incest* case, both psychiatrists testified that the defendant was suffering from a mental disease at the time he committed the anti-social acts, and that the etiology of his disturbance could be traced to early childhood. But, unlike the diagnosis in the housebreaking trial, neither psychiatrist claimed that the defendant had, at any time, shown evidence of psychotic behavior; nor was there any record of previous confinements to mental institutions, medical treatment, or personal and job instability. No mention was made of hallucinatory or delusional symptoms and there were no reports of violence against himself or others. The only term applied to the defendant's mental state was "psychoneurosis," or more explicitly "paraphiliac neurosis" or sexual perversion.

The verdicts for each trial will be presented separately in two tables. The first table will describe the individual verdicts, that is, the verdict reported by each juror on the questionnaire distributed immediately after the trial, and the second table, the group verdicts.

Tables 4 and 5 describe the individual and group verdicts in the housebreaking case.

TABLE 4. PRE-DELIBERATION VERDICTS IN THE HOUSEBREAKING CASE

Not guilty by reason of insanity	66%
Guilty	34%

Based on (12 × 30 =) 360 jurors

TABLE 5. GROUP VERDICTS IN THE HOUSEBREAKING CASE

Not guilty by reason of insanity	56%
Hung	27%
Guilty	17%

Based on 30 juries

The group and individual verdicts are similar. Before the deliberations, 66 per cent of the jurors believed the defendant not guilty by reason of insanity. Of the group verdicts, 56 per cent of the juries voted to acquit on grounds of insanity. If we divide the 27 per cent of the juries that hung into half acquittals and half convictions and add 13.5 per cent to the 56 per cent acquittals, we find that the group and individual verdicts were almost identical: 69.5 per cent not guilty by reason of insanity on the group level and 66 per cent on the individual level.

Tables 6 and 7 describe the individual and group verdicts in the incest case.

TABLE 6. PRE-DELIBERATION VERDICTS IN THE INCEST CASE

Not guilty by reason of insanity	33%
Guilty	67%

Based on (12 × 68 =) 816 jurors

TABLE 7. GROUP VERDICTS IN THE INCEST CASE

Not guilty by reason of insanity	13%
Hung	16%
Guilty	71%

Based on 68 juries

The differences between the individual and the group verdicts were greater in the incest case than in the housebreaking case. Even after we divide the hung juries and add half of the 16 per cent to the 13 per cent not guilty by reason of insanity verdicts, we still find that the per cent of NGI (not guilty, insane) verdicts on the individual level was higher by 12 per centage points (33% vs. 21%).

Dramatic as the differences in verdicts are between the two trials, we cannot generalize their implications. The housebreaking and incest experiments are two independent events. The jurors' verdicts on the two trials should not be compared with the aim of generalizing how jurors respond to a plea of insanity when the crime is a relatively mild offense in contrast to a heinous offense or when the defendant is patently insane or neurotic.

There are, however, a few comments about the nature of juries' verdicts that are common to both trials and that we believe would generalize to other cases as well:

(1) For about half the jurors (47 per cent in the housebreaking trial and 55 per cent in the incest trial) there was no conflict between the opinion they held before entering the jury room and the eventual group decision.

(2) Of the remaining jurors, 27 per cent in the housebreaking trial and 16 per cent in the incest trial ended up in hung juries. In the housebreaking trial 88 per cent and in the incest trial 76 per cent of those in hung juries voted the same way on their post-deliberation ballot as they did on their pre-deliberation ballot.

(3) Thus, in the two trials, slightly over 25 per cent of the jurors were in groups that reached decisions which opposed the jurors' pre-deliberation verdicts. Among those jurors, 61 per cent in the housebreaking and 66 per cent in the incest trial changed both their verdicts and their opinions. We measured this change by examining how the jurors voted on their pre- and post-deliberation ballots and compared it against the group verdict. Those jurors whose post-deliberation verdict matched the group's verdict but differed from their pre-deliberation ballot were apparently convinced by the group discussion.

Among the remaining jurors, 35 per cent in the housebreaking trial and 25 per cent in the incest trial voted with the group and, later on their post-deliberation ballots switched back to their earlier preferences. These were jurors who "went along with the group" rather than "hang" the jury. Slightly over 5 per cent of the jurors in both trials made what appear to be irrational decisions. These were jurors who went into the jury room agreeing with the group's verdict, but who, on their post-deliberation ballots reported opinions that differed from their pre-deliberation and group verdicts.

To summarize, about half the jurors had no conflict. Their individual preferences matched those of the group. Of the remaining jurors, 16 per cent and 27 per cent were in hung juries. Of those in hung juries, over 75 per cent retained their original opinions. Among the 25 per cent or so jurors whose individual preferences conflicted with those of the group, 60 and 66 per cent were persuaded by the group and changed their opinions. Most of the remaining jurors went along with the group's preference but were not convinced of its correctness.

The figures below show the details for each trial.

VERDICTS IN HOUSEBREAKING TRIAL

Pre-deliberation	Group	Post-deliberation	Per cent
1. NGI	NGI	NGI	40
2. NGI	NGI	Guilty	1
3. NGI	Guilty	Guilty	7
4. NGI	Guilty	NGI	3
5. NGI	Hung	NGI	13
6. NGI	Hung	Guilty	2
7. Guilty	Guilty	Guilty	7
8. Guilty	Guilty	NGI	0
9. Guilty	NGI	NGI	9
10. Guilty	NGI	Guilty	6
11. Guilty	Hung	Guilty	11
12. Guilty	Hung	NGI	1

VERDICTS IN INCEST TRIAL

Pre-deliberation	Group	Post-deliberation	Per cent
1. NGI	NGI	NGI	5
2. NGI	NGI	Guilty	2
3. NGI	Guilty	Guilty	15
4. NGI	Guilty	NGI	5
5. NGI	Hung	NGI	3
6. NGI	Hung	Guilty	3
7. Guilty	Guilty	Guilty	50
8. Guilty	Guilty	NGI	1
9. Guilty	NGI	NGI	4
10. Guilty	NGI	Guilty	2
11. Guilty	Hung	Guilty	9
12. Guilty	Hung	NGI	1

PART II

The Impact of the Experimental Variables on the Jury's Verdict

CHAPTER 3

The Jury's Response to Legal Rules in Defense of Insanity Trials

We turn now to an analysis of one of the basic questions in the study: What effect do legal rules have on the jury's verdict in defense of insanity cases?

Of the two rules of law that juries are likely to receive in defense of insanity trials the *M'Naghten* rule is the older and more widely used. Like the M'Naghten rule, the more recently formulated *Durham* rule has also aroused a great deal of criticism and discussion in the dozen years of its existence. Supporters of *M'Naghten* and *Durham* view the controversy over which rule the court should use as having two main dimensions.

The first dimension goes to the intrinsic value of the two formulations. Supporters of *M'Naghten* believe that its emphasis on cognition and morality are consistent with society's views about responsibility. Supporters of *Durham* argue that the "product" formula facilitates communication between law and psychiatry and permits medical testimony that is more in keeping with present-day scientific knowledge about the human mind and personality.

The second dimension concerns the applicability of the rule by a jury. This dimension is of great practical significance because it is the jury's interpretation of the rule that determines the defendant's fate. One of the primary functions of any rule of law is to limit the arbitrary element in legal decisions. In defense of insanity trials, a rule of law defines for the jury the criterion of responsibility that it is to apply in determining the guilt or innocence of the defendant. Supporters of the *M'Naghten* rule argue that the "right from wrong" formula reflects society's feelings about responsibility, and therefore the rule is easily communicated to a jury of laymen who in turn have little difficulty applying it. The *Durham* rule, on the other hand, is so vague as to be uninterpretable by a jury, or so its detractors argue. Opponents of *Durham* also claim that the expert's testimony is so prominent that the jury sees its own function as being little more than to serve as a rubber stamp to the expert.

Our empirical inquiry is not, of course, designed to resolve the policy debate. It represents no more than an effort to discover what the jury makes of the contending rules. But this is no small matter. Under present legal arrangements, the point at which the theoretical debate over criminal responsibility becomes operative in the real world is the point at which it makes a difference to the jury.

Verdicts and the rules of law: The housebreaking case

In the psychiatric testimony under *M'Naghten,* it will be recalled that the experts claimed that the ability to distinguish right from wrong had no meaning in their assessment of the defendant's mental state and refused to answer the crucial question about responsibility. Under *Durham,* the doctors equivocated but answered in a way that generally supported the defense. The *uninstructed on responsibility* version did not offer any specific basis for predicting verdicts because the experts were not asked for their opinion about a doctrine of responsibility.

Tables 8 and 9 describe the jurors' individual, pre-deliberation, and group verdicts under the three instruction versions. On the individual verdicts jurors who were exposed to the *uninstructed* version were most likely to acquit the defendant on grounds of insanity. Their verdicts differed significantly from the verdicts of jurors who were exposed to the *M'Naghten* instruction. Between *M'Naghten* and *Durham,* the jurors

TABLE 8.   PRE-DELIBERATION VERDICTS OF INDIVIDUAL
JURORS BY RULE OF LAW (HOUSEBREAKING)

	Per cent voting NGI
Uninstructed	$76_{(120)}$
M'Naghten	$59_{(119)}$*
Durham	$65_{(119)}$*

Uninstructed vs. M'Naghten: $X^2_{1d.f.}$ (.99) = 6.6; X^2 = 8.9, p. < .01
Durham vs. M'Naghten: $X^2_{1d.f.}$ (.95) = 3.8; p. > .05
* One juror in each version did not indicate his pre-deliberation verdict.

who were exposed to the *Durham* rule behaved more like the *uninstructed* jurors, but the difference between M'Naghten and Durham did not attain statistical significance.[1]

In the group verdicts, however, the *M'Naghten* juries behaved more like the *uninstructed* jurors than the juries who

[1] Throughout, we exposed jurors to different stimuli such as rules of law, expert testimony, and presence or absence of commitment information, and we compared jurors' responses, usually in the form of verdicts, to see if the stimuli produced differences. We needed a statistical test which would tell us whether the differences in verdicts under the three different sets of instructions were due to chance or were real differences. The chi-square (X^2) test differentiates between real and chance differences. The chi-square (X^2) is a statistic which measures the discrepancy between observed and expected frequencies. If the observed frequencies agreed completely with the expected, X^2 would be zero. X^2 increases in size as the observed frequencies depart more and more from the expected frequencies. The question is how large does the difference between the observed and expected frequencies have to be before it is considerd a real difference. The question is answered in terms of probability theory; a difference is considered statistically significant if the probability of its occurring by chance is less than 5 in 100 (p < .05). The smaller the p (probability) value, the larger the difference. When the p value is greater than .05 we can assume either that there are no differences or that the differences are due to chance; i.e. they are negligible. The degrees of freedom (d.f.) is a criterion used to determine the probability of the frequency of X^2. In Table 8 the differences in verdicts between jurors exposed to the *uninstructed* and *M'Naghten* versions is statistically significant because the probability of such a difference occurring by chance is less than 1 in 100 (p < .01).

TABLE 9. JURIES' VERDICTS BY RULES OF LAW
(HOUSEBREAKING)

	NGI	Hung	Guilty	Total Juries
Uninstructed	6	1	3	10
M'Naghten	7	1	2	10
Durham	4	3	3	10

were instructed under the *Durham* formula. But with only ten replications in each category, the numbers of jurors that the 60 or 70 per cent represent is too small to be given much significance.[2]

Any lack of clarity in the findings that arose as a result of the smallness of the sample could of course have been remedied by running more juries. But we decided not to extend the number of replications because there are weaknesses in the design of the housebreaking experiment relating to the rules of law that have nothing to do with the number of replications. These weaknesses were not imposed by the experiment. They are part of the record of the original trial.

In the first of the two *Durham* trials, in the Washington District Court, when the prosecutor asked the two psychiatrists whether in their opinion the defendant could distinguish right from wrong, the psychiatrists said that they had no opinion on the matter. The questions and answers that followed in the real trial were re-created in our transcript and appear *supra* page 48. When the case was tried a second time under the *Durham* rule, the psychiatrists answered the product question, but equivocally. Their responses appear *supra* page

[2] We did compare the pre-deliberation verdicts split between jurors who were exposed to the *M'Naghten* and *Durham* rules to see if the higher proportion of NGI group verdicts under *M'Naghten* could be explained by an odd distribution of pre-deliberating verdicts. That is, to see if under *Durham*, the initial majority favoring the NGI verdict was so thin that it could not translate itself into the group verdicts, or, if under *M'Naghten* it was so strong that it was able to win every doubtful decision. The distribution in the two versions could not explain the reversal in the proportion of NGI group verdicts between *M'Naghten* and *Durham*. The best explanation is the size of the sample.

49. Thus in neither the *M'Naghten* nor the *Durham* versions of the housebreaking trial was the rule of law clearly tested. It is important to emphasize that this is not an atypical occurrence. In the real world there is frequently a tie-up between instructions and record such that one is affected by the other.

In preparing the recorded version of the housebreaking trial we chose to retain the weaknesses of the original record because we wanted to present as realistic a re-creation of the original trial as possible. But after thirty replications it became apparent that the housebreaking experiment was not as good a vehicle for testing differences in juries' reactions to the *M'Naghten* and *Durham* rules as we had originally expected.

We think that most of the difficulties with the housebreaking experiment were remedied in the incest experiment. It turns out that the incest trial is a much better test case for examining differences in jurors' reactions to variations in legal rules.

Verdicts and the rules of law: The incest case

In the *M'Naghten* version when the psychiatrists were asked the crucial question about the defendant's ability to distinguish right from wrong they answered the question and they answered it in the affirmative. In their opinion the defendant could distinguish right from wrong. The psychiatrists answered yes to the "right from wrong" question after they testified that in their opinion the defendant was mentally ill and after they described some of the manifestations of his illness.

Under *Durham*, when the psychiatrists were asked the crucial question about the relation between the defendant's mental state and his crime, they explained that the criminal act was a product of the defendant's mental condition. In the *uninstructed* version, the psychiatrists were not asked whether the defendant's behavior met or failed to comply with a specific criterion of responsibility.

We see then that in the incest experiment the rules of law introduced a real difference in the trial record. According to the experts, under *M'Naghten* the defendant met the criterion of responsibility; under *Durham* he did not.

But it is exactly this fact, which we have taken to be a strength in the design of the incest experiment, that some may point to as its basic weakness. Ideally, the experiment should have been designed so as to have the psychiatrists respond to the crucial questions concerning responsibility in the same way under both *M'Naghten* and *Durham*. For example, under *M'Naghten* in the model and typical versions, when the prosecutor asks the psychiatrist, "Doctor, from all your examinations of the defendant, would you say that he was able to distinguish right from wrong," in one version the witness should have responded as he did, "Yes, I would say that he could distinguish right from wrong," while in another version he should have responded, "No, I would say that he could *not* distinguish right from wrong."

Then, under *Durham* when the defense attorney asks the psychiatrist, "Now, Doctor, did you come to the conclusion that the offenses which are complained of here were the products of the defendant's disease," in one version the witness should have responded as he did, generally affirming that the defendant's behavior was a result of his illness, and in another version he should have responded in the negative.

Had we carried out this pattern, instead of the three by two factorial design (three rules of law and two versions of psychiatric testimony) we would have had a three by two by two design with a total of twelve cells as compared to six.[3]

But we decided to sacrifice some degree of experimental rigor and precision for the sake of clinical and legal realism. Two factors determined our decision. The first was that in both the jury and the subsequent bench trials, in the original Claison King case, the psychiatrists answered both the

---

[3] Actually we would have had only ten cells because there would have been no additional variation introduced into the *uninstructed* version.

M'Naghten and *Durham* questions in substantially the same way as they did in the edited transcript.[4] Second, when our consulting psychiatrists reviewed the edited transcript they felt that a defendant with Jason Lunt's symptoms would probably be able to distinguish right from wrong. They also believed that his behavior was probably a result of his mental illness. In sum, we chose to adhere to clinical realism at the cost of some weakness in the rigor of our design. In so doing, we recognize that we may have loaded the dice against the defendant under *M'Naghten*. If we have, we played with the same dice one is likely to encounter in an actual defense of insanity trial.

Tables 10 and 11 describe the individual pre-deliberation and group verdicts under the three instruction versions.

TABLE 10. PRE-DELIBERATION VERDICTS BY RULES OF LAW (INCEST)

	Per cent voting NGI
Uninstructed	34(264)
M'Naghten	24(240)
Durham	36(312)

Uninstructed vs. M'Naghten: $X^2_{1d.f.}$ (.99) = 6.6; $X^2 = 8.8$, p. < .01.
Durham v. M'Naghten: $X^2_{1d.f.}$ (.95) = 3.8; $X^2 = 6.0$, p. > .05.

TABLE 11. JURIES' VERDICTS BY RULES OF LAW (INCEST)*

Rules of law	NGI	Hung	Guilty	Total Juries
Uninstructed	4	4	14	22
M'Naghten	0	1	19	20
Durham	5	6	15	26

* Counting the hung juries as half acquittals, M'Naghten vs. Uninstructed, $X^2_{1d.f.}$ (.95) = 3.8; $X^2 = 4.9$; p < .05; M'Naghten vs. Durham, $X^2_{1d.f.}$ (.95) = 3.8; $X^2 = 6.0$; p <.05.

[4] In 1956, the Circuit Court for the District of Columbia held that the "right from wrong" test could be used along with the *Durham* instructions. For further discussion of this point see *infra* page 212 note 20.

In the incest experiment, the pre-deliberation verdicts and the group verdicts were consistent. The proportion of NGI verdicts under *M'Naghten* was significantly lower than under the *Durham* or the *uninstructed* versions.[5]

Jurors who heard the *uninstructed* version behaved very much like the jurors who were exposed to the *Durham* rule. This is a surprising finding. When we talked with experienced lawyers and judges about the rules of thumb jurors were likely to use for assessing responsibility in the absence of instructions, most of them predicted that the jurors would fall back on the "right from wrong" formula. We had expected that verdicts in the *uninstructed* version would be much closer to the verdicts reported by the juries deliberating under *M'Naghten*.

The findings in the incest experiment demonstrate that under the *M'Naghten* rule, jurors are less likely to acquit the defendant on grounds of insanity than they are under *Durham* and the *uninstructed* versions. When jurors are permitted to deliberate in the absence of a court-defined criterion of responsibility, they are more likely to find in favor of the defendant, but no more likely than when they are instructed under the *Durham* formula. Juries' verdicts in the *uninstructed* and *Durham* versions are almost identical. The *Durham* rule produces a powerful difference in jurors' verdicts, but it must be noted that it does not produce a monolithic response. Not all the juries that deliberated under *Durham* found the defendant not guilty by reason of insanity. Indeed most of them found the defendant guilty. Having observed how jurors in the incest trial reacted to the rules of law, it would be interesting to try a variety of crimes and see if the rule differences hold.

Any conclusions about the effects of rules of law on the

---

[5] Even omitting the hung juries completely and just comparing the juries that reached consensus under each instruction version, we still find that *M'Naghten* juries are significantly less likely to decide not guilty by reason of insanity than either the *uninstructed* or the *Durham* juries.

jury should await further analysis. We have yet to examine how each of the rules fares under the two versions of psychiatric testimony. But before comparing verdicts by rules of law and type of expert testimony, there is still another dimension of the impact of the rules of law on the jurors: length of deliberations under the three instruction versions.

Relative length of deliberations by instructions

In the previous section we stated that some legal scholars opposed adoption of the *Durham* rule because they believed it would seriously limit the function of the jury, making it little more than a rubber stamp to the medical experts. We tested this belief empirically by comparing the amount of participation that the jurors engaged in before completing their task under the three instruction forms. If the fears about the influence of the *Durham* rule are valid, juries deliberating under

TABLE 12. MEAN BURSTS OF SPEECH PER JURY
BY RULES OF LAW*

Uninstructed	$496_{(13)}$
M'Naghten	$257_{(12)}$
Durham	$564_{(14)}$

M'Naghten vs. Durham, t = 4.3; p < .001; M'Naghten vs. Uninstructed, t = 3.7; p < .01.

* Once again we needed a statistical test to decide if the differences between the mean bursts of speech under the three different instruction versions were significant or due to chance, i.e., to fluctuations that occur in a particular sample or at a particular time. The "t" test is a statistical test that is used to compare means, rather than per cents. In Table 12 we were interested in testing whether the means are different from one instruction to another. Some fluctuation would be expected by sheer chance. Again we evaluated the magnitude of the differences between the means via probability theory. The smaller the probability the more likely it is that the difference between the three groups is real. Thus when p is less than .05 (and in Table 12 it is much less, i.e., .001) it is probable that real differences exist among the three groups.

Durham should have shorter deliberations. It seems reasonable to assume that the smaller the magnitude of the task, the less time it would take to complete.

Table 12 compares the lengths of the juries' deliberations under the three instruction versions.[6] Juries deliberated significantly longer under *Durham* than they did under *M'Naghten*. They also deliberated longer under the *uninstructed* version than they did under *M'Naghten*.[7]

But these differences that seem to be caused by rules of law could in fact have been caused by the differences in outcome of the verdicts. Table 13 compares the relative lengths of deliberations by verdicts and rules of law.

TABLE 13. MEAN BURSTS OF SPEECH PER JURY BY RULES OF LAW AND JURY VERDICTS

	Uninstructed	*M'Naghten*	*Durham*
NGI	$410_{(4)}$	—	$565_{(5)}$
Guilty	$470_{(7)}$	$239_{(11)}$	$486_{(6)}$
Hung	$768_{(2)}$	$454_{(1)}$	$721_{(3)}$

Separating juries by verdicts did not change the rankings reported above. In each instruction version, hung juries deliberated longer than juries that reached consensus; and juries that found the defendant not guilty by reason of insanity deliberated longer than juries that found the defendant guilty.

[6] These data on the relative lengths of the deliberations are based only on the incest case. The 68 deliberations were divided according to the three instruction versions. Deliberations were randomly selected from each category giving a total of 39 protocols. The 39 deliberations were analyzed for their content and interaction.

[7] If, instead of comparing the average number of bursts per jury, we compare the average number of pages, the order is still the same, although the difference is not as great:

Version	Mean number of pages in transcription
Uninstructed	43
M'Naghten	26
Durham	45

But in each group the deliberation under *Durham* is considered longer than under *M'Naghten*. Again we are struck by the similarity of responses between *Durham* and *uninstructed* juries.

The finding that hung juries deliberated longer than juries that reached consensus is another confirmation of the realism of the experimental juries. We might note in passing that in real cases, hung juries deliberate longer because the participants have a sincere desire to reach consensus and to save the county or the state the expense of trying the defendant a second time. The feeling that a hung jury is a waste of the taxpayers' money carries over into the experimental juries.

The data consistently indicate that deliberating under the *Durham* rule does not interfere with — but if anything increases — the involvement of the jury. Rather than lessen its responsibility, as many lawyers feared, the *Durham* rule causes the jury to assume greater responsibility.

In his article "The Distinction of Being Mad," Edward de Grazia, a Washington lawyer, made this point:

> . . . *Durham's* greatest impact upon future determinations of criminal responsibility may well be in the radical change demanded of the trial judge in his critical words to the jury.
>
> In the end, the *Durham* court looked to the much-abused, but indestructible jury to sift all the evidence on "mental disease" through "our inherited ideas of moral responsibility."

This reaffirmance by the *Durham* court of the importance of the jury in determinations of insanity in criminal cases holds further significance. By common law, the question of insanity originally was held to be a question of *fact* for the jury to decide. The *M'Naghten* rule erred by injecting into the jury's arena of deliberation a legal test which colored the evidence and disturbed the requisite judgement of fact. The error was for the court to instruct the jury on an issue of fact as if it were an issue of law. The jury was led to believe (for the court so instructed) that in order to acquit it had to decide that the defendant did not know the difference between right and wrong (a legal conundrum) rather than that the defendant was insane (as a matter of fact) . . . Thus the real vice of the *M'Naghten* rule was that it allowed the court to impede the jury in its determination of responsibility — allowed the court to intrude, if not actually usurp, the jury's rightful province.[8]

De Grazia concludes by noting that although it was not the primary purpose of *Durham*, the decision may have the effect of restoring to the jury its "rightfully predominant role" of determining who should and who should not be relieved of criminal responsibility.

In Chapter 9 we discuss jurors' reactions to the rules of law again by comparing which rules they are most likely to recommend that the courts use in the future. In the same chapter we also review jurors' reactions to the rules of law by comparing their responses to a series of items measuring satisfaction and preferences for a judge or a jury trial.

[8] De Grazia, The Distinction of Being Mad, 22 U. of Chi. L. Rev. 345-346 (1955).

CHAPTER 4

The Jury's Assessment of the Psychiatric Testimony

The last chapter dealt with what is generally for the lawyer the heart of the matter: the formal legal rules defining insanity. This chapter turns to what many psychiatrists think is the more relevant variable: the quality of psychiatric testimony. We are turning, therefore, from the question of what difference the rules of law make to the question of what difference the psychiatric experts make.

It will be recalled that a prominent feature of the design in the incest case concerned variations in psychiatric testimony, and it is arguable that the test of the rules of law begun in the last chapter will not be completed until we have examined their interaction with the psychiatric testimony. Accordingly, the principal business of this chapter is to report the results of the jury's reactions when both psychiatric testimony and rules of law were varied.

Two points about the design need to be re-emphasized. First, we have the variation in psychiatric testimony only for the incest case and not for the housebreaking case. Second, the point of the variation was to improve the quality of the testimony, at least as the psychiatrist sees it, so as to enhance its communicability to the jury.

Before reporting the results, a brief review of the role of the psychiatrist as an expert witness and the problems associated with that role are in order.

The psychiatrist as a witness

The practice of the courts of calling in experts to advise them on matters not generally known to the average person has been followed, certainly in English courts, for well over four centuries. Initially the experts were used as technical assistants to the court, rather than as witnesses. The judge summoned experts to inform him about technical matters; he then determined whether or not the information should be passed on to the jury. By the middle of the seventeenth century, when the finding of the facts had become the exclusive province of the jury, the practice of court-appointed experts reporting to the judge was abandoned; instead the experts were called as witnesses by the parties involved in the dispute.

The procedure commonly used today, focusing narrowly on criminal cases involving the defense of insanity, is for the defense to call one or more experts to testify as to the mental state of the defendant at the time of the crime. The state may or may not summon experts of its own. It is likely that the psychiatrist will have seen, but not necessarily examined, the patient before his appearance in the courtroom.

The law appears to have elaborate qualifications for experts, but in practice the accreditation of certain witnesses as experts is often carried out in a relatively casual manner. A witness is permitted to qualify as an expert if it can be shown to the court's satisfaction that he has knowledge and experience beyond the sphere of knowledge of the average layman. The practice of the courts has been to permit almost any person holding the degree of doctor of medicine to testify on any specialty, psychiatric or otherwise, in the field of medicine.

There is always something of a mystery about the distinctions between expert and lay testimony. An important formal difference between them is that the expert is allowed to give his opinion. The testimony of the ordinary witness is restricted to the recounting of facts. Theoretically, according to

Guttmacher and Weihofen, the basis for the distinction is the following.

> The expert is permitted to state his opinion in order to give the jury (or the judge, where he is trying the case without a jury) the benefit of his skill and experience in drawing the proper conclusions on matters about which the layman has insufficient knowledge to form a sound conclusion. On most facts presented in a lawsuit, the necessary inferences can be drawn by jurors whose only qualifications are that they are good men and true, but some matters call for special and peculiar experience in evaluating the significance of the evidence and in making the proper inferences.[1]

In criminal cases involving a plea of insanity, the major function of the medical expert is to offer technical testimony about the defendant's mental condition: whether in his opinion the defendant was "sane" or "insane" at the time of the crime. But the expert is not expected to render a decision on the issue of responsibility, because it is a legal matter to be determined by the jury in accordance with the rules of law. In the eyes of the law the universe of people who are mentally ill is larger than the universe of people who are mentally ill and not responsible. The law protects the distinction between persons who are mentally ill and persons who are not responsible by instructing the jurors that it is their duty to determine whether the defendant was of sound or unsound mind at the time of the crime and if the unsoundness was of a kind and a degree as to cause lack of responsibility in the eyes of the law.

The problem of differentiating the jury's task from that of the expert witness is particularly acute in a defense of insanity trial because on first glance it looks as if the expert is expected to decide the same issue that the jury has been instructed it must resolve. In addition to describing the defendant's mental condition, the expert is usually asked for his opinion under the same criterion of responsibility that the jury will use in deciding the case. Under *M'Naghten* the expert

---

[1] Guttmacher and Weihofen, Psychiatry and the Law 207 (1952).

is asked if the defendant could distinguish between right and wrong, and under *Durham* if the crime was the product of a mental disease.

The following is a representative instruction by the court to the jury on how the jury should treat expert testimony.[2]

> The important point of all this discussion of expert witnesses and opinion testimony is that you are not bound as jurors to accept the testimony of expert witnesses. You should certainly consider carefully the qualifications of the witnesses, their experiences, their observations of the defendant, their opportunity to observe, and all of the factors that they told you about in their lengthy testimony today. Then you are to give to their testimony as experts such weight as in your judgment it is fairly entitled to receive with full recognition of the fact that while you shouldn't arbitrarily disregard the testimony of any witness, yet, if you are satisfied that you don't accept the testimony of the expert witnesses you are not bound to do so.

One legal practice that is a great source of irritation to the psychiatrist is the lawyer's habit of asking him to respond to hypothetical questions in which the lawyer describes situations the expert believes has no bearing on the particular proceedings, or that illustrate points contradictory to the specific case. The psychiatrist claims that when he attempts to present a detailed report of the symptoms of the defendant who is actually on trial, it is objected to as irrelevant. In fact the expert may not refer to opinions or reports of other experts who have specialties complementing his own. For instance, a report by a biochemist that was helpful to the doctor in formulating his opinion on the case at hand may not be cited, but the witness may be asked for his opinion on matters unrelated either to his own area of expertise or to the nature of the case.

The adversary system is particularly upsetting to the psychiatrist. Dr. Philip Q. Roche, former president of the American Psychiatric Association and author of *The Criminal Mind*, has written: "As a man of science in search of truth, the psychiatrist has no place in the courtroom. The function of a

[2] It is the instruction used in the incest case.

criminal trial is to dramatize and publicly pronounce adherence to the existent values and prevailing ethical system of the society." [3] The courtroom resembles neither the examining room nor the laboratory. "A trial is not a scientific investigation, it is not a search for objective truth. The doctor who undertakes to go into court and testify as an expert witness must bear in mind that he is stepping squarely into the middle of a fight." [4]

In his relations with the public, the medical expert rarely hears his authority or his technical skill questioned. More specifically, in the patient-doctor relationship the doctor is expected to assume responsibility for the protection of his patients as well as for his own professional reputation. Many doctors claim that the system of partisan expert testimony produces such tension between their usual role expectations and those expected of them in court that they seek to avoid all courtroom appearances. "By our system of partisan expert witnesses we have alienated and deprived ourselves of the services of the best; and accepted, and at the same time criticized and have been shocked by the performances of the worst." [5]

Dr. Guttmacher, in his most recent book, *The Mind of the Murderer*, stated:

> More than ten per cent of psychiatrists refuse all courtroom employment and another twenty per cent refuse employment as partisan experts. They are only willing to testify when cast in the role of neutral advisors to the court. One can, of course, simply assert that that still leaves seventy per cent of the nation's psychiatrists to draw upon and that that is more than enough. The truth of the matter is that in this dissent there are to be found most of the leaders of American psychiatry. [6]

[3] Roche, The Criminal Mind 271 (1960). Dr. Roche was a recipient of the Isaac Ray Award in 1957.

[4] Guttmacher and Weihofen, Psychiatry and the Law, 205 (1952).

[5] Niles, Impartial Medical Testimony, 45 Ill. B.J. 282 (1957).

[6] Guttmacher, The Mind of the Murderer 119 (1959). Dr. Guttmacher was a recipient of the Isaac Ray Award in 1958.

But the adversary quality of the proceedings protects the jury's role because it leaves the jury in the position of choosing. The fact that psychiatrists sometimes disagree indicates that expert consensus does not always exist on the issues in question. It should be noted, however, that when there is disagreement between experts it is usually not on the technical medical issues but on the special questions that the law puts to them.

The adversary system is the lawyer's great institution and invention. He has profound distrust for anything that cannot be exposed to adversary scrutiny. The lawyer wants to expose the psychiatrist's testimony to the adversary system because he is fearful lest the psychiatrist's views of human nature and his beliefs concerning the genesis of deviant or criminal behavior be too far removed from the legal orientation and tradition.

Lawyers often have been dismayed by the open conflicts in the courtroom between proponents of "different schools of psychiatry." In major criminal trials heated intra-professional controversies between psychiatrists called by the opposing sides have occurred quite regularly.[7]

Lawyers also fear that unless the function of the expert is carefully delineated, the combined effects of his general prestige and his detailed technical knowledge can virtually dictate to the jury the outcome of the case. But, while lawyers may fear the potential influence of the psychiatrist, they are also somewhat skeptical of the "scientificness" of the discipline he represents. For many members of the bar, the problem remains one of control of power, even when it is in the hands

[7] At the present time at least twenty states have statutes which authorize the court to appoint experts. The same provision is also found in the Federal Rules of Criminal Procedure. As the practice of court-appointed experts becomes more general, perhaps one of the sources of difficulty, that of partisanship among the experts, will be substantially reduced. For a discussion of this see Guttmacher and Weihofen, *supra* note 1. There is a move toward impartial medical testimony in personal injury cases. See Zeisel, Kalven, Buchholz, Delay in the Court, c. 11 (1959).

of a benevolent holder.   Many lawyers want to have the expert available when needed, but clearly as a witness whose credibility is subjected to the usual scrutiny of the jury.

Verdicts, psychiatric testimony, and rules of law

Of the 68 juries who heard the incest trial, 33 were exposed to the model version and 35 to the typical version.   Tables 14 and 15 describe the jurors' pre-deliberation verdicts and the group verdict under the two versions of psychiatric testimony and the three rules of law.

TABLE 14.   PRE-DELIBERATION VERDICTS BY
PSYCHIATRIC TESTIMONY AND RULE OF LAW
(Per cent finding NGI)

	Uninstructed	*M'Naghten*	*Durham*
Model testimony	36%(264)	26%(240)	35%(312)
Typical testimony	33%	22%	37%

TABLE 15.   DISTRIBUTION OF JURIES' VERDICTS BY
PSYCHIATRIC TESTIMONY AND RULE OF LAW

	Uninstructed			*M'Naghten*			*Durham*		
	NGI	Hung	Guilty	NGI	Hung	Guilty	NGI	Hung	Guilty
Model testimony	2	2	7	—	—	9	2	4	7
Typical testimony	2	2	7	—	1	10	3	2	8

We had two expectations concerning the effects of the psychiatric testimony on the juries' verdicts.   We thought that the model version would result in a greater proportion of NGI verdicts and that the *Durham* rule in contrast to the *M'Naghten* rule would have a greater impact on the jury under the model version.   It is immediately apparent that both expectations were not realized.   The faint suggestion that the model testimony increases the number of NGI verdicts as shown by the *uninstructed* and *M'Naghten* versions disappears when we note the opposite effect for the *Durham* version.   In any case, given such small differences we must conclude that our effort to vary psychiatric testimony had no impact on the jury.

It remains possible that a more dramatic variation in psychiatric testimony might have an effect on the jury. It must be remembered, however, that the particular variation we introduced was drafted with highly expert advice. It represents, therefore, a measure of difference in psychiatric testimony which the psychiatrists themselves thought to be interesting to test. And equally important, it represents the maximum improvement in quality of testimony which they thought was likely to occur in the actual administration of the criminal law.[8]

We can add one postscript to this discussion. The jurors were asked a number of questions about the psychiatric testimony on the post-deliberation questionnaire. Table 16 describes their responses.

TABLE 16. JURORS' APPRAISALS OF PSYCHIATRIC TESTIMONY

Questions on post-deliberation questionnaire	Model testimony	Typical testimony	Combined
1. Did you believe that the language the experts used in testifying was too technical? *Answering No:*	81%	74%	77% (808)*
2. Did you want more information from the experts? *Answering No:*	64%	69%	67% (816)
3. Did you find helpful the testimony of the two psychiatrists called by the defense? *Answering Yes:*	74%	73%	73% (816)

* Eight jurors did not answer the question.

[8] Another explanation is theoretically possible: the changes in expert testimony may not have been made along the correct axis. Perhaps, if in one version we had the psychiatrists' comment extensively on specific aspects of the defendant's behavior at the time of the crime and in the other dwell primarily on the defendant's background and childhood, these variations would have resulted in significantly different

We see that the responses of at least two thirds of the jurors indicated that they were favorably impressed with the psychiatrists' testimony. Seventy-three per cent felt that it was helpful, 67 per cent did not want more information and 77 per cent did not believe the language the psychiatrists used was too technical. Exposure to the model and typical versions failed to produce significant differences in jurors' reactions on any of the dimensions tested.

We look finally at one more way of assessing the importance to the jury of the expert's testimony. We compare the jurors' responses to an item that appeared on the post-deliberation questionnaire in both the incest and the housebreaking experiments.

Jurors' choices between psychiatrists and jurors as decision makers

A pivotal point of controversy about psychiatric testimony is the fear that the psychiatrist's prestige would cause jurors to lose faith in their role in the proceedings. We asked the jurors:

> Which do you believe is the best way of deciding what should be done with a person who has committed a crime and pleads that he is insane?
> — He should be tried before a jury just like anyone else.
> — He should be tried before a judge.
> — He should be turned over by the court to a group of psychiatrists and they should determine what is to be done with him.

Table 17 describes the percentage of jurors who favored decision by psychiatrists.[9]

---

reactions. The changes that were made in the psychiatric testimony were introduced on the advice of medical experts with extensive courtroom experience. But it is clear that in this particular case the changes were not crucial, at least not to the audience for which they were intended.

[9] Less than 7 per cent of all the jurors in both trials chose a judge. The major comparison, then, is between the jury and the medical experts.

TABLE 17. PER CENT OF JURORS FAVORING DECISION
BY PSYCHIATRISTS

Housebreaking trial	$66_{(360)}$
Incest trial	$33_{(816)}$

( ) = Number of Jurors

These percentages of 66 for the housebreaking trial and 33 for the incest trial suggest that jurors would be more willing to delegate responsibility to medical experts when the case involves a relatively minor crime and/or when the defendant is psychotic or patently insane.

The data in Table 18 show that jurors who voted for acquittal on grounds of insanity on the pre-deliberation questionnaire favored decision by psychiatrists more heavily.

TABLE 18. PER CENT OF JURORS FAVORING
DECISION BY PSYCHIATRISTS BY VERDICT

	NGI	Guilty
Housebreaking trial*	$71_{(238)}$	$65_{(122)}$
Incest trial†	$41_{(269)}$	$30_{(547)}$

* $X^2_{1d.f.}$ (.95) = 3.8; X^2 = 6.4; p < .05.
† $X^2_{1d.f.}$ (.99) = 6.6; X^2 = 9.2; p < .01.

But as Table 19 shows, jurors who heard the model version were no more likely to favor decisions by psychiatrists than jurors who were exposed to the typical version.

TABLE 19. PER CENT OF JURORS FAVORING DECISION BY
PSYCHIATRISTS BY VERSION OF EXPERT TESTIMONY

Model testimony	$32_{(396)}$
Typical testimony	$30_{(420)}$

( ) = Number of Jurors

Once more the difference between model and typical psychiatric testimony fails to discriminate.

The proportion of jurors favoring the psychiatrists failed to vary with the three sets of instructions.

TABLE 20. PER CENT OF JURORS FAVORING PSYCHIATRISTS
BY TRIAL AND RULES OF LAW

	Uninstructed	M'Naghten	Durham
Housebreaking trial	$70_{(120)}$	$68_{(120)}$	$63_{(120)}$
Incest trial	$33_{(264)}$	$33_{(240)}$	$33_{(312)}$

Table 21 offers a last refinement of the data showing that
among jurors who heard the *uninstructed* and *M'Naghten*
versions there were no significant differences in the proportion favoring the psychiatrists between those who voted for acquittal on grounds of insanity and those who found guilty.

TABLE 21. PER CENT OF JURORS FAVORING DECISION BY
PSYCHIATRIST BY VERDICT AND RULE OF LAW

	NGI	Guilty
Uninstructed		
Housebreaking	$70_{(91)}$	$71_{(29)}$
Incest	$39_{(90)}$	$30_{(174)}$
M'Naghten		
Housebreaking	$70_{(68)}$	$65_{(52)}$
Incest	$29_{(58)}$	$34_{(182)}$
Durham		
Housebreaking*	$70_{(78)}$	$37_{(42)}$
Incest†	$46_{(112)}$	$24_{(200)}$

* NGI-Guilty: $X^2_{1d.f.}$ (.999) = 10.8; X^2 = 11.2; p <.001.
† NGI-Guilty: $X^2_{1d.f.}$ (.999) = 10.8; X^2 = 13.0; p < .001.

But under *Durham,* jurors who favored acquittal on grounds
of insanity were much *more* likely to support decisions by
psychiatrists, and jurors who found guilty were much *less*
willing to support decisions by psychiatrists than jurors who
were exposed to the *M'Naghten* and *uninstructed* versions.
On this issue of the jurors' preference for a decision by a lay
group or a body of experts, the *Durham* rule polarized jurors'
reactions more than the *M'Naghten* rule or the *uninstructed*
version.

We remember that it was only in the *Durham* version of both trials that the jurors had an opportunity to hear the experts make a judgment on an issue that the law considers crucial: that there was a relationship between the defendant's mental condition and the criterion of responsibility. Jurors who agreed with the psychiatrists — that is, jurors who believed the defendants were insane — were more willing to support a recommendation for a shift in responsibility, so that experts rather than laymen become the final arbitrators. But jurors who found the defendants guilty under *Durham* did so in direct contradiction to the experts' opinions. It is understandable that these jurors would be less enthusiastic about supporting a policy recommendation that would enhance the psychiatrists' influence over the final outcome.

The jurors' responses to the question concerning who should make the final decision in defense of insanity trials tells us something about how the jurors perceive the division of labor between themselves and the psychiatrists. The jurors are much more concerned about exercising their responsibility when a defendant has committed a heinous crime and is not patently insane than they are when the defendant has committed a relatively mild offense and is patently insane. In Chapter 8, which is devoted to the deliberations, there is a section on the jurors' reactions to the psychiatric testimony that deals primarily with the issue of the division of labor between the jury and the expert witness. From that discussion it is clear that the jury recognizes the importance of the information that the psychiatrists supply, but it is equally clear that the jury is not willing to relinquish its responsibility for deciding the case to the psychiatrist.

CHAPTER 5

The Jury's Response to the Commitment Instruction

In this chapter we examine the last of the experimental variables by testing the jury's concern with the consequence of an NGI verdict.

In ordinary criminal trials, the consequences of the jury's choice are relatively clear. It may find the defendant guilty of the crime for which he is charged, or in some cases of a lesser offense. Or the jury may acquit. If it does the former, the defendant may be fined, imprisoned, or even subjected to the death penalty. If it does the latter, the defendant will go free. There is little question that in most cases the jury understands the practical implications of its choice.

But there is a good deal of question as to how the jury sees its choice in criminal cases involving a defense of insanity. Even though the disposition of the defendant is theoretically no concern of the jury, there is a suspicion often voiced by the bench and bar that this question becomes a practical concern in the jury's deliberation. The jury probably assumes that in an insanity case a defendant found guilty receives the same treatment as in any other criminal case. The problem is: What does the jury assume about the defendant's future if it should find him not guilty by reason of insanity?

In most states and federal jurisdictions, a person who is acquitted on grounds of insanity will be confined to a mental institution until he recovers or is restored to sanity, and in many jurisdictions commitment is automatic.[1] According to Glueck, the rationale for automatic commitment was given in *Ragsdale v. Overholser* as follows:

> The Automatic Commitment procedure does not offend due process because of the reasonableness of the assumption that mental illness will not cure itself in a relatively short time and because of the danger involved in letting mentally abnormal persons who have demonstrated antisocial tendencies to be freed at once upon acquittal.[2]

Some states have an automatic commitment procedure, but the jury is not informed of it before it begins to deliberate. It is noteworthy that one year after establishing the *Durham* rule, the District of Columbia thought the jury's doubts about what happens to a defendant after a successful plea of insanity raised an important policy question. Accordingly, it adopted a rule that made it mandatory to instruct the jury that the consequence of an NGI verdict would be the automatic commitment of the defendant.[3]

The instruction has been highly praised. In an article in the *Yale Law Journal*, Abe Krash, a member of the District of Columbia bar, described the feelings of the bar when he wrote, "This instruction may have an enormous influence on the jury's deliberations, and it is clearly one of the most important developments in this field since *Durham* itself."[4] Krash continued:

> The consequences of a verdict of not guilty by reason of insanity are not commonly understood. The jury does not usu-

[1] Three require an independent jury trial to determine continuance of mental illness after the defendant has been acquitted on grounds of insanity. Eight states require the jury that acquits to indicate whether the defendant is still insane or has recovered. In the latter event, he is entitled to unconditional discharge. See Glueck, Law and Psychiatry 121-126 (1962).

[2] Id. at 120 n.55, discussing Ragsdale v. Overholser 281 F.2d 943 (1960).

[3] Tayler v. United States, 222 F.2d 398, 404 (D.C. Cir. 1955).

[4] Krash, The Durham Rule and Judicial Administration in the District of Columbia, 70 Yale L.J. 905, 937 (1961).

ally know that a defendant who is acquitted on insanity grounds will be confined in a mental institution. In the absence of this knowledge, "a jury, influenced by the spector of violent lunatics turned loose in the community, may convict despite strong evidence in insanity at the time of the crime." [5]

We have before us a question of practical concern to the administration of criminal law. Will the jury's verdict in an insanity case be affected by disclosure to the jury of information about commitment procedures? Since, as will be recalled, half of the juries in the housebreaking case received the commitment instruction, while the other half received no instructions on this point, we turn directly to the experimental results.[6]

Tables 22 and 23 describe the individual pre-deliberation and the group verdicts by the presence and absence of commitment information.

TABLE 22.   JURORS' PRE-DELIBERATION VERDICTS
BY COMMITMENT INSTRUCTION

Commitment instruction	In Per Cent		Total
	NGI	Guilty	
Given	67	33	100 (180)
Not given	65	35	100 (180)

TABLE 23.   JURIES' VERDICTS BY COMMITMENT INSTRUCTION

Commitment instruction	NGI	Hung	Guilty	Total
Given	9	4	2	15
Not given	8	4	3	15

The results are conclusive. The presence or absence of commitment information had no noticeable effect on the individ-

[5] Id. at 937. The quotes within the article are from the dissenting opinion in Tatum v. United States, 249 F.2d 129, 356 U.S. 943 (1948).
[6] In the incest case, all juries were informed at the end of the trial that the defendant would be committed to a mental institution if he was found not guilty by reason of insanity.

uals' or the juries' verdicts. The absence of information did not increase, to any significant extent, the likelihood that a jury would find the defendant guilty; nor did the presence of information enhance the likelihood that the jury would acquit the defendant on grounds of insanity. We can only conclude from the data that information as to disposition of the defendant is *not* a crucial consideration in the jury's decision. The results, however, are surprising and sharply contrary to the expectations of the bench and bar.

There is also some puzzle as to how to interpret the lack of differences between the two treatments. Perhaps the jury is after all not concerned with the defendant's disposition. Or perhaps the jury somehow determines by itself, in the absence of specific information, that the court will provide for some period of commitment before it allows the defendant to go free.

We have evidence bearing on both hypotheses. First, there are data from the deliberations which are relevant to whether the jury is concerned about the disposition of the defendant. Discussion of this topic is in Chapter 8. Second, there are data bearing directly on the jurors' expectations about commitment. In the housebreaking trial, the jurors were asked: "In a criminal case like this one, what do you think happens to the defendant when the jury returns a verdict of not guilty by reason of insanity?" The alternatives were:

☐ He is put in a mental institution for a period of time set by the court.
☐ He is put in a mental institution until, in the opinion of the psychiatrists, he is cured.
☐ He is put in prison.
☐ He is placed on probation.
☐ He is set free.

This question was put to all jurors, those who were given the commitment instruction and those who were not. Ideally, all jurors who were exposed to the commitment instruction version should have checked "He is put in a mental institution until, in the opinion of the psychiatrists, he is cured." We would expect a difference in responses to this question depending on the commitment instruction jurors received.

TABLE 24. JURORS' EXPECTATIONS ABOUT THE COURT'S DISPOSITION OF THE DEFENDANT BY COMMITMENT INSTRUCTION

IN PER CENT

Commitment instruction	Mental institution*	Prison	Probation or free	Combined
Given	$93_{(167)}$	$3_{(6)}$	$4_{(7)}$	$100_{(180)}$
Not given	$91_{(163)}$	$3_{(6)}$	$6_{(11)}$	$100_{(180)}$

* Of those respondents who checked "mental institution," 20 per cent (in both treatments) indicated that they believed the length of time defendant remained in the institution was designated by the court. The remaining 71 or 73 per cent of the jurors indicated that they believed the defendant "is put in a mental institution until, in the opinion of the psychiatrists, he is cured."

But Table 24 shows that 93 per cent of the jurors who received the commitment information checked the correct answer, and 91 per cent who did *not* receive the information also checked the "commitment to mental institution" alternative. Thus any mystery about the information in Tables 22 and 23 is solved. Jurors who did not receive the commitment instruction assumed correctly that the defendant would be committed. The data also afford a sidelight on the more general question of the extent to which jurors absorb instruction. The point concerns the jurors who were given the commitment instruction. Even though they were told that the defendant in case of an NGI verdict would go to a mental institution, $(3 + 4 =) 7$ per cent gave the wrong answer.

We got one final insight into the jurors' feelings about disposition of the defendant by asking: "If it were strictly up to you, what would you do with the defendant, Martin Graham?" The jurors were provided with a comparable set of alternatives: commitment to a mental institution, prison, probation, set free.

TABLE 25. JURORS' RECOMMENDATIONS AS TO THE
DISPOSITION OF THE DEFENDANT BY COMMITMENT
INSTRUCTION

		IN PER CENT		
Commitment instruction	Mental institution*	Prison†	Probation or free	Combined
Given	77(140)	19(33)	4(7)	100(180)
Not given	84(151)	15(27)	1(2)	100(180)

* The jurors could have checked "mental institution for life" or made defendant's release dependent on the psychiatrists' diagnosis. Less than 10 per cent thought defendant ought to be incarcerated for life.

† Jurors who checked "prison" also indicated the number of years. Less than 10 per cent thought defendant ought to be incarcerated for more than five years.

These percentages reflect the jurors' own preferences; they are not a reflection of the instructions they heard. Over 75 per cent of all jurors, those who received the commitment instructions and those who did not, favored the mental institution.[7]

Finally, we compared jurors' preferences with their verdicts.

It comes as no surprise that all the jurors who found the defendant not guilty by reason of insanity in both versions recommended commitment to a mental institution. What is surprising, however, is that about half the jurors who found him guilty, in both versions, also favored commitment to a mental institution over imprisonment.

[7] Some might argue that the housebreaking case is a poor test of the value of the commitment instruction since housebreaking is not particularly dangerous behavior, and therefore jurors will be less concerned about removing the defendant from society. We note, however, that even in the absence of a heinous crime over 90 per cent of the jurors expect the defendant to be committed and over 75 per cent believe that he should be committed. We conclude that the jury would favor committing any defendant whom it finds not guilty by reason of insanity no matter what the nature of the crime. In this sense, the housebreaking case provided a good test of the value of the commitment instruction because it demonstrates the jury's support of it even for a relatively mild crime.

TABLE 26. JURORS' RECOMMENDATIONS BY VERDICTS*

Commitment instruction	NGI Mental institution *(in per cent)*	Prison	Guilty Mental institution *(in per cent)*	Prison
Given	100	0	39	61
Not given	100	0	52	48
Combined	100 (237)	0 (0)	46 (53)	54 (61)

* The 9 jurors who would have placed the defendant on probation or allowed him to go free are not included.

The almost even division among the jurors who favored a verdict of guilty between imprisonment and commitment to a mental institution is an important point. It indicates that there are jurors who favor "treatment" for persons whom they believe are "responsible" within the formal requirement of the law. In Chapter 8, we quote a complaint repeated frequently in the jury room. It is a desire to find the defendant guilty, but in need of medical treatment; or as some jurors suggest, guilty but insane.[8]

In conclusion, we note that the jury's common sense is better than the law in some jurisdictions. In the absence of a mandatory automatic commitment instruction, the jury decided that anyone who commits a crime and is found not guilty by reason of insanity should not be unconditionally released. While the data show that a commitment instruction is not specifically needed, we do not offer these results as policy advice. Rather, we think it would be a useful precaution to include such an instruction under all circumstances and not leave it to the common sense of the jury. On occasion it can do some good and it can never do any harm.

[8] This is an interesting phenomenon which we pick up later in Chapter 8.

PART III

The Influence of Social Status and Attitudes on the Jury's Decisions

CHAPTER 6

Social Status Differences
Among Jurors

One way of approaching the materials in this chapter is to treat them as a second experiment. In the first experiment, described in Part II, we varied the trial record and the amount of information that was available to the jurors. In this part we hold the trial record constant and systematically vary the subjects who are exposed to it.

The theme of this chapter provides an unusual blend of two kinds of interests. It brings together the practical interests of the professional bar and the theoretical concerns of behavioral scientists. Lawyers are interested in socio-economic status as a practical matter. They have accumulated a good deal of lore about the qualities and characteristics of different types of jurors from their courtroom experiences. Before each trial they have the opportunity to select and challenge jurors and it is important that they be able to identify persons who are likely to be sympathetic to their side. Selecting a jury with the right combination of social characteristics, they believe, can mean the difference between winning and losing a case. Behavioral scientists are interested in the problem because the jury offers an excellent forum for testing the influence of social status on attitudes and decisions. Jurors are selected from almost all layers of society and represent a great diversity of social and cultural backgrounds.

The first section of this chapter discusses the theoretical

concerns of the behavioral scientists; the second section reviews the professional lore which the bar has accumulated about juror selection. In the third section, the findings are reported.

The theory

In every complex society there is some system of stratification which locates its members along a hierarchy that measures power and prestige. In most modern industrial societies stratification is closely related to the division of labor. A person's position in the occupational sphere affects his power, prestige, style of life, and general values. A central theme in public opinion and attitude research is that persons of different social statuses will respond differently to a great variety of public and private issues.[1]

The theory is that even in a society such as ours, with its relatively fluid class system and its considerable opportunities for movement, the beliefs, attitudes, and values that persons hold are not homogeneous throughout; nor are they randomly distributed across age, sex, class, religious, or ethnic lines. The positions that persons occupy, either as a result of ascriptive qualities such as sex or of achievements such as education and occupation, will influence, and on some issues even dictate, the values and beliefs that they express.

We can illustrate the interrelationship of status components with several examples from our juror population. For the first example we use two status components to predict a third. The respondents in Table 27 are male jurors who participated

---

[1] See, for example, Berelson, Lazarsfeld, and McPhee, Voting: A Study of Opinion Formation in a Presidential Election (1954); Stouffer, Communism, Conformity, and Civil Liberties (1955); Sears, Maccoby, and Levin, Patterns of Child Rearing (1957); Hollingshead and Redlich, Social Class and Mental Illness (1958); Jones, Life, Liberty and Property (1941); Kinsey, Pomeroy, and Martin, Sexual Behavior in the Human Male (1948); Niebuhr, The Social Sources of Denominationalism (1954).

in the experimental civil or criminal juries. We classified them by occupation and education and compared median incomes in these different categories.

TABLE 27. MEDIAN MONTHLY INCOME BY EDUCATION AND OCCUPATION

	Grade school	1-2 years high school	3-4 years high school	College	Combined
Proprietor	$543_{(49)}$	$486_{(61)}$	$533_{(94)}$	$712_{(287)}$	$633_{(491)}$
Clerical worker	$393_{(39)}$	$411_{(62)}$	$440_{(124)}$	$428_{(157)}$	$426_{(382)}$
Skilled laborer	$417_{(128)}$	$474_{(108)}$	$462_{(136)}$	$469_{(95)}$	$454_{(467)}$
Labor	$377_{(208)}$	$388_{(111)}$	$402_{(136)}$	$380_{(39)}$	$386_{(494)}$
Combined	$410_{(424)}$	$437_{(342)}$	$454_{(490)}$	$573_{(578)}$	$478_{(1834)}$

Looking first at the last column, we find, as one might expect, that average income decreases as one moves down the ladder from proprietors ($633) to unskilled laborers ($386). Moving across the bottom row we see that education also is related to income, although less so than the job a man holds. If we follow all the columns down, and all the rows across, we note that the relationship between education and income exists primarily for proprietors, but the occupation-income relationship holds true for all educational levels.

Finally, if we turn from the income figures to the number of jurors in each group, we note that in the top two rows the number of people in each cell grows as we move to the right, but in the bottom two rows this pattern does not continue. That is, persons holding white-collar jobs are more likely to have a college education, and persons in blue-collar jobs are more likely to have a grade school or high school education. Thus, the table shows that a population can be distributed along several dimensions such as education, occupation, and income, and that the interrelationships among the dimensions are not random. They can on occasion allow a real insight into the structure of society.

In a second illustration we take this type of analysis one step further. We ask how socio-economic characteristics are related to voting preferences. In Table 28 the respondents are male jurors who participated in the experimental *civil* trials.

TABLE 28. PER CENT PREFERRING DEMOCRATIC PARTY BY OCCUPATION AND EDUCATION*

	Grade school	High school	College	Combined
Proprietor	$58_{(12)}$	$51_{(39)}$	$34_{(82)}$	$39_{(133)}$
Clerical worker	$74_{(15)}$	$67_{(82)}$	$54_{(61)}$	$63_{(158)}$
Skilled laborer	$77_{(47)}$	$76_{(86)}$	$73_{(12)}$	$76_{(145)}$
Laborer	$78_{(84)}$	$81_{(107)}$	$58_{(38)}$	$76_{(229)}$
Combined	$75_{(158)}$	$72_{(314)}$	$48_{(193)}$	$66_{(665)}$

* The question on which these data are based is: "I generally consider myself to be: — Republican; — Democrat; — Third Party Supporter; Which? ——————— "

As the figure in the lower right-hand corner indicates, 66 per cent of all jurors preferred the Democratic Party. But among proprietors the figure reaches only 39 per cent in contrast to 76 per cent among the skilled and unskilled laborers. Note that the greatest difference in political preference occurred between proprietors with a college education and laborers with a grade school education (34 vs. 78 per cent).

Looking at the column totals, we note that between grade- and high-school-educated persons there was little difference in party preference, but that the college-educated respondents were considerably less enthusiastic in their support of the Democratic Party.

Tracing the percentages down any one of the educational categories, we note that the percentage favoring the Democratic Party increased from proprietors to skilled and unskilled laborers. Similarly, looking within an occupational category across education, we note a decrease in Democratic preferences as education increases.

We presented Tables 27 and 28 for two reasons. First, to indicate how such status charatceristics as education and occupation are useful in predicting another status component, namely the amount of money a person is likely to earn, and in predicting an attitude, namely the political party that a person is likely to support. Second, and more important, to demonstrate that such status distinctions as occupation and education are meaningful predictors of *jurors'* attitudes and behaviors. In other words, the jurors' behavior contains the same general regularities that we have learned to attribute to all human behavior in our society. The question is: Can we use these statistics as an index of jury decision-making?

The lore

In a talk before the New York County Lawyers' Association some years ago on the art of the jury trial, Louis Nizer observed:

> There are two schools of thought on the selection of the jury. One school says that it is best, once you have satisfied yourself that the jury does not know counsel or litigants and has no surface prejudice on the case, to waive further examination and with a grand gesture say: Jury satisfactory.
>
> Many good lawyers do that. They hope to profit from the fact that the jury will say, "He has great confidence in his case, because he doesn't question as much."
>
> And then there is the other school, the school which says it is not given to you in other fields to pick your judges. You can't pick them in the state court, in equity trials, or in federal court. But the law gives you an opportunity to pick the judges of the facts. It is a precious opportunity and it should be used with all the resourcefulness at your command.
>
> I cast my vote for the second school.[2]

Most lawyers agree with Nizer on the importance of juror selection. Most of them also take great pride in their skill. We shall not attempt to recapitulate all of the words of counsel and caution that lawyers have written on the subject of juror selection. We shall sample only a few of the more famous bits of

[2] Nizer, The Art of the Jury Trial, 32 Cornell L.Q. 59-72 (1946).

advice and hope that the following quotes will illustrate the skills and subtleties involved in the art of juror selection.

Over eighty years ago, J. W. Donovan, an experienced trial lawyer, gave this advice to his colleagues on the selection of a jury:

> Mark their candor, age, humor, intelligence, social stand, occupation, and let your eyes choose the most friendly, liberal and noble faces, young or old but better young than old — better warm than cold faces; better builders than salesmen, better farmers than inventors. Avoid doctors, lawyers, and petti-foggers. There is a little man deformed, narrow, selfish, opinionated; yonder is a captious, caustic, witty man, of stale jokes and street corner argument; and further on is a hard man, grim faced and cold, grey look, white blood and glassy eyes. Rule them all off, if possible. The world has used them ill. They will spread their misery for company's sake.[3]

On the subject of women on the jury, Clarence Darrow said, "I formed a fixed opinion that they were absolutely dependable, but I did not want them." [4] Others suggested: "If you are representing a personable young man, try to seat kindly old ladies in the jury box. If you are representing an attractive young woman, have as many male jurors, old or young, as possible." [5] And, "In all cases where the trial lawyer would seek the more emotional and sympathetic types of jurors, he should also be willing to accept women jurors. Women jurors are considered as good jurors in that they usually pay more attention to evidence, and are serious, and strive to do their duty." [6]

The occupation of prospective jurors elicited the following comments from lawyers:

> As a rule, clergymen, school teachers, lawyers and wives of lawyers do not make desirable jurors. They are too often sought out for advice and tend to be too opinionated.

[3] Donovan, Modern Jury Trials and Advocates 227 (1887).
[4] Darrow, Attorney for the Defense, Esquire 212 (May, 1936).
[5] Appleman, ed., Successful Jury Trials 119 (1952).
[6] Goldstein, Trial Technique 158 (1935).

Retired businessmen are usually fair but disinclined to render wild verdicts. A reasonably well-educated laboring man is not to be despised. Generally railroad men and their wives are excellent jurors. They are solid, substantial citizens who work hard, are frugal in their personal living, yet have the opportunity to travel and to play more than their fellows.[7]

Also, "It is generally known that ex-policemen, ex-sheriffs, and ex-justices, with other like ex-officials, have imbibed a deep-seated prejudice for the plaintiffs, whom they have served so long; while laboring men prefer their kind." [8]

On the matter of a juror's nationality and religion, we hear again from Clarence Darrow:

In criminal cases, I prefer Catholics, Episcopalians and Presbyterians to Baptists and Methodists, because the tenets held and the disciplines practiced by the latter set higher standards of human conduct and make them less tolerant of human frailty.

The Irishman and the Jew, because of their national background, will put a greater burden on the prosecution and prove more sympathetic and lenient to a defendant, than an Englishman or a Scandinavian whose passion for the enforcement of the law and order is stronger.[9]

And according to Goldstein, another authority, "The prosecution in criminal cases will seek the Nordic type of jurors: German, Englishmen, Scandinavian and, in general, a juror of Irish, Jewish, Italian, French, Spanish or Slavic descent will be more sympathetic to a defendant." [10]

We see from the above that a good deal of the bar's lore is proverbial, contradictory, and extravagantly specific. But there is an impressive repertoire of hypotheses about the importance of the kinds of stratification that are of interest to the

[7] Appleman, ed., Successful Jury Trials 127 (1952).

[8] Donovan, Modern Jury Trials and Advocates 227 (1887).

[9] Darrow, quoted by Busch, Law and Tactics in Jury Trials 198 (1959).

[10] Goldstein, Trial Technique 156 (1935).

social scientist. This study, as a by-product, offers an opportunity to test in a highly limited context the practitioner's lore against systematic observation.

The findings

We think we found a better method for determining the relation between status and verdicts than lawyers have because we can trace the course of each juror's decision. The lawyers have only the jury's final verdict, and if they wish to take the time and effort, they can obtain dubiously reliable accounts by individual jurors about how each of the other jurors voted. Our method also has the advantage of allowing us to distribute jurors' verdicts by any of the components of status that we are interested in examining.

But before we look at the data there are several aspects of the jurors' task in general, and in defense of insanity cases in particular, that are worth underscoring.

First, the jurors have to make a concrete decision; they are not asked for their attitudes or opinions in general.

Second, in a case involving a defense of insanity, they have to make an *atypical* legal decision. They are not faced with the choice of either finding the defendant guilty or acquitting him outright.[11] The jurors' task is to determine whether the defendant is capable of assuming responsibility for his behavior. If they believe that he is capable of such responsibility, they must find him guilty. If they believe he is not, they can acquit him on grounds of insanity.

Finally, the defense of insanity introduces a complication in the expected relationship between social status and defendant-proneness. There is the equally plausible counterhypothesis that jurors of higher socio-economic status will have a greater degree of psychiatric sophistication and therefore a greater willingness to find the defendant not guilty by reason of insanity. The traditionally pro-defendant jurors, on the other hand, may find that they have no underdog with whom

[11] Technically, of course, the jury could find the defendant not guilty.

to identify because they are more likely to view manifestations of mental illness in moralistic terms. They might react by rejecting the defendant for being weak and queer, as well as crazy.

The nature of the crime might be an important discriminator of jurors' verdicts. Housebreaking is a crime against property. It is likely, therefore, to be more threatening to persons who have accumulated greater amounts of material possessions. Jurors whose occupational status gives them more property might react more harshly against those who threaten the safety of property. Incest, on the other hand, is not as likely to arouse anxiety proportional to the socio-economic status of the jurors. If this is so, then occupational status or other standard demographic variables will be of little help in explaining jurors' responses in the incest case.

The illustration at the beginning of the chapter shows that jurors' education is related to political affiliation and to income; more educated jurors are politically more conservative and earn more money. This finding is consistent with the trial lawyer's expectations about jurors' behavior in traditional criminal cases. He views education as one index of socio-economic status and expects that the less educated jurors will be more likely to favor the defendant. But the plea of insanity could alter that relationship.

In Stouffer's study *Communism, Conformity, and Civil Liberties,*[12] he found that the more educated respondents had greater tolerance for political deviation and were more accepting of nonconformity. Other studies support Stouffer's finding that the more educated the respondent the less authoritarian, the more tolerant, and the more accepting of nonconformity he is likely to be. If insanity is viewed as another manifestation of nonconformity, then we would anticipate a positive relation between education and pro-defendant verdicts. Finally, we would expect persons with more education to have greater knowledge and understanding of mental illness, and therefore to be more sympathetic to the defense.

[12] Stouffer, Communism, Conformity, and Civil Liberties 107 (1955).

Table 29 describes the relation between education and verdicts.

TABLE 29. VERDICTS BY EDUCATION*

	Housebreaking	Incest
	(Per cent NGI)	
Grade school	73 (95)	35 (175)
High school	71 (171)	34 (429)
College	56 (86)	25 (210)

* Eight jurors in the housebreaking case and two jurors in the incest case did not state their levels of education.

Housebreaking: $X^2_{2d.f.}$ (.95) = 6.0; X^2 = 7.4; $p < .05$.
Incest: $X^2_{2d.f.}$ (.95) = 6.0; X^2 = 6.3; $p < .05$.

The jurors' verdicts in both trials followed the pattern expected for the traditional criminal case. Jurors with a college education were *less* likely to acquit the defendant on grounds of insanity. The findings do not support the results reported in studies of social and political attitudes.

What about the relation between occupation and verdicts? If we base our predictions on the beliefs of the trial lawyers, we would expect jurors in lower status occupations to have a higher percentage of not guilty by reason of insanity verdicts than jurors in higher status occupations. We would also expect a steeper gradient for the housebreaking case than the incest case.

TABLE 30. VERDICTS BY OCCUPATION*

	Housebreaking	Incest
	(Per cent NGI)	
Proprietor	58 (38)	30 (145)
Clerical worker	64 (111)	29 (221)
Skilled laborer	58 (57)	35 (152)
Laborer	75 (85)	37 (168)
Housewife	71 (65)	21 (108)

* Four jurors in the housebreaking case and 22 jurors in the incest case either did not answer the question or said they were unemployed or retired.

The differences among occupations are small but in both cases they are in the direction expected for the traditional criminal case. Laborers favor acquittal on grounds of insanity more than businessmen. The gradient is steeper in the housebreaking case than in the incest trial.

The findings in Tables 29 and 30 are surprising. Related studies of social and political attitudes led us to expect that higher educated jurors would be more sympathetic toward a plea of insanity. But the findings in Table 29 state explicitly that college-educated jurors are less likely to acquit on grounds of insanity and the findings in Table 30 do not show any significant differences. We then checked on the possibility that the relation between verdicts and education was confounded by another status variable such as occupation. Table 31 describes the impact of education within different occupational categories.

TABLE 31. VERDICTS BY EDUCATION AND OCCUPATION

| | INCEST TRIAL ONLY | | |
	Grade school	High school (Per cent NGI)	College
Proprietor	20 (15)	44 (39)	26 (91)
Clerical worker	35 (17)	32 (147)	21 (57)
Skilled laborer	37 (35)	35 (92)	32 (25)
Laborer	39 (71)	35 (84)	38 (13)
Housewife	31 (32)	24 (55)	0 (21)

We note that even under more controlled conditions there is no consistent evidence that the more educated jurors are more likely to sympathize with a defense of insanity. The jurors responded as the trial lawyers expected them to and as the voting studies would have led us to believe. A finding of guilty is a more conservative verdict than a willingness to accept a defendant's plea that he was not responsible for his criminal behavior.

The behavior of the housewives in the two trials is interesting. In the housebreaking case, the housewives voted like laborers, that is, they revealed a high propensity to vote NGI, but in the incest case they were more punitive than even the proprietors, who were most apt to bring in a verdict of guilty.

By examining the data in Table 32 we can determine whether the housewives' verdicts generalize to all women on the jury.

TABLE 32. VERDICTS BY SEX*

	Housebreaking	Incest
	(Per cent NGI)	
Men	$62_{(213)}$	$33_{(547)}$
Women†	$73_{(145)}$	$30_{(269)}$
Housewives	$71_{(65)}$	$21_{(108)}$
Non-housewives	$75_{(80)}$	$35_{(161)}$

* Two jurors in the housebreaking case did not answer the question.
† This category includes all the women jurors, housewives, and women who worked outside the home.

In both trials the difference between men and women is not great. But in the housebreaking case the housewives' verdicts reflect the verdicts of the women jurors generally and show that they are more sympathetic to the defendant than the men. In the incest case, the housewives' verdicts would not generalize to the working woman. An overt violation of the incest taboo is probably even more threatening to housewives than it is to women in other social roles because housewives bear a disproportionate share of the responsibility for the emotional stability of the family. It may be that housewives would be more punitive than other jurors toward all sex offenders.

The jurors were also divided into high and low income categories as in Table 33.[13]

[13] Income was coded according to the categories used by the 1960 United States Census. About half of the jurors fell into the below $450 per month category.

TABLE 33. VERDICTS BY INCOME*

	Housebreaking	Incest
	(Per cent NGI)	
$450 or less	$71_{(178)}$	$33_{(362)}$
More than $450	$62_{(163)}$	$31_{(417)}$

* Nineteen jurors in the housebreaking case and thirty-seven in the incest case did not answer the question.

The differences are small especially in the incest case, but they follow the pattern of occupation and education; lower income jurors are more defendant prone.

Finally, we examined the combined effects of occupation, education, and income on jurors' verdicts and found that the cumulative index provided no more information than that which we obtained by looking at each variable separately. Since the latter results could be presented more neatly, we have not included the combined tables.

For defense counsel in the ordinary criminal case, the lawyers' lore would recommend jurors of minority ethnic and religious affiliation on the theory that such persons are likely to view themselves as potential victims of society and particularly of law enforcement institutions. The expectation, therefore, is that they would be more likely to identify with the defendant than would persons from the majority ethnic or religious community. Once again our concern is: How does the insanity case fit this pattern? Will the expectations based on traditional criminal cases apply?

TABLE 34. VERDICTS BY RELIGION*

	Housebreaking	Incest
	(Per cent NGI)	
Protestant	$66_{(169)}$	$32_{(479)}$
Catholic	$68_{(156)}$	$31_{(286)}$
Other and none	$59_{(34)}$	$31_{(51)}$

* One juror in the housebreaking case did not answer the question.

TABLE 35. VERDICTS BY ETHNICITY*

	Housebreaking	Incest
	(Per cent NGI)	
Negro	$85_{(26)}$	$52_{(42)}$
Southern and Eastern Europe	$65_{(110)}$	$32_{(176)}$
Central Europe	$68_{(76)}$	$29_{(157)}$
Scandinavia and Britain	$74_{(34)}$	$35_{(160)}$
U.S.A. (3 or more generations)	$56_{(96)}$	$30_{(255)}$

* Eighteen jurors in the housebreaking case and twenty-six jurors in the incest case belonged to "other" ethnic categories or did not answer the question.

Negroes vs. others (Housebreaking): $X^2_{1d.f.}$ (.95) = 3.8; X^2 = 6.1; p < .05.

Negroes vs. others (Incest): $X^2_{1d.f.}$ (.99) = 6.6; X^2 = 7.8; p < .01.

Table 34 describes the relation between religion and verdicts, and Table 35 describes the relation between ethnicity and verdicts. The differences in both cases between Protestants and Catholics are so small that they are not worth discussing.

As for ethnicity in both cases, the differences between most minority ethnic groups and the U.S.A. category were not statistically significant. But Negro jurors are more willing to acquit the defendant on grounds of insanity than are jurors in all other ethnic categories. Negroes are our most visible minority group. They are also more likely than other minority groups to see themselves as victims or potential victims of the police and other law enforcement institutions. Most lawyers believe that in the traditional criminal trial Negroes will identify with the defendant.[14]

Finally, studies have shown that older persons are politically more conservative and less tolerant of non-conformity than are younger persons.[15] But as Table 36 demonstrates this relation-

[14] Obviously, this relation would not hold in criminal trials with racial overtones.

[15] See Stouffer, Communism, Conformity, and Civil Liberties 107 (1955).

ship was not present to any noticeable extent in either the housebreaking or the incest case.

TABLE 36.   VERDICTS BY AGE*

	Housebreaking	Incest
	(Per cent NGI)	
Under 35	80 (66)	36 (161)
35-54	61 (220)	31 (434)
Over 55	71 (72)	31 (221)

* Two jurors did not answer the question in the housebreaking case.

In the housebreaking case, there was a smaller propensity for jurors in the middle age category to find the defendant NGI. This lesser willingness to find NGI may be a reflection of property differences.   By and large middle-aged persons own more property and have more money.[16]

We introduced this section by suggesting two alternative hypothesis concerning the relationship between social status and verdicts.   The jurors could have reacted as trial lawyers would have expected them to in a traditional criminal case. If they did, lower status jurors would be more likely to favor the defendants.   On the other hand, the fact that the defendants introduced pleas of insanity could have altered the relationship so that the more educated, higher status jurors would be more likely to favor acquittal on grounds of insanity. The relationship between status characteristics and verdicts was not powerful in either case, but when a relation was found, it always supported the expectations that trial lawyers have about jurors in traditional criminal cases: lower status jurors are more likely to favor the defendant.[17]

[16] In addition to the characteristics discussed above, we examined such factors as marital status, presence or absence of children, church attendance, and political affiliation, and found no relationship in either case to verdicts.

[17] Selective status characteristics such as education and occupation were also compared against the experimental variables (rules of law and expert testimony).   In the housebreaking case we found a glimmer of evidence which suggested that higher status jurors (proprietors and

Social status and influence[18]

We examined three clues for measuring jurors' influence: the selection of the foreman, the relative participation by sex and occupation, and the frequency with which a minority of the jurors succeed in persuading a majority to shift their verdicts.

At the outset of every deliberation, the jury was told to select one of its members as foreman. Almost always the foreman is selected very quickly, and usually without a formal vote. Table 37 compares the distribution of foremen's occupations with the relative representation of each occupation in the over-all jury population.

TABLE 37. OCCUPATIONAL STATUS OF 39 JURY FOREMEN

	*Expected**	*Observed*
Proprietor	7	17
Clerical worker	11	15
Skilled worker	7	1
Laborer	8	4
Housewife	5	0
Retired/unknown	1	2

* Computed under the assumption that the occupation of the foremen will be proportional to the distribution of the occupations among all jurors in the sample.

---

jurors with a college education) were more likely to differentiate among the three instruction versions and were more likely to acquit under the Durham version. When the same variables were tabulated in the incest case there was no support for the thesis that higher status jurors were more responsive to differences in the rules of law. Jurors in every status category were more likely to find in favor of the defendant under Durham than under M'Naghten and to report similar verdicts between Durham and uninstructed version. We also compared the reactions of jurors in different occupational and educational categories to the model and typical testimonies and found no difference by either characteristic. Somewhat to our surprise the model version did not prove more supportive of the defendant's case to jurors of higher socioeconomic status.

[18] The data in this section are based solely on the incest case.

As Table 37 demonstrates, the results are not as random as the process might suggest. There is a marked propensity in favor of the election of higher status male jurors. Proprietors, for example, have more than four times better chance of being elected than laborers although their proportion among the jurors is about the same. Housewives were never elected and only half as many laborers were elected as their frequency in the population would have led us to expect.

Time in the jury room is a common but scarce commodity. How a jury chooses to allocate this resource among its participants may yield a measure of the relative influence of each of the members in the group. In most studies of small group interaction, a subject's power and participation are positively related to his status in the larger community. In the jury, there is a presumption of equality which is reinforced by the institutional requirement of verdict unanimity. But, even in the jury, previous studies have shown that the status gradient of the larger community differentiates individual jurors' performances.[19] These patterns were observed in juries that considered civil actions and in which there was a stronger relationship than we found between social status and verdicts.

Although the incest case verdicts were not greatly differentiated by jurors' positions on the status hierarchy, their statuses could influence participation.[20] For example, men might participate more actively than women, and businessmen more than laborers, if only because men generally, and those with higher status particularly, have acquired greater skill and experience participating in task-oriented groups.

We compared first, the participation of foremen and non-

[19] See Strodtbeck, James, and Hawkins, Social Status in Jury Deliberations, 22 Am. Soc. Rev. 713-719 (1957); James, Status and Competence in Jury Deliberations, 64 Am. J. Soc. 563-570 (1959); Strodtbeck and Mann, Sex Role Differentiation in Jury Deliberations, 19 Sociometry 3-11 (March, 1956).

[20] If participation in jury deliberations were apportioned equally, each juror would use $8\frac{1}{3}$ per cent of the total time ($8\frac{1}{3}$ x 12 = 100 per cent).

foremen and, as expected, found that jurors who were elected foremen talked significantly more than other jurors.

TABLE 38. PARTICIPATION OF FOREMEN AND
NON-FOREMEN

	Mean per cent participation
Foremen	31.1 (39)
Other jurors	7.5 (429)

Foreman vs. other jurors: $t = 2.8$ p $< .01$.

But the foreman's greater participation may be due to several factors. The demands of his job might be such that he has to participate more actively, calling for votes, mediating procedural questions, etc. Or other members of the jury might defer to the foreman more than they do to anyone else in the group, thereby giving him more of an opportunity to voice his opinion. We have shown already that persons who are elected foreman have the social characteristics that would make them high participators irrespective of their formal position in the group.

Having shown the disparity in participation between foremen and non-foremen, and the greater likelihood of high status male jurors occupying that position, we next compared participation rates among non-foremen. As between men and women there was no difference.

TABLE 39. PARTICIPATION OF MEN AND WOMEN

	Mean per cent participation
Men	7.5 (288)
Women	7.5 (141)

Males vs. females: $t = .06$ n.s.

This finding is in sharp contrast to that reported for civil juries, in which women participated significantly less than men.[21] One guess is that women participate more actively in criminal cases generally, but especially in criminal cases involving crimes of violence or sexual crimes. We found that in the housebreaking case women participated more than they did in the civil juries but not as much as in the incest case.

When occupation and participation were compared, we found that businessmen spoke more than laborers. And

TABLE 40. PARTICIPATION OF JURORS IN DIFFERENT OCCUPATIONS

	Mean per cent participation
Proprietor	9.1 (73)
Clerical worker	7.7 (110)
Skilled laborer	7.6 (95)
Laborer	6.1 (96)
Housewife	7.6 (52)

when these rankings were compared with those based on the civil juries, we found that not only did the occupational categories follow the same order from higher to lower status, but that the participation gradient was no steeper in the civil juries than in the criminal juries.

TABLE 41. PARTICIPATION BY OCCUPATION* IN CIVIL† AND CRIMINAL JURIES

	Civil juries	Criminal juries
Proprietor	8.9 (112)	9.1 (73)
Clerical worker	7.0 (173)	7.7 (110)
Skilled laborer	6.3 (108)	7.6 (95)
Laborer	5.9 (169)	6.1 (96)

* Data from Strodtbeck, James, and Hawkins, note 19 *supra,* at 716.
† Only male jurors are represented in the civil juries. The criminal juries combined men with women who are not housewives.

[21] See Strodtbeck and Mann, Sex Role Differentiation in Jury Deliberations, 19 Sociometry 3-11 (March, 1956) and Strodtbeck, James, and Hawkins, Social Status in Jury Deliberations, 22 Am. Soc. Rev. 713-719 (1957).

The status differences of the larger society may not have intruded so as to significantly differentiate jurors' verdicts in the incest case, but their influence was clearly felt in the distribution of participation.

As for the third measure of jurors' influence, in only six of the 57 juries that reached consensus did jurors who were in a minority position on their pre-deliberation verdicts succeed in persuading the majority to their point of view. In five of those juries the minority was composed of five members, in one jury it was composed of four. There was no instance in which one juror or even two held out against the other ten or eleven and finally persuaded them to their position. We compared the statuses of the jurors who composed these successful minorities against the other jurors and found that businessmen and skilled laborers were over-represented and laborers and housewives under-represented.

TABLE 42. JURORS IN THE "SUCCESSFUL" MINORITY
BY OCCUPATION

	Expected	Observed
Proprietor	5.2	8
Clerical	8.1	7
Skilled	5.5	8
Laborer	6.1	3
Housewife	4.1	2
Retired	—	1

When educational levels were compared there was no greater likelihood that the more educated jurors would compose the successful minority position — if anything, it showed that college-educated jurors were slightly under-represented.

Thus, on our most direct measure of jurors' influence, we

TABLE 43. JURORS IN THE "SUCCESSFUL" MINORITY
BY EDUCATION

	Expected	Observed
Grade school	6.1	7
High school	12.4	17
College	7.5	5

found no consistent evidence that the opinions of jurors in higher socio-economic statuses carried more weight than the opinions of lower status jurors.

Concluding remarks

It is extremely difficult to predict the response or behavior of a given individual to a concrete situation on the basis of such gross characteristics as occupation, education, sex, or age. In any situation what a person thinks or does is a function of who he is, the exigencies of the situation, how strongly he feels about the problem, and a host of other factors. In comparing jurors' verdicts by various status components we were not trying to predict concrete decisions. We were estimating the probability that some jurors would be more favorable to the defendant than others.

One is particularly tempted to study how background and status components affect decisions in the jury because members of a jury represent almost all layers of society and a great diversity of social and cultural backgrounds. If we could show that background and status components have an important impact on the jury's decision, this finding would probably generalize to many other situations.

One practical finding that emerged from our investigation of the effects of social status on verdicts is that the lawyers' lore about the defendant-proneness of lower status jurors generalizes, although in a somewhat weakened form, to jurors' behavior in criminal cases involving a defense of insanity. Specifically, our results were that: Negro jurors are more willing to vote for acquittal on grounds of insanity than jurors of majority ethnic background, and jurors of higher social status, as measured by educational attainment, are more likely to vote for a guilty verdict. Another practical finding, not directly anticipated by the lawyers' lore, is the greater punitiveness of housewives, as opposed to both other women and to men, toward the defendant in the incest case. Finally, a finding that should interest lawyers but about which there is little lore, is that while male jurors who hold important positions in the larger society talk more in the jury room and are more likely to be elected foreman, they do not appear to wield more influence, at least when influence is measured by the ability of the members of a minority faction to persuade the majority to their point of view.

CHAPTER 7

Jurors' Attitudes Toward Mental Illness, Psychiatry, and Related Topics

In his pre-trial examination of prospective jurors, a lawyer's interest is not limited to the juror's background or social status. He is equally interested in the opinions and attitudes that the juror holds. For example, in a personal injury case the lawyer might be interested in the juror's attitudes toward insurance, wealth, and health as possible indicators of his propensity to side with the injured plaintiff. In a case involving a Negro or a member of some other minority group, he will try to learn something about the juror's attitudes toward that group. In criminal trials involving a defense of insanity, the prospective juror's attitudes toward psychiatry and his ideas about mental illness could be important predictors of how the juror will respond to the issues in the trial he is about to hear.

But the lawyer's inquiry is sharply limited both by etiquette and law. Thus, persistent questioning about attitudes toward insurance is as a rule even legally improper. More important is the role of etiquette, which restrains, for instance, the direct inquiry about political affiliation or religion. And although there might be an oblique connection for instance between attitudes toward homosexuality and the propensity to acquit in criminal cases, the practice generally prohibits such questions unless they are directly relevant to the particular case.

However, this study was not bound by the same principles

of social decorum that bind the trial lawyer, since we asked questions in wrting, hence in private, and not as part of a public trial. Through the use of the pre-trial questionnaire, we could ask the jurors about almost anything that might possibly relate to their verdicts; and we could then attempt to tie the jurors' responses to their verdicts. We could thus pioneer an attempt to predict jurors' verdicts from personality tests. We were able to investigate jurors' attitudes towards the following three topics: mental illness, psychiatry, and the legitimacy of various forms of sexual expression.

Jurors' responses on the questionnaire are reported below in two stages. We first report the jurors' attitudes toward the particular issue; then we relate those attitudes to the pre-deliberation verdicts actually reported.[1]

Attitudes toward the mentally ill

There were four items about attitudes toward the mentally ill, selected from a larger set known as the "Custodial Mental Illness Ideology Scale."[2] This scale has been tested many times and has been shown to differentiate reliably between humanistic and custodial attitudes toward persons who are mentally ill.

The theoretical assumption is that the "humanistic" response will be more sympathetic to mental illness and therefore more favorably disposed toward accepting the defense of insanity.

The jurors' responses to each of the four items are shown below.

---

[1] The discussion in this chapter is based on the incest case alone, because the personality measures were not developed at the time of the housebreaking experiment.

[2] The CMI scale was constructed by Doris C. Gilbert and Daniel J. Levinson and is reported in Custodialism and Humanism in Mental Hospital Structure and Staff Ideology, in Greenblatt, Levinson, and Williams, The Patient and the Mental Hospital 20-35 (1957). We selected the four items that differentiated most sharply.

TABLE 44. JURORS' ATTITUDES TOWARD THE MENTALLY ILL

	Agree	Disagree
	(In per cent)	
1. We should be sympathetic with persons who are mentally ill; but we cannot expect to understand them.	79	21*
2. A person who is mentally ill still makes decisions about everyday living problems.	43*	57
3. We can make some improvement, but by and large, the conditions of mental hospitals are about as good as they can be considering the type of people living there.	24	76*
4. Unless you spend a good deal of time with mentally ill people, it is hard to tell them from normal persons.	69*	31

* An asterisk indicates the "humanistic" response.

If the lawyers in the incest case had put these questions to the prospective jurors during the voir dire, would they have been useful in distinguishing jurors' verdicts? Table 45 describes the relation between attitudes and verdicts.

TABLE 45. JURORS' VERDICTS BY RESPONSES TO THE "MENTALLY ILL" ITEMS

	Humanistic alternative	Custodial alternative
	(Per cent NGI)	
1. We should be sympathetic with persons who are mentally ill; but we cannot expect to understand them.	29 (171)	32 (645)
2. A person who is mentally ill still makes decisions about everyday living problems.	32 (351)	30 (465)
3. We can make some improvement, but, by and large, the conditions of mental hospitals are about as		

	Humanistic alternative	Custodial alternative
	(Per cent NGI)	
good as they can be considering the type of people living there.	^{32}(195)	^{29}(621)
4. Unless you spend a good deal of time with mentally ill people, it is hard to tell them from normal persons.	^{32}(563)	^{30}(253)

The results are strikingly negative. For each of the four questions the percentage of NGI verdicts of those selecting the "humanistic" alternative and those selecting the "custodial" alternative is virtually the same. Thus we can only conclude that this particular effort to discover discriminating juror attitudes failed.

Jurors' attitudes toward various forms of sexual expression

Jason Lunt violated a basic sexual taboo. How prospective jurors respond to milder forms of sexual perversion and exhibitionism may offer useful clues about how they would respond to a defendant who committed incest. We expected that persons who were more permissive and who seemed to have less difficulty managing their own sexual feelings might react more leniently toward the defendant. Listed below are the jurors' responses to eight questions which we designed with the incest case in mind.

TABLE 46. JURORS' ATTITUDES TOWARD FORMS OF SEXUAL EXPRESSION

	Yes	No
	(In per cent)	
1. Do you believe that there is more improper and immoral sexual activity going on than most people realize?	81	19*
2. Do you think homosexuality between adults should be punishable by law?	66	34*

	Yes	No
	(*In per cent*)	
3. Should pregnant women in bathing suits be seen on public beaches?	16*	84
4. Do you think that a lot of the paintings or sculptures of nude figures that pass as works of art are an excuse for the distribution of obscene or pornographic material?	26	74*
5. Do you approve of the present trend toward scanty bathing suits and plunging necklines in evening dresses?	27*	73

	Indifferent	Ill and/or angry
6. What are your reactions when you see or hear of men with feminine mannerism in their speech, dress, walk, etc.?	69*	31

	Mother-son; father-daughter	Mother-daughter; father-son	Both daughter; both son
7. In families where there are sons and daughters, is the mother more likely to favor the son or the daughter? Is the father more likely to favor the son or the daughter?	52*	32	16

	Favor	No opinion	Oppose
8. What is your opinion of nudism?	2*	30*	68

* An asterisk denotes the more permissive response.

The responses reveal strong puritanical leanings. Over two thirds would restrict pregnant women in bathing suits from public beaches, disapprove of scanty bathing suits and plunging necklines, believe that there is more improper sexual activity going on than most people realize, oppose nudism, and believe homosexuality should be punishable by law. We suspect that the choice of response is influenced by the subject's perception of the attitudes that are appropriate to the role of a juror. The respondent probably feels that in his role as a juror it is incumbent upon him to endorse puritanical values. But the division of opinion is sufficient to allow us to test whether the attitudes are related to the jurors' verdicts.

We expected that jurors who made the more permissive responses would be more likely to find in favor of the defendant.

TABLE 47. JURORS' VERDICTS BY RESPONSES TO
SEXUAL EXPRESSION

Items	Permissive	Repressive
	(Per cent NGI)	
1. Do you believe that there is more improper and immoral sexual activity going on than most people realize?	31(155)	32(661)
2. Do you think homosexuality between adults should be punished by law?	32(277)	30(539)
3. Should pregnant women in bathing suits be seen on public beaches?	48(131)	29(685)
4. Do you think that a lot of the painting and sculpturing of nude figures that passes as works of art is an excuse for the distribution of obscene or pornographic material?	29(604)	34(212)
5. Do you approve of the present trend toward scanty bathing suits and plunging necklines in evening dresses?	33(220)	31(596)
6. What are your reactions when you see or hear of men with feminine mannerisms in their speech, dress, walk, etc.?	31(563)	30(253)

Items	*Permissive*	*Repressive*
	(Per cent NGI)	
7. In families where there are sons and daughters, is the mother more likely to favor the son or the daughter? Is the father more likely to favor the son or the daughter?	$32_{(424)}$	$32_{(392)}$
8. What is your opinion of nudism?	$38_{(260)}$	$29_{(556)}$

The results are disappointing again. With one interesting exception (jurors' responses to the item asking about pregnant women in bathing suits),[3] attitudes offered no practical guide to verdicts.

While the jurors' responses to the pregnant women item are intriguing, they do not provide much encouragement, since we had no expectation that this question would be a better indicator than the other questions about sex, all of which failed conspicuously. There is, therefore, a theoretical difficulty in interpreting this particular answer; and in the absence of a theoretical foundation, one cannot attach much significance to it.

Jurors' knowledge and attitudes about psychiatric interpretations of motivations and behavior

We turn finally to our third set of attitudes. It seems reasonable to assume that a prospective juror who has knowledge about and is positively disposed toward psychiatric interpretations concerning why people behave as they do would be more sympathetic to the defense than to the prosecution. Table 48 reports the jurors' responses to items that test knowledge and acceptance of psychiatric interpretations.

[3] Lawyers, take note!

TABLE 48. JURORS' KNOWLEDGE OF PSYCHIATRY

(In per cent)

	Relationship $\left(\begin{array}{l}\textit{More likely}\\\textit{or less likely}\end{array}\right)$	No relationship
1. Do you think there is a relationship between intelligence and mental disease?	54	46*

	Good cue for how he feels	Just a mistake — no meaning
2. When a person makes a "slip of the tongue" do you think it is an indication of how he really feels about the subject he is discussing?	49*	51

	Yes	No
3. Do you believe that most people know why they act as they do?	48	52*

	Relationship $\left(\begin{array}{l}\textit{More likely}\\\textit{or less likely}\end{array}\right)$	No relationship
4. Do you think there is a relationship between too much brain work and mental disorder?	55	45*

	$\left(\begin{array}{l}\textit{Do not}\\\textit{care}\\\textit{about}\\\textit{people}\end{array} \; or \; \begin{array}{l}\textit{Conflict}\\\textit{within}\\\textit{own per-}\\\textit{sonality}\end{array}\right)$	No significance
5. Do you think that the tendency some persons have for not remembering the names of people they meet has any significance?	20*	80

	Yes	No
6. Do you believe doctors can learn anything from their patients' dreams that they could not more easily obtain by direct questions?	38*	62

* An asterisk denotes the more knowledgeable response.

	Physical disorder	Emotional disorder
7. Does stuttering usually occur as a result of some physical disorder or as a result of some emotional disorder?	25	75*

	All, most, or many cases	Few or no cases
8. Do you believe that cases of mental disorder may arise from lack of will power?	50	50*

* An asterisk denotes the more knowledgeable response.

Table 49 reports what relationship there is between verdicts and psychiatric sophistication.

TABLE 49. JURORS' VERDICTS BY RESPONSES TO ITEMS ON PSYCHIATRIC EXPLANATIONS

Items	Jurors who agreed with psychiatric explanation	Jurors who disagreed with psychiatric explanation
	(Per cent NGI)	
1. Do you think there is a relationship between intelligence and mental disease?	31 (375)	31 (441)
2. When a person makes a "slip of the tongue" do you think it is an indication of how he really feels about the subject he is discussing?	32 (400)	31 (416)
3. Do you believe that most people know why they act as they do?	33 (392)	30 (424)
4. Do you think there is a relationship between too much brain work and mental disorder?	31 (367)	32 (449)
5. Do you think that the tendency some persons have for not remembering the names of people they meet has any significance?	34 (163)	30 (653)

Items	Jurors who agreed with psychiatric explanation	Jurors who disagreed with psychiatric explanation
	(Per cent NGI)	
6. Do you believe doctors can learn anything from their patients' dreams that they could not more easily obtain by direct questioning?	33'(310)	30(506)
7. Does stuttering usually occur as a result of some physical disorder or as a result of some emotional disorder?	31(612)	33(204)
8. Do you believe that cases of mental disorder may arise from lack of will power?	31(408)	32(408)

Table 49 demonstrates that a defense attorney would have gained no advantage for his client by subjecting the jury panel to such inquiries — and probably would have incurred the displeasure of the court for having taken up so much of its time.

Concluding remarks

The sharp lack of findings reported in this chapter rival in interest any data we have. Three efforts were made to relate attitudes to verdict and each ended in failure. The distribution of percentages in Tables 44, 46, and 48 demonstrates that people do hold different attitudes toward the issues in question; and the 66-34 per cent verdict split certainly suggests differences in verdicts. The puzzling fact is that there is no relationship between the two sets of results.

Had we reported the responses to the attitude items separately and not compared them with the jurors' verdicts, we think that most researchers would have expected and would have been prepared to use them as good predictors of verdicts. It may be some comfort to the trial lawyer who is prevented from asking these kinds of questions to learn that such information would give him no advantage.

PART IV

The Jury Deliberates

CHAPTER 8

The Sound of the Jury

Introduction

The data in this chapter offer a novel approach to the understanding of juries' behavior because they report the actual content of jury deliberations. For the first time we can hear what the jury sounds like. In the first part we reported the effects of the experimental variables on verdicts. In the next part we reported findings from the questionnaires. This part provides still a third source of data about the jury.

The materials in this chapter should be thought of as an anthology of jury observations; as an informal, non-quantified content analysis of the jury's main ideas. We think that the comments quoted represent the jury's thinking. But we make no pretense about having sampled the jury in any technical sense. What we did was to submerge ourselves in the deliberations by listening to the tapes and reading the typed protocols.[1] We think that there is a latent representativeness in the

[1] We could have done a formal content analysis, but our previous efforts with this technique in the housebreaking experiment did not prove very interesting or fruitful. After we had categorized an entire deliberation in which every burst of speech was coded into a system of mutually exclusive categories we did not feel that we had captured either the specific contents or the tone of the deliberation. Perhaps we should have spent more time trying to improve our formal content system rather than switch to the technique employed in this chapter. But very quickly we began to see results from this less systematic technique that were much more useful. For a detailed description of the formal content system and of the results it yielded see: James, Status and Competence in the Jury Deliberations, 64 Am. J. Soc. 563 (1959); James, People v. Martin Graham, unpublished Ph.D. thesis, University of Chicago (1957).

excerpts we have included, but we can offer no scientific guarantee that someone else could not have studied the same deliberations and have come up with a different set of quotes. All we can say is that we are doubtful.

Two general criteria influenced our selection of specific excerpts.[2] We looked for the jury's discussion of problems that the *law* expected the jury to discuss before reaching consensus and for problems that the jury discussed most frequently, irrespective of their legal salience. Substantively, the chapter is divided into the following five topics:

1. The jury's use of the record,
2. The jury's understanding of the insanity plea,
3. The jury's concern about the norm for non-responsibility,
4. The jury's evaluation of the psychiatrists' testimony,
5. The jury's feelings about imprisonment as opposed to commitment.

1. *The jury's use of the record*

The impression that comes through most clearly about the jury's discussion is its utilization of the record. The jurors are concerned about the details of the case. Their point of departure is the trial record, not abstract philosophical ideas. The information that gets through most clearly to the jury are facts about the defendant: his childhood, his work record, his relations with his wife, and his day-to-day behavior.

The wife's role

The defendant's wife is the mystery character in the Lunt script. Mrs. Lunt did not appear as a witness, nor was any mention made of her presence in the courtroom. But other

---

[2] Thirty-nine of the 68 deliberations in the incest case were transcribed. The 39 were distributed into the following verdict and instruction categories: 12 M'Naghten juries, 1 hung and 11 guilty; 13 uninstructed juries, 4 NGI, 2 hung, 7 guilty; and 14 Durham juries, 5 NGI, 3 hung, and 6 guilty.

witnesses referred to her many times in the course of their testimony. The youngest daughter, for instance, described a
scene in which her father asked her to have sexual relations
with him. The daughter reported that her mother said: "No,
have relations with me, not with her." The daughter testified
that when the father refused, the mother made no further pro-
tests. There is ample evidence that this was not the first occasion on which it was made known to the wife that her husband
was having sexual relations with their daughters.

Neither the defense nor the prosecution tried to use the
mystery of the mother's role in the family for its own advantage. But it is obvious from the number of times that the
mother was the topic of discussion that the jurors did not allow
her to pass unnoticed. Many jurors stated explicitly that they
would like to try the mother as well as the father. In one jury,
several jurors commented:

> She is equally to blame.
> She should have reported it to the police right off the bat.
> Like I say, they have the wrong person on trial. He should
> have been placed in a mental home and she should have been
> put on trial.
> At least she could go into the bedroom and get a gun and
> shoot him.

In another jury:

> You would think the very first time it happened the mother
> would have taken it to the police right away.
> The unfortunate thing is that it isn't the mother that is be-
> ing tried.

One woman declared: "The mother was more insane than he
was. It is just like murdering her daughter. Even if she were
half crazy, she should still fight for her child. No matter what
she had to do to her husband, she should have stopped it!"
Some jurors offered half-hearted excuses for the wife's behavior, suggesting that she might have been too frightened of her
husband or too ashamed of scandal to intervene. One juror
suggested:

Now I would assume that this mother, though she knew this thing was a terrible hurt to her daughters, it was a hurt to her, she was fearful for herself. She was fearful of what may happen to her by him; and, of the embarrassment that would have been brought upon the entire family by having those acts revealed.

The women jurors, especially the housewives, had the greatest difficulty understanding the mother's seemingly passive acceptance of the situation.[3] One juror asked of a woman juror:

Well would you stand by and see your husband do that to your daughter?
Absolutely not!
You would hit him with a chair.
That is right.
So would any normal person.

In another jury a woman commented: "As the mother of five daughters of my own, I am sure I would not have stood by with a man like that." One man turned to the men on the jury and said: "Any of you men here has got daughters, I am sure your wife would die defending her daughters against any such act."

In sum, the jurors' main reactions to the wife were a feeling of having been cheated because they could not punish her directly and a failure to understand how any woman could permit such a situation to continue over a period of time (that is, more than once). Some of the jurors seriously questioned the wife's sanity more than they did the defendant's. On the whole, the jurors' perceptions of the wife's attitude about her husband's behavior worked against the defendant because it suggested that his behavior was part of the family pattern. They had to believe that everyone in the family was insane or assume that the defendant's behavior was no more perverse than anyone else's.

---

[3] We recall from Chapter 6 that the housewives had the highest proportion of guilty verdicts.

The defendant's employment record

During the trial the jurors heard that the defendant was able to perform his duties in the fire department so as to merit two promotions: one from private to sergeant, and another from sergeant to lieutenant. He held the latter position for the three years prior to his arrest. They heard also that he received efficiency ratings of 99 per cent and 95 per cent on two civil service examinations. The defendant's ability to perform adequately as a lieutenant in the fire department was at odds with the jurors' conceptions of a mentally incompetent person.

One of the jurors, the wife of a fireman, spoke as follows:

My husband is a lieutenant with the department. I know what the tests are and I know you have to know what you are doing. If you are mentally disturbed you could never compete with the tests that are put up to the fire department. They are not easy questions and you have to have your wits about you. You are given a mental test when you take your examination, and you have to weigh the right and the wrong in answering each question. If you do not you do not get the promotion. Here is a man that wound up eighth on the list of 108 men. So, he had what it took to answer those complicated questions.

Later in the same deliberation she had this to say about the defendant:

He progressed in the fire department. If he had lost his job because of his inability to think that would be different. Besides, he was an officer in the department. He had to lead his men. He had to think for his men. So, if his mind was not alert, he certainly would not have kept that job because it is his duty as a lieutenant or a sergeant to lead his men into a fire. And it is his duty to keep his men out if he thinks they should not be in there.

In other juries, the facts that the defendant maintained his position in the fire department and performed well on examinations were important behavioral criteria for evaluating his mental health and social adjustment. As one juror said:

> The key to this case is that he maintained a normal position. That is it. That is the law's definition of sanity or insanity. It is whether or not you are able to carry out your normal activities or not. I think if this man had gone from job to job and exhibited behavior that might be considered abnormal or neurotic, if he had been a drifter and so forth, that might throw a different complexion on this case.

The defendant's relatively stable employment record was a major factor working against him. That, along with the evidence that he used contraceptives, weighed very heavily against his plea of insanity.

The defendant's use of contraceptives

During the trial the jurors heard the prosecution read the following admission from the defendant's statement to the police: "During the period over which these acts occurred I made all efforts to avoid pregnancy with my daughters and such never occurred. The following contraceptives were used: diaphragm, vaginal douche, suppositories, and prophylactics." The fact that the defendant acknowledged using contraceptives proved to be the single most important item of testimony against him. The defense attempted to interpret his use of contraceptives as exhibitionistic and therefore as a good clue of his insanity. But most of the jurors interpreted it as a clear indication of his deliberate intent and, hence, a good clue of his sanity. As one juror said:

> I think that any possible crime of violence that occurs on the spur of the moment might be excusable on grounds of insanity. But, when a person thinks about it, plans something like he certainly did by using contraceptives, to me that means he was responsible and sane.

In one jury, the amount of time devoted to discussing the availability and means of procuring contraceptives suggests that the jurors had found rewards in such a discussion, other than the presumed one of facilitating consensus. Their discussion is partially reproduced below:

1-1 If he was out of his mind, he would not give a tinker's damn who it was that got pregnant.

12-1 And to go to such precautions as the, as . . . .

1-12 The diaphragm, vaginal douche, suppositories, and prophylactics.

12-1 Diaphragm, douche, yes and all of that.

1-12 He had to go out and buy those . . .

12-1 He had to buy those things.

2-1 His daughter could not, that's for sure.

1-2 No, his daughter could not.

12-1 He had to go into the store and buy them.

8-8 Sure, it was a premeditated sex act.

1-1 Sure, it was premeditated.

12-1 And the girl had to go out and be fitted for that diaphragm. Heavens, they all knew what they were doing. The girl had to be fitted for that diaphragm. She could not walk into a dime store and buy it off the counter.

8-1 She had to get it at a pharmacy . . .

12-12 Unless things have changed, I don't know. [Laughter.]

1-8 What?

8-1 You have to get that from a regular pharmacist.

1-8 Yes, but a youngster could not go in and buy it.

12-1 No, a youngster could not.

8-1 No, I know that.

12-1 A youngster could not walk into a drugstore and ask for a diaphragm and . . .

1-12 In other words, it indicated here, that she had to be fitted for the diaphragm. The vaginal douche and the suppositories her mother could buy. He might even buy the prophylactics. But, nonetheless, it is the diaphragm that she would have to be fitted for.

12-1 And over a period of five years . . .

1-12 And over a period of five years, she had to have more than one.

12-1 More than one, see.

8-8 That has to be taken out and recleaned.

1-1 Now you cannot tell me that that is an insane man.

12-12 That was premeditated. The man is no good. He knew what he was doing.

6-12 It might have not necessarily been the act of the man, it might have been the act of the mother. She might have done it.

12-6 Now wait, we are not allowed . . .

3-12 I can see your side of it too.

12-3 That is what I mean. Now would a person who is insane go into a store and buy those things?

8-12 They could.

12-3 Not a diaphragm.

3-12 We do not know who bought them. The mother may have.

12-3 Who bought them? The girl had to be there. A diaphragm is fitted isn't it? The prophylactics a man can walk into the drugstore and buy.

8-4 This girl I knew had to have it fitted. They are fitted, you have to go to a doctor. But it has to be a size for a youngster like that. A diaphragm has to fit the child. There are all different sizes.

1-12 Suppositories?

12-4 I lost track.

12-1 I've been out of circulation for eight years so I don't know.

4-4 Maybe the mother did all of that. Maybe she was afraid.

12-4 It has to fit. So it was all premeditated. It was all premeditated.

1-1 I don't know how those things are done, whether they come in small, medium and large, or what.

4-1 Small, medium, and large!

12-4 Do they?

3-3 No, they don't.

1-3 What? What did you say?

8-8 I know from a girl that worked with me. I worked for a pharmaceutical house. And we went to a convention. We had got some stuff for putting things up in them. But she did say she had to go and have one made for herself, personally.

1-1 I understand that you have to.

The evidence concerning the use of contraceptives made the strongest impression on the jury. More than any other piece of information, it indicated that the defendant was not out of touch with reality, that he was not living in the private world of the psychotic, and that he was aware of the social and moral demands of his community. If the defendant had attacked a stranger on the streets; if he had raped a child; even if he had committed the same acts with his daughter but without regard for the consequences, then his sanity might have been more seriously questioned. The use of contraceptives symbolized to the jury the defendant's concern for the future, his fear of public condemnation, and his ability to manipulate his environment so as to maximize his immediate gratifications and to minimize the possibility of public exposure.

Turning briefly to the housebreaking case, we note that, like the jurors in the incest case, these jurors also stressed the defendant's behavior at the time of the crime rather than his childhood or other events in his past. They also asked: Were his acts premeditated? Did they seem purposive and rational? Were they goal-directed? The specific facts that they cited most frequently to support their belief that the defendant was insane were the items that he attempted to steal. The fact that they were small and of little value indicated that the defendant was not robbing for profit, i.e., that there was no rational purpose behind his behavior. One juror put it this way: "If you were going to go out and break into someone's house, would you take the chance of breaking into somebody's house and getting caught and spending a couple of years in jail just to steal a cigarette lighter or a pair of cuff links?"

A second factor frequently cited by jurors in the housebreaking case was the defendant's position when the police found him. One juror described it as follows:

> The defendant was hiding in such a childish way, in a corner holding something over his face like an ostrich. His failure to resist arrest by fighting or running away was not the behavior of the normal criminal, who would have been aware of his situation and the consequences of being caught.

It is interesting that jurors who argued in favor of finding the defendant guilty emphasized essentially the same facts as the NGI jurors: the defendant's behavior at the scene of the crime and the items he attempted to steal. But when the jurors who decided to vote guilty reviewed Graham's behavior, they noted:

> If in broad daylight, with people watching him, he had thrown a brick through the window and then tried to enter the house, that would have indicated insanity. But here, we have a case in which the defendant broke into an empty house in the middle of the night by fiddling with the lock.
>
> When he entered the house, he did it so quietly and at a time when any ordinary burglar would think it safe to break in. Once he was in the house, he didn't turn on any lights, which again is normal for a burglar; and he was selective in the articles he stole; that is, he took small pieces that were easy to carry and negotiable.

In both trials the jurors focused on the defendant's behavior immediately preceding and following the crime. Details about his background, his early childhood, his adolescence, and his family life were of much less interest to the jury.

The defendant's background

The psychiatrists in the incest trial testified that the defendant's father either died or deserted the family when the defendant was very young and that a strong emotional dependence developed between mother and son which was sharply severed when a stepfather appeared on the scene. The defendant was then six years old. The stepfather was described as a cold, rejecting person who made little attempt to relate to the young boy. When the defendant was between three and six years old, he had an opportunity to observe patrons of his mother's dance hall engage in perverse sexual acts. During this same period boys employed by the mother in her confectionery business introduced him to the practice of masturbation by so engaging themselves in his presence.

From the traditional perspective of criminal law, environmental influences such as poverty, broken homes, maternal separation, and deprivation are not expected to totally overwhelm the individual, although the law recognizes that they may exert some influence on his behavior. In general, the jurors' attitudes reaffirmed the traditional view of the law. They agreed that discussion of the specific environmental factors was helpful in understanding the defendant's behavior, but that the circumstances of his childhood did not excuse his behavior as an adult.

The following is an excerpt from a jury that heard the typical psychiatric version under *Durham:*

> His background, it does not seem to me, should justify his becoming the type of person he has become. Not that he was not unhappy: his childhood, his experiences, a stepfather, threats, improper sex acts, but that should not have any effect on his becoming unbalanced to the point of being excusable for what he has done. I do not doubt that he was a borderline case, but I cannot see that he should be found not guilty and excused for his acts because I am sure he understood what he has done. In my opinion it is a matter of being able to determine right from wrong.

Jurors who were exposed to the model version shared similar feelings. One juror argued:

> All right now, this gentleman over here brought up the question of Leopold and Loeb a while ago. You keep basing your opinion because this fellow did not have a father. I was raised without a father, so was that man. [Referring to another juror.] Loeb and Leopold came from wealthy families. They were millionaires. They had all the physical comforts and the stuff that money could buy; but there was something lacking in their early bringing up, in the understanding of their parents and in their family and friends.

Another juror responded: "Well, can you take any one of the twelve of us here and say absolutely that man there was raised with everything he needed? He had his own mother, his own father? You can't with any of us." The first juror agreed: "No. Yet, we are not so maladjusted that we go out of our way to commit a crime of this sort. I think everybody had had a lot of disappointments and had been deprived of stuff at some time or other in their childhood, but it did not make them into a criminal."

In another jury that was also instructed under the *Durham* rule, a juror suggested: "He is to be pitied because he was brought up in terrible surroundings. He probably did not understand the decent things of life, not as well as most people do. He was not brought up in a decent respectable house." But another juror responded:

> But he still knew the difference between what is generally recognized as right and wrong. The fact of having been brought up in poor surroundings, okay, we will recognize that as a fact, but people can rise above their surroundings. Sometimes they will turn to hate their surroundings and they will do the opposite.

Another juror commented along a somewhat different vein:

> Throughout his life he keeps calling attention to what a hard life he had. He said when he was young he saw indecent acts in the place where his mother ran her business. I think that was being used to direct sympathy. If he saw an indecent act when he was at that age, why didn't he walk away from it? But he evidently stayed there. He watched what was going on because he followed suit shortly afterward. His mind was not affected then. He watched and he did. That is his statement. I do not see how a three-year-old can remember what took place when he was three years old. I do not. Do you remember anything when you were three years old?

On the whole, the jurors were not impressed with the account they heard of the defendant's childhood; at least not so impressed that they were willing to excuse his behavior because of it. They placed great emphasis on an individual's responsibility for controlling his own destiny and for rising above difficult surroundings. Many jurors argued that a man always has the opportunity to choose between good and evil. In failing to exercise that choice in the direction of good, the defendant demonstrated a weakness of character — not a mental disease. Some jurors suggested that, if anything, a difficult childhood should serve as an incentive for self-achievement.

To summarize, we think that the jury's use of the record shows that it believed that no crime, not even incest or cannibalism, is prima facie evidence of insanity. No matter how bizarre or perverse the crime itself, the jury will still go back and review all the homey details surrounding the case. It will trace and re-trace all aspects of the defendant's behavior, and if it finds some logical consistency or rationality about it, it will be strongly inclined to find the defendant sane.

2. *The jury's understanding of an insanity plea*

Some jurors believe that the plea of insanity is a popular defense and that it is especially popular among persons charged with unusually heinous or violent crimes. They believe also that the juries' verdicts in such cases generally favor the defendant.[4] Believing this, some jurors sought to convince their colleagues that it was their responsibility to protest this practice by finding the defendant guilty, and to articulate their opposition to society's increasing willingness to excuse socially and morally delinquent behavior by labeling persons who engaged in such behavior as "sick." One juror, deliberating under the *Durham* instructions, expressed his feelings as follows:

> There is too much here of late being said about insanity and sanity. The more publicity this sort of thing gets through the newspapers and everything else, the more it is a hiding place for people to run when they get caught. A lot of people use this plea of insanity as a hiding place from jail. They would rather be put into an institution for a much lesser period of time and then get back into society to do the same thing over again. I have always said this and felt this way. There is not enough emphasis on right and wrong. We just do not have a line which we can point to and say that distance and no further and automatically expect to receive punishment for anything above that standard. That is why we will always have somebody pleading a certain way according to what their attorneys says and he gets away with it. Then, the

[4] In fact, considering the whole range of criminal cases that are heard by juries in state and federal courts each year, the percentage of defense of insanity trials is only about 2 per cent. Some data and a more detailed discussion of this topic may be found in Chapter 10.

next man tries the same thing. Well, now this insanity plea, in this case is just a bunch of hooey, that is all. The man was just pure ornery because he prepared the daughter for the purpose every time and went through with it with two separate children until he finally got caught with the last one. Then he comes up with an insanity plea. After all this time, there is no need to talk about insanity. It is done!

In another deliberation, a juror made the same point more tersely: "The first thing that any person who commits a crime pleads is insanity and their need for psychiatric treatment. Everybody does that because they get off so easily now-a-days. This does not happen in foreign countries and it should not happen in this country."

In another deliberation, a juror warned:

It seems to me that what we have to think about is that every man is responsible for his own actions. We have to start from there. This defense of insanity can be an out too, just as well as it can be a fact, you know. It can be just something to draw a red herring across the trail; and it frequently is at a lot of these trials. And I think that the first place that you have to go to start with is the fact that every man is responsible for his own actions. If he is not, well, then, you get kind of an anarchy existing, see!

Jurors also referred to newspaper accounts and stories they had heard about persons who committed crimes after they were released from mental institutions to which they had been committed after having been acquitted on grounds of insanity.

We had a fellow by the name of John Gray in the stockyards. Every time he wanted to kill somebody, one of his enemies, he would go and get pretty well loaded up on liquor and go out with a gun and kill them. He had good lawyers and they pleaded he was insane. They put him away for a year or two, then he came right back out and on the same corner he pulled the same thing. Every time he wanted to kill somebody, he became temporarily insane. That stuff is all right; they get away with it.

In the past few years, it seems to me that with all the art of psychiatry and with everything else that has been pushed forward, I think at the present time we have about the highest criminal rate. Too much is given to mental illness. You find that on juries like ourselves, they are too prone to waive a person's crime just on the basis that they say he is mentally ill. There has also been a great many cases that I have read about in the newspapers. I have heard of instances where people have been released from these institutions and have gone right back and committed the same crimes over again.

A few of the more zealous jurors acted as if they had exposed a hitherto unknown but pervasive deviant practice which if allowed to continue would seriously weaken the society's moral code. These jurors felt that it was their responsibility to prevent any further extension of this social cancer and they viewed a verdict of guilty as the first act in their program of reform.

If a person can commit a crime like this with impunity, without any thought of having to pay for his sins, why then I think the world would be flooded with this type of crime. Maybe not this particular type, but very similar types of other sexual crimes. Just because there are people who live like animals that does not keep them from being responsible like humans; because they know the difference.

In the same deliberation, another juror added: "The only way that acts like this can be prevented, the only way that society can be protected from all kinds of serious offenses, is by suitable punishment. I mean, I am not saying that we will stop it, but I think it will be worse if we do not have it." From another deliberation: "I do not feel that whether this person (the defendant) goes to jail or not is going to help him too much. But, it might square away somebody else who learns about it and finds that he cannot get away with this kind of bunk, and, that's the important point."

Several jurors confessed that their first reaction upon hearing that the charge was incest was: The man must be crazy. It was only after they listened to the details of the case, particularly the number of times the acts were committed, the defendant's use of contraceptives, the facts about his employment record, and the steady advances he made in his position that they began to doubt their initial reaction.

For instance, the following discussion was taken from a *Durham* deliberation:

> The point is you can have a quirk and still be a member of society as long as you have the mental sense not to allow your quirk to break the law. But, if you break the law, because you have this quirk and still have the mental capacity to know what you are doing and go ahead and do it deliberately, then you are not insane. Then it is no excuse or alibi that you have a quirk. The judge's instructions say that if you think he has a mental illness then you should judge this man insane. If I cut my finger am I ill? I have damage to my body, but is that an illness? I mean is it to the degree that we are trying to judge here. My argument is that the expert testimony does not associate a mental illness to this man that has significance in terms of insanity. They have associated what is known as a neurosis. If we had a medical dictionary here I think you will see that neurosis means where you think a little differently than the average man. But it does not mean that you have lost control over your senses; even when you are indulging in your neurosis.

In another jury, the following exchange occurred:

8-2   But would any normal man do anything like that if he did not have a mental disturbance?

2-8   He is not normal to begin with, but that does not mean he is insane.

5-5   There is a drawing line. But where do we draw the line?

7-7   That is the point.

2-7   I just told you.

7-2   No, you have not told me yet.

2-7   Yes, I have. Listen to me. If a person can live among average people in an average society without doing anything toward them, without harming them in any way, you understand what I mean?

7-2   Uh huh.

2-7   And have an occupation, be employed, and live among society then he is considered sane. The minute he does some untoward act toward society, in other words if he rapes, robs, kills, murders, or does other things that are not according to the social norm, or an accepted social norm, then he is considered insane.

7-2   Well, he did these things, didn't he?

2-7 But he did it in his home.

5-5 He is considered sane then?

7-2 I do not think where he did it makes any difference. You have not defined insanity for me.

2-7 I mean he was able to keep a house and everything. I mean, he did not hurt anybody, did he?

7-2 You mean he was sane because he did it in his home, and if he would have done it outside some place he would have been insane?

2-7 No, I mean he had a lucrative job. He kept a household.

4-4 I think the definition was fine except for the last statement that you have to commit a robbery or a murder, or, you are not insane . . .

2-4 Not robbery. I do not mean robbery. I mean something that is against, I mean, let's say, what is that, ahh . . .

9-2 A crime against nature.

2-9 That is right, something like that. Yes. This is really a crime against society. It is not a, it's more than just a judicial crime. You wouldn't call it . . .

9-2 That is not a natural thing to do.

2-9 That is right. That is right.

Both of these discussions suggest that the kinds of symptoms the jurors associate with insanity are violence, irresponsible behavior, and an inability to carry out ordinary day-to-day activities such as those involved in doing one's job.

For some jurors the problem became one of distinguishing degrees of insanity. One juror said:

> Well, I still think that any individual who in the commission of wrong doing, understands the consequences of that wrong doing, and takes precautions; all that indicates that the man to that extent, is in his right mind. He is thinking. Whatever the act, he was certainly aware of what would happen. He was aware of the wrongness of the act. He felt the guilt, he felt the remorse. When a person is insane, it seems to me, he is completely, would you say out of this world. His mind does not function that way. And when his mind is completely malfunctioning, he is retained in an institution.

Another juror reacted:

I think we should all try to look at this and try to pinpoint the key factors to determine whether or not this man should be judged guilty or not guilty. The whole thing could be summed up by pointing out the difference between a psychosis and a psychoneurosis: a psychosis being a form of mental disease which puts the person out of touch with reality. A psychoneurosis is what practically everybody has to a more or less degree. I think it was pretty well established that he is not psychotic, that he is not out of touch with reality, and that he is not insane in the manner that we think of people being insane; who are confined to mental institutions. If this man is let go, then that places practically every one of us on the same basis. If I go out and rob a bank, I could plead insanity. There are probably some behavior characteristics in my life which could be judged not exactly according to normal in the way a psychologist would define normal. And neither is this, sexual perversion, that of course is not normal. Therefore, if this man is freed then we would have to re-examine the whole legal system.

And another:

It is just incredible to me that anyone should be as rational as this fellow is all the time, whenever anyone talked with him; and not be responsible for his acts. I mean his answers are sensible, his reasons are logical; they may be criminal but they follow a pattern. How can you live like that and not be responsible? Then perhaps only one million out of 160 million could really be considered responsible for their acts. There would be mighty few.

One juror supplied a personal analogy:

He had a mental disorder, but was it of such a magnitude that the man was not responsible for his acts? Can a man have a mental disorder and still have enough free will to make up his mind whether to commit an act or not? You follow me? I mean suppose I like to go out and get drunk on Saturday nights and I love to and I do it lots of Saturday nights. But as long as I make a mental decision ahead of time that that is what I am going to do, and make it, say, in a reasonably sound mind, then I am responsible for going out and getting drunk on Saturday night. I mean, I make the decision of my own free will, I use what is normally deemed as a normal mind to make the decision, because after I am drunk I no longer have a normal mind. But did this man have free will? What I am trying to differentiate is whether this mental disorder or emotional disorder, depending on which man you want to listen to, was such that it denied this man free will in making a decision. If the mental disorder denied him the free will, then he cannot act like an average person on making a decision. See what I am trying to say? If the act of having a neurosis, and the psychiatrists can tell if a neurosis, is a type of mental disorder that takes away your free will? As long as a person can make a rational decision then the neurosis is not sufficient to say that a man is not guilty of a crime?

In essence, many of the jurors were saying that when all aspects of the defendant's life were examined, his behavior appeared no less rational than their own except for his incestuous relations with his daughters. They found no other evidence that would support exempting the defendant from responsibility unless the commission of the act itself was sufficient grounds for declaring him mentally incompetent; that criterion they were unwilling to accept.

The symptoms that the jurors most frequently associated with insanity were indulgence in spontaneous emotional activities that seem pointless to a "normal" observer and that were generally carried out with little or no concern for consequences. One juror observed:

> He is too methodical to be insane. I mean, he did it too regularly. If it would have happened the first time and then the girl told on him, to me this would have made a difference. But this was periodically, I mean this was forthright. He planned it. I mean if a man gets emotionally upset one day or something like that, that is possible. Then he gets caught at it and that is the end of it. I believe that the man could be emotionally upset at one time, but here is a man that does it periodically, and then goes back and forth from one daughter to the other.

Another juror remembered the ages of the daughters, and commented:

> If he had been insane, well, I think that probably he would have started on his daughters at an earlier age. But he waited

until they were about eleven or twelve years old. Any of us that have daughters know that is when your daughter starts performing more like a woman. That is when actually he started getting after those girls. If he had been insane he would have attacked them when they were four or five years old, or six or seven.

Other jurors had similar reactions:

Let us look at it from this standpoint. If the man was insane at the time the act was committed, if he did not know what he was doing, then he might have grabbed your daughter or my daughter if we were living nearby and do the same thing, when this passion would come on him. But here he got artificial respiration [probably means contraceptives] and all this protection and controls against the act, against the very germ of pregnancy, let us put it that way. If he had enough control over himself to shun your daughter and my daughter and just use his daughter, the man was just pure ornery.

Many jurors found troublesome the defendant's consistency, as manifest by his having sexual relations only with his daughters, and only after they began to mature sexually. For example:

If he had done it five different times with five different girls in the community that would be grounds for insanity. If it were different girls at different times, or if he had just grabbed the girls and carried them into an alley. I mean, if you were downtown and got an urge, you are downtown amongst all the people, if you get enough control of yourself to go out of there into a certain district, you have enough control not to do it, period. Now that is that. So this man here is not insane. Every act was in his house. And he used birth control methods. Let us use the words, because that is exactly what it was. That is something some of us that are purely sane, do not even use.

In another deliberation:

Here is what I cannot hardly conceive of. The fact that in his testimony, he said that during the period over which these acts occurred, he made every effort to avoid pregnancy. Have you seen a diaphragm, vaginal douche, suppositories, and prophylactics? If that man was nutty or insane and over a period of nineteen or twenty times, if that man would have forced his daughter or beat his daughter or his wife. He says his wife was not sexually inclined. Well so what? Why does he have to take it out on his girl, right in his own house? He did not beat her, he did not harm her, he did not do anything. When a man is insane, or even on the borderline of being insane, they go out and get what they want and get it in any manner in which they want to get it. Now you read in the paper, you read in magazines, in periodicals and in the like about these different things. These boys that are insane, they just, they just rape them out in alleys and everywhere else. Well what I'm trying to bring out is this, one time in their testimony they will say one thing and pretty soon they will go haywire and will try to punch somebody or something like that, but this man was a gentleman all the way through.

The fact that the defendant "was a gentleman" was another source of disturbance for many jurors. They mentioned over and over again that there was no evidence that he used physical violence on members of his family, that he failed to provide for them, or that he failed to maintain a respectable job and place in the community. Many of the jurors doubted that an insane person would be able to present such a consistently reasonable front. They were willing to grant that a person does not have to be mentally defective, that he does not have to be a raving, hallucinating maniac before they could find him not guilty by reason of insanity; but the picture of calmness, detachment and, respectability that characterized Jason Lunt was too much for most of them.

About half of the jurors assumed that there is a relationship between cognitive functioning and mental illness. A few suggested a positive correlation between insanity and high intelligence, but most maintained that it is *sub*-normal intelligence and insanity that are positively related.

For instance when a juror commented that the defendant must have been intelligent "considering how well he scored on his tests," another replied: "His IQ must have been good. Experts on the subject will say genius is akin to madness." In another jury, when the discussion came around to the defendant's performance on the civil service examinations: "Yes, but, then I think that you will find that in most cases where a person is insane, that on a test, his mental capacity is much stronger. That is, he gets better grades than other people that are not. You will find a lot of these geniuses . . ." Juror 1 interrupted: "Well, they claim that it's a step from genius to insanity."

But the following kinds of comments were more frequent:

> The man held quite a responsible position with the fire department. He was a lieutenant. Now, if a man has that much knowledge and assuming that he has average intelligence, first of all to get out of high school then, all of a sudden to go off the deep end and commence to do something like that, which is, well as wild as I have ever heard of, I think he just cannot be screwy to hold that kind of a position.

Juror 8: Well, the thing that makes it so unusual, so unbelievable is the fact that he is an average man who can read and write and who has an average education. And he is a fireman, that is what makes it so unusual.

Juror 9: Well, actually he was above average.

Juror 8: That's it. If he was somebody else, somebody who did not know how to read or write, and his wife did not know how to read or write and they were Indians, or something, somewhere. But she must, she went to school with him, high school.

Juror 9: Well, I do not know that she went very far in school.

Juror 8: Well, she did too, she went to high school with him.

Juror 9: She did not get much out of it then because she certainly was not very intelligent.

The rest of the jurors acted as if they assumed that the relationship between intelligence, cognitive functioning, and mental illness was more complicated than could be described by a simple correlation between the quantity of intelligence and mental illness. For example, in response to the following statement: "I do not know if any of you folks have passed a civil service test, but this disease or whatever they want to call it, he must have been fairly sane because those were not easy tests that he had to pass. He had to have a sort of sanity in mentality." Juror 3 explained: "As I understand it, you can be perfectly sane in some subjects and entirely off in others." Juror 4 agreed: "That is right because intelligence and insanity or lack of insanity have nothing to do with each other."

In other juries:

> I don't think being able to pass a test has anything to do with insanity. As far as his mental knowledge is concerned, he can have all kinds of knowledge about certain subjects, but it does not make him sane.
>
> Did you ever see any of these patients in mental hospitals? There are lots of them, that are pretty well. If you saw them anywhere else, you would not think they were insane. And they are not dumb either. Lots of them are not dumb. You can really teach them something like anyone else, and boy, they can be pretty smart at it. They are not a bit dumb.

As we read and listened to the deliberations, we were surprised at how easily the jurors described accounts of mental disturbance involving their most intimate family members to a group of strangers. These accounts provide the clearest understanding of the jurors' image of mental illness and of their attitudes toward persons so afflicted. Indeed, if we were asked to name the one factor that was most influential in determining a juror's verdict, the extent to which the defendant resembled or failed to resemble someone whom the juror knew to be mentally ill would rank extremely high. A few of these accounts are described in detail on the following pages.

The first account is from a deliberation in which it was revealed that two of the jurors had a parent in a mental hospital. In his first comment, Juror 2 told the group:

> My father died in an institution. He had had a stroke and his mind was affected. Most of those patients, most of the time, are abnormal and insane. Sometimes they act just the same as we do; but very seldom. Most of the time they are off, really off.

Juror 2 had no more than completed his remarks when Juror 4 announced:

I have to disagree there. My mother is in _____ right now. She has been there for the last eighteen years. Of course hers was from change of life. We have people visit her and she tells everybody that the children do not want her home, that she is all right. Now we all know that they would not keep them there if they were all right and yet my mother is normal. We take her home every once in a while. You would never think anything is wrong, but yet she is there.

Juror 2: That is what the doctors told us too, we could take my dad home for a weekend but he would never be responsible.

Juror 4: But they are judged insane. You would never think now in my mother's case, that there's anything wrong. She has her nieces, aunts and others visit her and they say —

Juror 2: Do they always find her that way though?

Juror 4: Well, as a rule I guess they find her that way.

Juror 2: One day we would go there and my dad would be real nice and then, the next day, he —

Juror 4: Of course, I know, because when I am with my mother more than two hours on Sunday, she starts hearing voices. People are talking about her and things like that. But these people are there maybe for a half an hour and they go away. She does not get any disturbance from that much.

Later in the same deliberation Juror 4 continued:

I do not know now whether I should bring this up again but I have been seeing my mother for 18 years, oh, maybe once a month on Sunday and there is never anything wrong. But I get all kinds of reports about what she does during the week. Sometimes they all get into a fight or beat the nurses and yet I would swear if I was in court that there is never anything wrong. She has never harmed anybody while I was there; never even tried. Now how do you account for that? That is 18 years and every time I, or any of the family see her she is normal. They certainly would not keep her there for 18 years if she was all right. These relatives that visit her they say her children do not want her. That they want to leave her in there. They all believe that she is sane and we kids do not want her home, that she is too much trouble. Now how do you explain that?

Juror 2 commented: "That is another thing about insane people. They behave much better when doctors and nurses are around than they do with their own family." Juror 3 added: "I talked to a man once in an institution, a private institution, for three hours and thought he was one of the attendants. I found out later he was hopelessly insane." Juror 4 told about having his mother committed:

> I am talking now about the time before we had her committed; and this happened for over a year. I never suspected it. Things she said or did; and this was going on over a year. Finally I started looking back over it and started putting it all together. One night she puts on her coat and she goes out. It was pretty cold. We lived at 5300 West _____ and I got into my car and I followed her. She walked across to _____ that's 4400 West. Walked all the way there and I just watching to see what she was going to do. She turned back and that is when I picked her up to come back home. Now that had gone on for years and none of us suspected that she took a daily walk. She walked around and she accused people of things. She accused this woman of howling at her out in the alley. Maybe it did happen. You do not put these things together when everything is normal. When I go back over these things, she was off for a year without our suspecting it. So I followed her one day. I asked her where she was going. She could not give any reason. That is what convinced me. A whole year and none of us knowing. Now who would have known what to call her then at that time, if anything had happened?

Juror 7 observed: "When you stopped your mother, she did not know where she was going. She did not know where or what she was doing. But when this fellow was caught he knew that he was being observed. He got frightened and he ran off. He knew he was doing something wrong." But Juror 4 added: "My mother was smart too. She did things wrong and we never caught on." Juror 7: "But she did not realize that she was doing anything wrong. She was just doing them over and over." Juror 4: "But she was hiding it. She was able to hide it — that is what I'm trying to say."

In another deliberation, a juror described a less personal experience:

> I have been down to _____. A doctor friend of mine was superintendent there for a few years. And I talked to one man who was in the criminally insane cells — it is not part of the institution really, it is part of the state prison, but it is administered by the hospital for the insane. This man was an expert cabinet maker and he committed a murder. But he works down there in the cabinet shop and does the most beautiful work. I tried to talk to him, because I am interested in that sort of thing. And he talked just as rationally as you or I. And the doctor told me that he does talk just as rationally most of the time, but, every now and then, something happens; and he goes off on a binge and then they have to get doctors and I do not know, shock treatments, whatever they do. Then he comes out of it and he is all right for a little bit of time. And then there was a woman there in the hospital, an old woman, that was just as quiet and docile a creature as you would want to see, sitting there talking to the woman next to her. And she talked with me, and finally she said, "Could I kiss you?" Well, I said, I do not think that is part of the regulations. Well, she said, "I like you." Well, she was off on a binge there for a few minutes, and pretty soon she forgot all about it and was all right again. Well, I went down there several times and I talked to several like that, and there would be times when they would be perfectly normal. And when they are you would swear that they are just as normal as any of us — during those periods. I think that in this case it appears that this fellow [the defendant] had mental disturbances from the time — almost from birth. From the time he was three years old or earlier. But from my observations, that can happen to certain people, and still they can be normal and lead a normal life with respect to their relationship with others, probably most of the time. Then suddenly something happens, and they go off. Something goes wrong with them at the time. And the fact that he apparently has no remorse for what he did indicated that there was an abnormality there that probably never could be corrected. It indicates to me just as clear a case of something wrong mentally as though he were very apparently insane. I would be inclined to think that he is better off in an insane hospital than he would be if he was adjudged guilty as an ordinary criminal.

In other deliberations, jurors told these stories:

> Well, we have a friend in an institution and yet you would
> never know, you would not think that he really belongs there.
> All he really does is write checks when he has not got sufficient
> money in the bank. Yet when he gets this attack that is what
> he does. He writes checks. He calls people up at 2 o'clock in
> the morning and disturbs them. Yet, he would not hurt any-
> body. But his people know that when he gets that way, he is
> on one of these maniacs, I think they call it. I mean it comes
> on fast, and they cure him fast. But, yet, you take, I mean
> somebody that did not know him, they would take that person
> and put him in prison and what he really needs is a doctor's
> care. If his family did not hurry up and take care of him and
> take him to the institution when he needs help, well naturally
> these people that got those checks and the checks bounced
> back, he would be in prison. Of course, he takes care of it,
> after he comes out. He takes care of those checks then.

> Insanity is not always detectable at any particular time. I
> know a case of an army officer, who had a fairly high rank for
> a number of years. All of a sudden out of the clear sky, it de-
> velops that he is unsuitable to continue as an officer. So he
> got a discharge. I think they call it a section 8 or what. Now,
> that had never shown up in all of his career. He had reached
> a fairly high rank as an officer, had all of the tests, mind you,
> and was supposed to be capable of holding his rank. He got
> his promotions and all that. There was something there that
> did not come out at a certain time, but it had been there for a
> while.

Another juror asked him: "Did he receive his section 8 because of insanity or something that did not make him suitable
as an officer?" He responded: "Well, the state of the unbal-
ance was such that it was decided that he was not mentally
competent. I do not know exactly what type of discharge he
got, but they put him in a mental hospital. And yet, he had
conducted the business of the battalion."

In one jury, Juror 12 held the attention of the others for
about ten minutes with these stories:

> Well, I have two cases. One is a very close friend and the
> other is a relative. First I will start with the friend. I feel

this very deeply. The man in this particular case was brilliant. He was called in the second World War, to go down to _____ University. He was a pioneer in dehydration, you know, of food stuffs. So you know how brilliant he was. Nothing in his background that would tend or lead anyone to thinking that he would get anything like that. But he got it, he became mentally ill. He has been down to Wisconsin, I will not mention the name of the town, you all know where it is. He has been down there about, at least 8 times, going through shock treatments. In between the first treatment and the third treatment, he tried to, he did not get a young girl, but he got an older girl. Now he was not that type of individual. See? And as I say, he took about eight treatments. The man is okay as far as we can see; but he is not the man he was before he became mentally ill.

Juror 7 asked, "You say you think he is completely normal now?"

Juror 12: Well, he is not, but he is very good. He had to retire, but his firm has taken care of him. Nobody thinks ill of him. You need not be ashamed of it if somebody has to go to a psychiatrist. All right — number two is a girl. She was at that time twenty-seven or twenty-eight years old. Nicest kid you ever want to lay your eyes on. Wonderful background, parents wonderful, and it started about I would say, eight to ten months before anyone actually knew what was happening, before you could see it coming. You know what I mean? She was suspicious of everything and everybody, you know. She was trying to say so and so, some man had taken her out, and all that. She was a single girl. It did not happen, but it was in her mind. She was getting worse and worse and worse. One of our noted physicians got hold of her, not a psychiatrist. He got hold of her, and then he in turn called in a psychiatrist and then they in turn between the two of them, sent her to this place in Wisconsin. Have you ever seen a victim of that shock treatment? You would never want to see them again if you ever have. I happened to see this, in particular. I went down there to see her. I would not want to see it again. That shock treatment is something. It has been going on now for four years. She lost her job. She was head bookkeeper for one of the big concerns here, getting a good salary, I mean, she was tops. You bucks would have liked to have had her as a wife. I mean she is that type of girl. Well, here about six months ago, they let her out for a while. She called up two friends of ours that are doctors, that she knows very well, not at the same time, but different intervals. Wanted to see them. Well, she got them down and then she says, "Can we take a ride out in the country?" Boy, I am telling you, she was sexually off balance, too. I do not know why it rides in that direction, but that is what it is. So I am just telling you what I know is true. I had this case in mind when I was thinking about what I would do with this fellow [the defendant]. I tell you, you do not know when it is going to strike your own family. Boy and I am telling you, it is a heartache to anyone of us. When you see that happening, there is not a thing you can do to stop it.

Juror 7: You mean it happens over a long period of time, or it —

Juror 12: Yes, this man happened over a period of two years. This girl over a period of, I would say, maybe a year and four or five months. You could see it starting to unravel.

In exposing his own experience to the scrutiny of others, a juror not only provided the group with more concrete information about mental illness, but in many instances he obtained therapy for himself. The opportunity to describe one's own involvement with someone who is mentally ill in an atmosphere that is both impersonal and supportive permits expressions of ambivalence about one's own participation. Such expressions served two functions. They relieved some of the juror's guilt about his own behavior vis-à-vis the spouse or parent whose commitment he was responsible for, and they reduced some of his negative affect toward the defendant. These results were especially apparent in the case of the juror who described the events leading up to his mother's commitment.

3. *The jury's concern about the norm for non-responsibility*

A suspicion frequently voiced about the jury is that it pays no attention to legal rules either because it does not understand them or because it decides they are irrelevant or unimportant. Our interest here is to find out what rule or criterion, if any, the jury referred to in deciding whether the defendant was responsible for his behavior.

Of the thirty-nine transcribed deliberations, twelve were instructed under *M'Naghten,* thirteen were *uninstructed* and fourteen were instructed under *Durham*. Eight of the twelve juries who heard the *M'Naghten* instructions considered explicitly the defendant's ability to distinguish right from wrong. In addition, seven out of the thirteen *uninstructed* and seven out of the fourteen *Durham* juries also considered the defendant's ability to distinguish right from wrong. In other words, even though only 31 per cent of the juries were formally instructed along the lines of the *M'Naghten* criterion, 56 per cent of all the juries considered the right-from-wrong formula in their assessment of the defendant. Most jurors seemed to feel that the ability to distinguish between right and wrong should have been internalized as part of one's basic personality, and that anyone reared in this society or for that matter almost any society should have learned that incest is wrong.

The following discussion which we think illustrates this perspective occurred in a jury that was instructed under the *Durham* formula and therefore had heard no reference by the court to "right from wrong." Juror 8 was speaking:

> If you say that a man is insane because he does something wrong, something that he knows is wrong, as in this case, then you could say the same thing about a burglar or a robber or anyone. Are they insane when they commit these acts? Our society brought us up in such a way as to believe that these particular acts are wrong; as any sexual perversion is wrong. Going back to Cleopatra's day, why brothers and sisters got

married and had children; and it was not considered wrong. But we have been brought up to believe that it is wrong. Now in his (the defendant's) mind he knew that it was wrong according to our society's teachings, but that doesn't make him insane or mentally unbalanced. Being wrong is guilty.

The following excerpt is another instance in which the right-from-wrong criterion was considered extra-legally, that is, by juries not instructed along the lines of the *M'Naghten* formula. The discussion occurred in an *uninstructed on responsibility* jury.

Juror 12: Well, sometimes, years ago, when families lived on farm communities . . . Well, say that a man lived in an isolated area, he and his family, that is, where there were brothers and sisters in families. In isolated communities there have been cases of incest. It had taken place and the people that were involved were not insane, they were not emotionally disturbed. It was part of their growing up and dicovering life. There was nobody else around and they just . . .

Juror 2: Well, I would call that just being brought up in ignorance. No training.

Juror 12: That is ignorance. But this man was in a community. He lived in a city and with society about him: and he knew he did something wrong.

Juror 2: Well I still say that I cannot imagine anyone performing anything like that unless there was something wrong with his mind in some respect.

Juror 1: Well, I don't know if this is true or not, but I have heard that the morals of the people in the different countries vary. It could be, it was not brought out what nationality this man was, but it could be that the morals of his country were a little bit lower than ours.

For most jurors, the defendant's admission that he knew that what he was doing was wrong proved that he was guilty and not insane. The fact that in most jurisdictions the legal norm for determining responsibility inquires as to the defendant's ability to distinguish right from wrong illustrates a convergence of legal norms and popular sentiments.

But there were some jurors who questioned whether the

principle of right from wrong was the proper criterion for determining non-responsibility. Strangely enough, in a jury deliberating under the *M'Naghten* rule one of the jurors argued: "Well, just because you can tell right from wrong does not mean that you are not insane. Why, I have known people who were affected by insanity and they did know right from wrong."

But the paradox is that while most of the *uninstructed* juries referred to the right-from-wrong principle during their deliberations, they reported verdicts that were much closer to the verdicts of juries that deliberated under *Durham*, not *M'Naghten*. We would have expected just the opposite. Having heard that the *uninstructed* juries use the right-from-wrong formula in determining the defendant's guilt, we guessed that the verdicts of the *uninstructed* and *M'Naghten* juries would be very similar. Instead, it is the verdicts of the *Durham* juries that match those of the *uninstructed* juries.

4. *The jury's evaluation of the psychiatrists' testimony*

The psychiatrists' testimony was reviewed in almost every deliberation. Many of the discussions focused on the problem of distinguishing between the expert's function and the jury's responsibility. The question that the jury considered over and over again was: Who should have the final say about what happens to the defendant — a jury of laymen or a group of medical experts? The following excerpts capture the general tone of those discussions.

> Is there anybody in this room who doesn't believe in psychiatry? That is the whole thing in my estimation. It is whether or not you are going to take the word of these two men, who are well-known and are admired in their field, and have excellent jobs. They are impartial. They are working for the county hospital. Are you going to take their word, or are you going to sit there and say that we know? We don't even know this man. They worked with him, they both say that he is mentally disturbed. If you don't take that as proof, I don't know what you are going to do. I mean, to me, in

other words, if you don't find him not guilty by reason of insanity, you are sitting here disregarding the two psychiatrists in the case.

A juror disagreed:

Just because these two people are educated and they are way up over our heads we don't have to accept what they say as truth and that is it. In other words, they would be deciding for us. We would not be deciding for ourselves what is right in this particular case.

A third juror interrupted:

If that is the case, this case shouldn't ever have gone to a jury. I mean that we should have to depend upon men specialized in the field of psychiatry to judge this man. But the judge said that we could disregard their testimony, if we wanted to. After all you can't base your whole opinion on the fact that these people have degrees.

Another juror continued: "That is right, you don't need a jury if you are going to take two doctors' words and say that this man is insane. Why do you need a jury?" In one jury, a juror complained: "They should have gotten a bunch of psychiatrists to decide this case." Another asked:

May I inject a joke in the proceedings please? This is like the story of the two psychiatrists who passed one another on the street. One said good morning. The other psychiatrist walked about two steps past, then paused and said, "I wonder what he meant by that?" But, seriously, you understand that there are apparently four different schools of psychiatry, all of whom claim their school is right and the other school wrong. And although they have made progress in psychiatry, I don't think they have identified it as a precise science as yet.

In another deliberation, a juror enlightened his colleagues about psychiatry by explaining:

I think psychiatrists are the first to realize that there is a spread of an area, lying above and below and there is no definite point where a person is sane here and insane there. Freud said everything was sex. Adler and Jung came along and they said, well it is not so much that everything is sex; there are other factors that enter into it. Now Freud is discredited by many. His theory has been junked. But in the past they used to say, well, if there is anything wrong with you it is because you were in love with your mother at the age of three weeks, or something like that, see. Now they don't stress sex so heavily, and all the things that are in it. But still, as you say, they don't come out definitely and say this man is insane or he is not insane.

In general, the psychiatrists fared better among jurors in the housebreaking case than they did in the incest trial.[5] One juror in the housebreaking case summed up his feelings with this illustration:

I don't know anything about this technically, but if a doctor said you had appendicitis, and you said no, I have not got appendicitis, who would you believe? Now, it is true that you might go to another doctor, but if he said the same thing, who would you believe? Your own feelings that you had a pain in your side, or the doctors', that you had appendicitis?

The jurors' chief criticism of the experts' testimonies was the psychiatrists' refusal to answer questions pertaining to those areas which the court has reserved for the jury: questions bearing on the defendant's sanity or insanity and his responsibility or lack of responsibility. Some of the jurors recognized that the psychiatrists' refusal arose from their desire to adhere to the distinction established by the court between the function of the expert and that of the jury, but most were impatient and annoyed by it.

Well, these doctors didn't say he was insane.
They didn't say he was sane, either.
No, that's why the doctors aren't helping us at all. They left us out on a limb.

[5] When jurors in the housebreaking case were asked to choose between a jury and a group of psychiatrists, 66 per cent favored the psychiatrists over the jury. In the incest case, only 33 per cent favored the psychiatrists. See Chapter 4.

In a *Durham*-typical jury that eventually hung, the experts' reluctance to respond in the language of the law was interpreted as follows:

As I remember it the doctor stated that this man had no emotional display, he didn't have the normal sense of guilt; but, the doctors didn't verify the man as being insane. It seems to me that in all the technical testimony, each doctor hedged away from the question of insanity. The term they were using was psychosis, the technical term, let's say, that is more commonly associated with the word "insane." But none of the three doctors tagged this man as psychotic. They tagged him in technical jargon covering his habits. But in my opinion no testimony indicated that he had a mental disorder. Part of the thing that bothers me about this is that everyone of us to some degree has a mental disorder. Anybody that likes the Cardinals but doesn't like the Browns[6] has a mental disorder because I like the Browns, you follow me? Or, for example, I raise my children differently than my neighbor raises his children, so there's something wrong with my neighbor. My only point is that in the realm of the mind there is lots of room for differences of thinking and behavior. Technically, none of the experts crossed the line and said that this man is insane. They said he had a mental disorder. Another thing that bothers me is in the judge's instructions. I believe he used the word that if he had a mental disorder, he is judged not liable for his acts. Well, basically, in my opinion, the judge's instructions are using contradictory terms to where virtually anybody who does anything wrong — from a kid stealing an apple off a push cart to a man committing murder — they judge as having a mental disorder, and as not being responsible for their acts.

In another *Durham* jury, a juror explained:

Here, in this statement by the superintendent of the hospital who examined him, he said, "We conclude that Mr. Jason Lunt is suffering from a mental illness of long standing and that the crimes with which he is charged were the products of this mental disease." He does not mention anything about the defendant being insane.

[6] Current and former St. Louis baseball teams.

Some of the jurors, however, did recognize the distinction that the psychiatrists were trying to maintain, as witness the following discussion in a *M'Naghten*-model jury: "I think if you will recall that when the psychiatrists stated that they were giving the reasons for his actions, they said that he did know right from wrong, that he was coherent, and that he knew the degree to which he was performing these acts." Another juror asked: "Were they asked whether or not they thought he was insane?" The first replied: "Yes, but they refused to answer in that word." A third juror added: "That's not in their province to answer whether he was insane or not."

The following discussion occurred in a *Durham*-typical jury:

> According to the findings of the doctors, he was not psychotic. He was, what do you call that, neurotic, disturbed.
>
> Okay, he had a psychoneurosis, but that doesn't make him insane.
>
> No, by the doctors' own testimony, that doesn't make him insane, completely.
>
> Well, the doctors said he was insane.
>
> No, they didn't say he was insane.
>
> Well, they didn't say he was sane, but they didn't say he was insane either and they are qualified. They hesitated to use the term insanity. That one doctor that was director of the institution, Dr. Fairchild, made the statement that the word "insanity," as far as psychiatry is concerned, is too ambiguous. A term to be applied only in a legal sense, and they did not feel qualified to make a legal interpretation of that word.

In the incest trial, the technical term which the psychiatrist used to describe Jason Lunt's condition was "paraphiliac neurosis," or a neurosis that manifests itself in sexual perversions. At no time did they find any evidence that Jason Lunt was psychotic. Although it happens rarely that a defendant who is not psychotic pleads insanity, the law does not have any requirements as to the severity of the defendant's disturbance before it will entertain such a plea. Many of the jurors, however, were skeptical about the legitimacy of the insanity defense in the absence of a more patent disturbance. For example:

> The part that bothers me is the difference between psychosis and neurosis. Does a neurosis technically come under the heading of insanity? I don't believe that in either the expert testimony of the defense or the prosecution, did they give this man a psychosis. In their language they used the word psychosis the way we use the word insanity; but they said he had a neurosis. This one doctor pointed out that he was treating people from the outside world who had neuroses who were carrying on their everyday business. Neurosis is not an abnormal mental situation. Most people are neurotic for one reason or another.

In a *Durham*-model deliberation, a juror noted:

> He is just a psychoneurotic, he is not a psychotic. There are so many psychoneurotics walking around you would be surprised. They go to psychiatrists yet they are able to conduct their everyday life and business normally. But they still have emotional disturbances and moments of stress and anxiety.

> Didn't that one doctor testify that he had an outside practice and in fact his whole practice consisted of mental patients? Now would you say all those mental patients should be committed? They are all neurotic and it was pointed out that this fellow was neurotic but not actually, legally insane. This doctor testified that his whole practice, practically, was of people who had neurosis. They are nervous, jumpy, maybe they do funny kinds of things; but you don't see his patients locked up in some institution, do you? Well, say this fellow's got a neurosis, or say he has a mental illness. These other people have a mental illness and they go to their psychiatrist and get treatment but you don't see them doing irrational acts and maybe breaking windows or robbing stores.

One of the jurors in an *uninstructed* version juxtaposed mental and emotional diseases and observed:

> Paraphilia was the word that one of these psychiatrists used.
> I think it was Dr. Howard Grant.[7] He described or defined it

---

[7] The psychiatrists who testified briefly for the prosecution without having examined the defendant.

not as a mental disease, he called it an emotional disease, as against a mental disease. Now by mental I would presume, that you could construe the man to be insane. We all have emotional disturbances. You come home from the office and maybe your youngster breaks all the dishes on the coffee table, or something like that and you have to count ten before you reprimand him. Or, maybe Mary Jones next door is going to have a party and she doesn't invite you, or something like that. It will disturb you emotionally. You will wonder what's happened. But that's, that's very far from this case here.

Another juror picked up the analogy:

That's right, emotions! Say you come home for supper and you don't like what your wife has fixed for supper. You yell at her: "What the hell did you make that stuff for, I don't like that." You see, you are emotionally disturbed. But, if you let these emotions get the best of you, to the point where you pick up the bread knife and slice her throat, then I would say you were insane.

For many jurors the most positive evaluation which they could make of the psychiatrist's testimony was that they sympathized with the difficulties of his role. By sympathize we mean they understood that the psychiatrist was performing under restrictions placed upon him by the court and they believed that if the court removes those restrictions his testimony would be more candid and more relevant. But most of the jurors were not as tolerant. They were irritated and frustrated by the incompleteness and non-pertinence of the psychiatrist's testimony. They wanted more guidance from the expert than the court permitted the expert to give. The jury wanted to hear the expert say what he would do if the decision was in his hands.

Perhaps the expert could serve both the court and the jury better if as part of his testimony he would be permitted to make something analogous to a closing statement in which he would give the jury his view of the case. The obvious danger of such a procedure is that the jury would become little more than a rubber stamp to the expert's opinion. But from everything we have seen of how the jury functions we doubt that this would occur. The jury is too impressed with its importance as an institution and with its responsibility to the court and to the community at large to relinquish its decision-making powers.

5. The jury's feelings about imprisonment as opposed to commitment

In his most recent book, *The Urge to Punish*, Henry Weihofen, a long-time advocate of reform in our penal institutions, remarked:

> The unconscious helps explain not only why criminals behave as they do but also why the rest of us behave as we do toward the criminal. Our righteous indignation against wrongdoers is more often than we consciously realize an expression of our own strong but repressed aggressive impulses. The urge to punish in others the misconduct we repress in ourselves is probably the main obstacle to the adoption of a rational penal code.[8]

It has become almost a commonplace for writers of fiction as well as fact to describe a jury as a group of angry citizens whose motivations are strongly colored by their desires for vengeance and retribution. Certainly in a case involving a charge of incest, justification at the expression of such feelings would meet with understanding.

But one of the most surprising facts to emerge from our study of the jury is that we found little evidence to support this image. We are not suggesting that the jury does not have an urge to punish, or that it does not have a need to differentiate itself sharply from the offender. But important factors are left out of this all-too-frequent characterization of the vengeful jury. These factors are the jury's recognition of its representa-

[8] Weihofen, The Urge to Punish 13 (1956).

tive role and its sense of responsibility to society. Both serve to temper the feelings of righteous indignation that Weihofen and others describe as characterizing the reactions of the law-abiding community. The following excerpts are offered to document these impressions:

> The law is not meant to punish, but it is meant to correct the situation. I mean we are not helping his family or him or society by putting him in a prison. The only possible way of helping him and his family and society is by putting him where he can be helped and that is in a mental institution.

A second juror remarked: "No matter how you feel about this man it is not your duty to punish him. It is our duty to weigh the evidence in accordance with the laws that are given and written down here." In another jury:

> I personally do not believe that putting people into jail helps anything or will satisfy the people that are involved. I think mentally sick people should be treated as such. There are places where they are taken care of in some manner, that would make them somewhat useful instead of letting them sit and rot in jail, where a lot of them get even worse.

Even among jurors who advocated imprisonment, one could hear a message that tempered punishment with a concern for rehabilitation. For example:

> If you say this man is sane, you can give him a jail sentence. I think it is your duty to condemn this man, make him serve a sentence for the act that he did and try to help him so he can become a better citizen after he is released. You are not going to send this man up for life, after five or ten years he can come out.

Many of the jurors after hours of discussion were still uncertain as to which alternative, imprisonment or commitment, was more likely to secure the results they were most anxious to attain: rehabilitation for the accused and security for society and for the defendant's family. The jurors voiced indignation, disgust, and anger at the defendant's behavior, but, in most instances, these feelings did not serve as directives for action. The jurors did not begin to approach the feelings recommended by an eminent British jurist when he wrote some seventy years ago:

> I think it is highly desirable that criminals should be hated, that the punishment inflicted upon them should be so contrived as to give expression to that hatred and to justify it as far as the public provision of means for expressing and gratifying a healthy natural sentiment can justify and encourage it.[9]

Some jurors wanted the defendant to receive medical treatment, even though they were reasonably satisfied that he was guilty.[10] They seemed to be searching for a compromise between the two verdict alternatives provided by the law — guilty or not guilty by reason of insanity. They were unwilling to find the defendant *not* guilty by reason of insanity because they were too impressed both with the heinousness of the crime and with the rational, calculated manner in which, to their minds, the defendant carried it out. On the other hand, for almost the same reasons, they were uneasy about having the defendant treated as an ordinary criminal. An ideal solution, and one which they seemed to be searching for, would have allowed them to find the defendant guilty, but in need of medical treatment. The defendant would then be committed to an institution that was neither prison nor hospital but which had the facilities of both.

For example, in one deliberation a juror asked: "Well, now, this man, if he is found guilty and sane while he committed these crimes, will he get any medical care? He needs medical care."

Another juror reassured him: "If he goes to the penitentiary and they find that something is definitely wrong with him,

[9] 2 Stephen, History of the Criminal Law of England 81-82 (1883).

[10] In Table 26, Chapter 5, we reported that half of the jurors in the housebreaking case who believed the defendant guilty recommended that he be committed to a mental institution. Unfortunately we did not ask comparable questions of the jurors in the incest case. If we had, we doubt that the proportion of jurors would have been as high.

they will put him in an institution. They do that right out here in ———— City. If there is anything wrong with him there, they have an institution right there."

It is interesting to speculate why some of the jurors, including a few of those who believed that the defendant was guilty, argued so insistently for the defendant's commitment to a mental hospital. What images did the mental hospital evoke in those jurors? Did they believe that the defendant could be cured? Did they think that a person suffering from a mental disease would respond to treatment in the same way as a person who has pneumonia or appendicitis? Or did they regard someone who is mentally ill as being more similar to a person with a coronary condition — he might improve, but he is chronically ill?

Even those jurors who argued most forcefully for commitment to a mental institution had little hope that the defendant would be cured. The alternatives as they saw them were between an indeterminate stay in a mental hospital and a predetermined (although unknown to them) period of imprisonment. The jurors tried to estimate the probable length of the defendant's prison term. Most of them believed it would not exceed five years; some suggested two; a few thought it would be for life. As most jurors saw it, the realistic choice was between about a five-year prison term and an indefinite confinement to a mental institution. Jurors who advocated commitment to a mental hospital emphasized that if the defendant was found not guilty by reason of insanity he would be removed from his family and from society for a longer period of time than if he was convicted.

We do not wish to give the impression that the jurors were totally without regard for the potential treatment or curative possibilities in mental institutions. For example, one juror argued:

> They didn't bring out whether the asylum could cure him or not. If the asylum cannot cure him, then it does not make a darn bit of difference whether he is in the asylum or in jail.

He is still under confinement where he cannot get at people and do any more damage. Now, if the asylum can cure him, that might be a point. That is not a legal point, but it might be a humanitarian point to consider.

Later in the same deliberation, during a conversation about the crowded conditions of jails and mental institutions, another juror inquired heatedly: "Are you going to put him where they have the most room for him, or where it will do him and society the most good?"

And in another deliberation:

Well, I feel he should be given a chance to be cured! You know, an even chance. If they found that he cannot be cured they will keep him in this mental institution which would be equal to being in prison. But I think he would have a chance of being cured in an institution, whereas if he was sent to prison, there would be absolutely no help for him.

The popular image of the jury as a group of vengeful, punitive men as suggested by films such as "Twelve Angry Men" received little support from our study of actual deliberations. But Weihofen's point about the unconscious desire for punishment is much more difficult to dispose of. Many jurors admitted frankly that they found the problem which the court had placed in their hands an extremely difficult one and that they were anxious to arrive at a verdict which would fulfill, to an optimal degree, the expectations of the community and the law. Statements such as these do not preclude the possibility, however, that unconsciously the jurors were motivated by a desire to punish. In so far as their overt behavior was concerned, the jurors claimed that they were seeking a verdict that would best prepare the defendant, his family, and the community for the day when the defendant would eventually return to society. They did not have much faith in the curative powers of mental hospitals or the rehabilitative effects of prisons. At best, they recognized a slight balance in favor of the mental hospital as a potential opportunity for treatment, and a slight shift in favor of the prison as a place of deterrence.

In the final assessment, most of the jurors were unwilling to give the defendant the benefit of the doubt. There were a few who believed that the defendant was malingering, and for them there was not even a shadow of a doubt about his sanity. But most of the jurors saw and were affected by a shadow. In the end, however, the shadow was not strong enough to relieve the defendant of his responsibility to society. After all it is the court and not the jury that limits the choice between imprisonment and commitment to a mental hospital. Given those alternatives, the jury did not believe the defendant was sick enough to warrant commitment to a hospital.

Concluding remarks

We emphasize again that the materials in this chapter are an anthology of jury observations and not a formal, quantitative content analysis of the deliberations. We think that the conversations that have been included in this anthology represent the main current of jury thought, but we stress that the quotes were not selected systematically — they are not a sample in the usual statistical sense.

There are four major findings that emerge from our inventory of jury reactions. The first and perhaps most important observation is the jury's concern with the case. The jurors relied very heavily on the record. They reviewed every piece of evidence presented during the trial [11] and they placed particular emphasis on the details surrounding the defendant's

[11] The best analogy we can find to the way the jurors go about piecing together the evidence is the way most of us fit together the pieces of a jigsaw puzzle. The jurors frequently jumped from a consideration of the testimony of witness A to a discussion of witness X, who appeared much later in the trial. They might continue to discuss witness X for some time, but before the deliberation is over they return to witness A and to a consideration of all the intervening testimony between witnesses A and X.

behavior at the time of the crime. The opinions they formed about the defendant were developed in reaction to the particular circumstances surrounding the crime. They did not stem from general philosophical ideas about how criminals should behave or how perverts should be treated. The parts of the record that were of most interest to the jury were the defendant's use of and acknowledgment of his use of contraceptives, his job and his capacity to meet the demands of his job, and his wife's passive acceptance of the situation.

The jury's dependence on the record demonstrated that it would be very loath to declare anyone insane on the basis of the act itself. No matter how bizarre or perverse the defendant's behavior appeared, we think that the jury would still insist upon reviewing the specific details surrounding the crime.

A crucial distinction between most criminal cases and a criminal case involving a defense of insanity is that in the latter case jurors are not asked to decide if the law is trying the right man or if the defendant is guilty or innocent. The question before them is: Should a defendant who admits committing the acts for which he is charged be subject to the same demands that society places on any other criminal? The law offers the jury some guidance on this matter when it instructs them that the presence of a mental illness or aberration should not by itself excuse the defendant. It is the jury's task to decide whether the particular manifestation of mental illness which the defendant exhibits meets the norm of non-responsibility specified by the rule of law. In other words, the jury's first job in deciding a defense of insanity case is to understand that the presence of mental illness cannot by itself excuse the defendant. Its second job is to decide whether the defendant meets or fails to meet the requirements stated generally in the rules of law.

It is on this particular point that many experienced lawyers and judges are most critical of the jury. They appreciate the delicacy of the distinction that the law asks the jury to make and they believe that most juries lack the intelligence for doing so. Our findings dispute the practitioner's judgment. We think that the data demonstrate that the jury recognizes the distinction between a clinical diagnosis and the application of a moral legal criterion, and that they understand it is the latter which they must use in deciding the case.

It is partly because the jury recognizes the separateness of the clinical and the legal questions that they are most frustrated by the psychiatrist's testimony. The jury realizes that the expert is emphasizing only one aspect of the problem, the clinical part, and that his testimony contributes little or nothing to the main dilemma facing the jury — that of placing the clinical or purely medical facts about the defendant into a moral-legal context. In their annoyance at the psychiatrist for his failure to be more responsive, some jurors discount or discard much of what the psychiatrist does say. A possible solution to their dilemma would be for the court to permit the psychiatrist to comment on the evidence during the trial. For example, in the incest case, it might have been instructive for the jurors to have heard a doctor comment about the defendant's ability to perform responsibly on his job in light of his mental condition. Or to have heard the doctor's explanation for the defendant's elaborate account of his use of contraceptives. The expert could offer these comments in the form of a closing statement, and the court could instruct the jury to receive them in much the same way that it instructs the jury to receive the opening and closing statements of the two attorneys.

The obvious danger of this kind of innovation is that it might place too much power in the hands of the experts and it might make the jury a rubber stamp to their opinions. But we think that this is not very likely. The jurors were sometimes puzzled about their role; what exactly is it that the law expects them to do? But most of the jurors, most of the time, recognized that the final responsibility for the defendant's fate rested with them. The jurors were both proud of and a little awed by this responsibility, and one thing is very clear, they did not seek ways of avoiding it. We think that if the court permitted the expert to communicate his opinion about the case to the jury, his value as a witness would be increased without detracting from the jury's role as final arbiter.

We have two other observations about the jury. One, we were surprised at how freely the jurors shared with each other some extremely personal and revealing accounts of their experiences with mentally ill relatives and friends. These experiences probably influenced a juror's verdict as much as his exposure to the particular details surrounding the defendant's behavior.

Two, we noted that the jurors were concerned about the defendant's fate. Many of the jurors felt constrained by the verdict limitations placed upon them by the court. They would like to have a way of easing the choice between acquitting the defendant on grounds of insanity and finding him guilty. The former designation goes further than they want to go in distinguishing the defendant from the ordinary criminal, and the latter allows for no distinction. In many instances the jury would have liked to declare the defendant guilty, but insane. That kind of verdict would permit the jurors to condemn the defendant's behavior and at the same time to grant him a special dispensation.

Part of the jurors' criticism of the verdict choice stemmed from their desire to commit the defendant to an institution that both punished and treated. Some were satisfied that the modern prison served both functions, and that anyone in need of medical treatment would receive it. Most jurors did not see that commitment to a mental institution could be a form of punishment, although they had little faith in how effective mental hospitals are in curing persons who are mentally ill.

In general, however, our image of the jury differed significantly from the popular one which describes the jury as a group of indignant, angry citizens seeking vengeance even at the cost of justice. We saw the jurors' urge to punish tempered by a sense of responsibility and socialized by the expectations which they believed were placed upon them by the judicial system.

PART V

A Look to the Future

The Jurors' Appraisal of Legal Rules

In this chapter we take advantage of the special opportunities afforded by the experimental procedures to do a miniature study of law and public opinion. In brief, we were able to poll our juror population on how they felt about the *M'Naghten* rule and the *Durham* rule as a matter of public policy. Our purpose here is to report the results of that poll.

The relationship between law and popular sentiments is not a simple one. If we think for a moment of the vast numbers and types of laws to which members of the society are subject, we are impressed with the complexity of the relationship. Some laws, like the first ten Amendments to the Constitution, are explicitly intended to protect minorities against public opinion. Indeed, that a rule of law should not be responsive solely to the passing and frequently changing waves of popular sentiment has been generally recognized and finds expression in the requirement of independence for the judiciary. But that there is a need for some interchange between legal formulations and lay sentiments is also recognized as essential for the long-term functional integration of a society. Thus, the relationship between law and public opinion is not only complex, it is ambivalent.

For example, in some instances a rule of law seeks directly to incorporate popular consensus. In laws pertaining to negligence actions, a criterion like "reasonable care" is designed as a measuring rod that members of the community may apply for determining verdicts. The law in such cases asks the community through its representative, the jury, to define the salient criteria.

But in between these two extremes, where the law seeks to incorporate public opinion in the very definition of the rule and where public opinion is irrelevant, there is a range of laws that have a tolerance for, but are not determined by, public opinion. The criteria embodied in defense of insanity instructions are illustrative of this third type. In such cases the courts have sought to establish some formal criteria such as "the defendant's ability to distinguish right from wrong." But within the boundaries determined by these formal definitions, the courts have shown a willingness to listen to and to be affected by public opinion.

In this study we asked jurors to recommend the rule of law they would like the courts to use in the future. The jurors' responses may be compared to the opinions solicited in a community survey, except that the respondents in this survey were specially informed. Their opinions cannot help but reflect the information and the insights gained by virtue of their jury experience. Frequently in a community survey it is necessary first to educate the respondents and to arouse their interest before they have acquired enough information or are willing to express a meaningful opinion. The qualities of a "forced conversation" that characterize many interviews in survey research were lacking in the jurors' responses.[1] The preferences expressed by this public are thus more securely based than those obtained from the typical opinion survey.

All our respondents were exposed to one rule of law. That rule was read to them by the presiding judge before they began their deliberation. It was also given to them in writing for their use during the deliberation. On the post-deliberation questionnaire the jurors were then asked to read two paragraphs. One summarized the instructions they were

[1] For a more detailed discussion of this idea, see Blum and Kalven, The Art of Opinion Research: A Lawyer's Appraisal of an Emerging Science, 24 U. of Chi. L. Rev. 1-69 (1956).

given by the court for their deliberation; the other summarized an alternative rule of law on the defense of insanity.

Obviously the exposure that jurors have to a rule they receive from the court before they deliberate is greater than the exposure they receive simply by reading a paragraph describing the rule after the deliberation. But since we exposed all jurors to both rules of law in the same manner, the bias they might have for the rule they were given at the outset of the trial has been controlled.

The jurors were asked to give their opinion about which rule of law the court should adopt for future usage in defense of insanity trials. Their alternatives were thus limited to the instructions they heard and to one other rule of law.

In total, 1176 jurors were involved in the experimental runs of the two trials.[2] The jurors listening to each set of instructions were distributed as follows:

INSTRUCTIONS HEARD BY JURORS IN BOTH TRIALS

Uninstructed	M'Naghten	Durham
	(Per cent of 1176)	
$33_{(384)}$	$31_{(360)}$	$36_{(432)}$

When the jurors' pre-deliberation verdicts in both trials were combined, the proportion of NGI verdicts among jurors who were instructed under *Durham* was 8 per cent higher than the proportion instructed under *M'Naghten*.

PER CENT FINDING NOT GUILTY BY REASON OF INSANITY ON THE PRE-DELIBERATION VERDICT BY JURORS JURORS IN BOTH TRIALS

Uninstructed	M'Naghten	Durham
46	35	43

[2] We examined the responses to each case separately and when we found no differences that could be attributed to the nature of the cases, we merged the data and analyzed the full set of 1176 responses simultaneously.

But the proportion of jurors whose verdicts remained constant before and after the deliberations was similar for all three instruction versions:

PERCENTAGE OF VERDICTS THAT WERE UNCHANGED ON THE PRE- AND POST-QUESTIONNAIRES BY JURORS IN BOTH TRIALS

Uninstructed	M'Naghten	Durham
79	75	75

And, among the 25 per cent or so of jurors who did shift their verdicts the direction of the shift was the same under the three instruction versions. *Uninstructed* jurors shifted 14 per cent from NGI to Guilty and 7 per cent from Guilty to NGI; *M'Naghten* jurors shifted 17 per cent from NGI to Guilty and 8 per cent from Guilty to NGI; and *Durham* jurors shifted 21 per cent from NGI to Guilty and 4 per cent from Guilty to NGI. In reviewing the jurors' recommendations we examined only the responses of those jurors whose verdicts remained unchanged in the pre- and post-deliberation questionnaires. In contrast to the jurors who shifted their responses, the recommendations of these jurors should be less affected by the substantive issues in the trials and by whether they were "moved" by the group to change their opinion. The responses of the unchanged jurors are, therefore, more likely to reflect attitudes toward the instructions per se. The facts that the percentages are relatively constant across the three instruction forms and that the number of jurors involved comprises over 75 per cent of the total sample support our decision to limit the responses to these jurors.[3]

[3] In this first section of the chapter we shall examine only the responses of jurors who were exposed to the *M'Naghten* and *Durham* instructions and asked to choose between them. Among the jurors who heard the *uninstructed on responsibility* version, half were asked to compare that version with the *M'Naghten* rules and others with the *Durham* rules. The responses of the *uninstructed* jurors are examined separately later in this chapter.

Jurors' policy preference between M'Naghten and Durham

The following paragraph appeared on the questionnaires of the jurors who had been exposed to the *M'Naghten* instructions:

IN THE CASE YOU JUST HEARD, THE JUDGE GAVE YOU INSTRUCTIONS ALONG THESE LINES:
 I. If you believe the defendant was unable to tell right from wrong at the time he committed the crime and the criminal act *was the result of his not being able to tell right from wrong,* you must find the accused not guilty by reason of insanity.

IT HAS BEEN PROPOSED THAT JURIES BE INSTRUCTED ALONG THESE LINES:
 II. If you believe the defendant was suffering from a mental illness at the time he committed the crime and the criminal act *was the product of the mental illness,* you must find the accused not guilty by reason of insanity.

For jurors who heard the *Durham* rule, the instructions under I and II were reversed. For all jurors, the question that followed was:

Which instruction do you think the court should use in the future?
 — The instruction that I heard.
 — The proposed alternative.
 — It wouldn't make any difference.

Table 50 describes the jurors' preferences.

TABLE 50. JURORS' RECOMMENDATIONS FOR
FUTURE USAGE

Rules of law	*Per cent recommended*
M'Naghten	33(192)
Durham	36(213)
No difference	31(184)

Neither instruction attained a clear advantage over the other. About one third of the jurors failed to see any difference, and the other two thirds were divided almost evenly between *M'Naghten* and *Durham.*

In addition to reporting the jurors' preferences between the two rules of law, another and related purpose of this study was to locate the sources of the opinions and to show how certain factors influenced those opinions. We examined three possible sources of influences: (1) the jurors' prior exposure to a rule; (2) the jurors' belief that one rule is more favorable to the defendant than another; and (3) the jurors' belief that one rule is more consistent with their verdict preferences than another.

On most surveys, when respondents are given a choice between a known commodity or idea and an unknown one, they are more likely to choose the commodity with which they are familiar or more familiar. The jurors in this situation were given the choice between a rule of law that they were familiar with by virtue of prior usage and exposure, and a rule of law that they might have been hearing for the first time.

Table 51 describes the relationship between prior exposure to a rule and jurors' recommendations.

TABLE 51. INSTRUCTION RECOMMENDED FOR FUTURE
USAGE BY PRIOR EXPOSURE

INSTRUCTION RECOMMENDED
(in per cent)

Prior Exposure	M'Naghten	Durham	No difference	Total
M'Naghten	37	26	37	$100_{(270)}$
Durham	28	45	27	$100_{(319)}$

As expected, Table 51 shows that the jurors who were instructed under *M'Naghten* were more likely to recommend *M'Naghten* and the jurors who were instructed under *Durham* were more likely to recommend *Durham.* But the margin of preference was slightly larger for *Durham* (45 per cent who heard and recommended *Durham* — 28 per cent who heard *Durham* but recommended *M'Naghten* = 17 per cent) than it was for *M'Naghten* (37 − 26 = 11 per cent). And the proportion of jurors who had no opinion concerning future usage was more heavily represented in the *M'Naghten* category than in the *Durham* category — 37 compared to 27 per cent.

Jurors were also asked to choose the rule of law that they would request the judge to read to the jury if

> you were the defendant's attorney, and wanted to obtain a verdict of not guilty by reason of insanity.

The jurors were given the same alternatives as those listed under the future usage question and their responses were distributed as follows:

TABLE 52.   INSTRUCTION JURORS BELIEVE FAVORABLE
TO DEFENDANT

Rules of law	Per cent
M'Naghten	$19_{(112)}$
Durham	$49_{(293)}$
No difference	$32_{(184)}$

The *Durham* rule received a clear advantage. Almost half of the jurors believed that it would be more favorable to the defendant. In contrast, only 19 per cent believe that it would be more advantageous to argue the defendant's case under the *M'Naghten* rule. Like the responses on the future usage question, slightly less than one third of the jurors saw no difference between the two instructions.

We can tell by inspection that previous exposure did not significantly influence jurors' choices because the jurors were exposed to the different instructions in approximately equal numbers, and the 49 to 19 per cent is a sizable difference. This finding indicates strongly that jurors really can perceive differences between rules.

To what degree are jurors' policy recommendations affected by their desire to have a rule favorable to the defendant? Table 53 describes the relationship between their belief that a rule favors defendant and their recommendations for future usage.

TABLE 53.   INSTRUCTION BELIEVED FAVORABLE TO THE
DEFENDANT BY INSTRUCTION RECOMMENDED FOR
FUTURE USAGE

Instruction believed favorable to defendant	INSTRUCTION RECOMMENDED			
	M'Naghten	Durham	No difference	Total
M'Naghten	69	20	11	100(112)
Durham	31	58	11	100(293)
No difference	13	13	74	100(184)

Table 53 shows that 69 per cent of the jurors who believed the *M'Naghten* rule was more favorable to the defendant recommended it for future usage and 58 per cent of the jurors who believed the *Durham* rule was more favorable to the defendant recommended it for future usage.   In this matter, the margin of preference was larger for the *M'Naghten* rule (69 — 20 = 49 per cent) than it was for the *Durham* rule (58 — 31 = 27 per cent).   Seventy-five per cent of the jurors who reported no difference in response to one item reported no difference in response to the other.

In each instruction version there was a relatively stable percentage of jurors (75 per cent) whose verdicts were unchanged on the pre- and post-deliberation questionnaires.   The distribution between not guilty by reason of insanity verdicts and guilty verdicts for those jurors looked like this:

TABLE 54.   PER CENT NGI AND GUILTY VERDICTS
AMONG UNCHANGED JURORS

Pre-deliberation verdicts	Post-deliberation verdicts	M'Naghten	Durham
NGI	NGI	25(68)	36(115)
Guilty	Guilty	75(202)	64(204)
		100(270)	100(319)

Like the over-all jury population, jurors with stable verdicts reported a greater percentage of NGI responses under *Durham* than under *M'Naghten* (36-25 per cent). But the salient question now is the relationship between verdicts and recommendations for public policy. We would expect that jurors who found the defendant not guilty by reason of insanity would be more likely to recommend the *Durham* rule over the *M'Naghten* rule and that jurors who found the defendant guilty would be more likely to recommend *M'Naghten*. Our short-hand phrase for describing these expectations is to refer to them as the jurors' desire for verdict consistency. Table 55 describes the relationship between verdicts and recommendations.

TABLE 55.   RECOMMENDATIONS FOR FUTURE USAGE
BY VERDICTS

	M'Naghten	Durham	No difference	Total
NGI-NGI	22	55	23	100 (183)
Guilty-Guilty	37	28	35	100 (406)

Table 55 shows that 22 per cent of the jurors who found not guilty by reasons of insanity recommended *M'Naghten* and 55 per cent recommended *Durham*. Among the jurors who voted guilty, 37 per cent recommended *M'Naghten* and 28 per cent recommended *Durham*. Among the NGI verdict jurors the margin of preference was (55 — 22 =) 33 per cent in favor of *Durham*. Among the guilty verdict jurors the margin of preference was (37 — 28 =) 9 per cent in favor of *M'Naghten*.

The 24 per cent difference between the NGI verdict jurors who recommended *Durham* and the guilty verdict jurors who recommended *M'Naghten* may be interpreted in several ways. One, it may mean that the *Durham* rule is perceived as a stronger weapon for the defense than the *M'Naghten* rule is for the prosecution. Two, it may mean that the NGI verdict jurors have a greater need than the guilty verdict jurors for consistency between their verdicts and the rules they recommend. This interpretation is supported not only by the 55 — 22 per cent difference as opposed to the 37 — 28 per cent difference but by the higher percentage of "no difference" responses among the guilty verdict jurors.

To sum up, we found that about one third of the jurors recommended the *M'Naghten* rule, one third the *Durham* rule, and one third said it made no difference. We then looked at three sources of influence on the jurors' recommendations: prior exposure, favorableness to the defendant, and verdict consistency. We found that 37 per cent of the jurors who were exposed to the *M'Naghten* rule recommended *M'Naghten* and that 45 per cent of the jurors who were exposed to the *Durham* rule recommended *Durham*. The margin of preference was slightly greater for *Durham* than for *M'Naghten*. When asked which rule they would prefer if they were the defendant's attorney, 49 per cent of the jurors selected *Durham* and only 19 per cent selected *M'Naghten*. About one third saw no difference. Among jurors who believed *Durham* favorable to the defendant, 58 per cent recommended it for future usage and among jurors who believed *M'Naghten* favorable to the defendant, 69 per cent recommended it for future usage. The margin of preference was greater for *M'Naghten* than for *Durham*. Finally, when verdicts and recommendations were compared, jurors who voted for acquittal on grounds of insanity were more likely to recommend the *Durham* rule as opposed to the *M'Naghten* rule. Jurors who favored a guilty verdict preferred *M'Naghten* but not as strongly.

Now we turn to the recommendations of jurors who received "no instructions."

Recommendations of jurors who were exposed to the uninstructed version

Half of the jurors who deliberated under the *uninstructed on responsibility* version were asked to compare the version they heard with the *M'Naghten* rule; the other half with the *Durham* rule. They were told:

IN THE CASE YOU JUST HEARD, THE JUDGE GAVE YOU INSTRUCTIONS ALONG THESE LINES:

> If you believe that the defendant was insane at the time he committed the acts of which he is accused, then you must find the accused not guilty by reason of insanity.

IT HAS BEEN PROPOSED THAT JURIES BE IN-STRUCTED ALONG THESE LINES:

The alternatives were either:

> If you believe Lunt was suffering from a mental disorder at the time he committed the crime and the criminal act *was the product of mental abnormality,* then you must find the accused not guilty by reason of insanity.

or:

> If you believe Lunt was unable *to tell right from wrong* at the time he committed the crime and the criminal act was the result of his not being able to tell right from wrong, you must find the accused not guilty by reason of insanity.

Which instruction do you think the court should use in the future?

Table 56 describes the jurors' choices between instruction heard and instruction recommended.

TABLE 56.   RECOMMENDATIONS FOR FUTURE USAGE BY INSTRUCTION HEARD

Instruction recommended for future usage	INSTRUCTION HEARD: UNINSTRUCTED VERSION COMPARED WITH:		
	M'Naghten *(in per cent)*	*Durham*	*Combined*
Uninstructed	45	42	44 (132)
M'Naghten	31	—	33 (101)
Durham	—	35	
No difference	24	22	23 (70)
Total	100(151)	100(152)	100 (303)

Forty-four per cent of the jurors recommended the version

they heard and 23 per cent saw no difference between that version and *M'Naghten* or *Durham*. In other words, two thirds of the jurors, either directly, or indirectly by their failure to note a difference, recommended an absence of instructions.

The jurors' responses may be interpreted in several ways. We could interpret them as meaning that the jurors do not believe they need a formal legal criterion of responsibility in order to do their job. We saw, earlier, that the absence of a rule of law did not prevent them from arriving at a decision. In other words, we are suggesting by this interpretation that jurors have shown they can determine the defendant's guilt or lack of responsibility from the evidence, the experts' opinions, and the experiential knowledge that they bring with them into the courtroom. Failure to instruct from the jurors' point of view is not crucial.

Another interpretation, and one that does not speak quite as well for the jurors' resourcefulness, is that the jurors failed to recognize that they had not received an instruction from the court, or that they saw no qualitative difference between the proposed instruction with its criterion about right from wrong or product of mental disease and the "instruction" they heard.

A third interpretation goes to the form in which the problem was posed to the jurors. Perhaps the distinctions we are asking the jurors to make are too subtle to be captured by the usual instruments of survey research. In other words, we are suggesting, on the basis of the jurors' performances in other spheres, that a higher proportion of the jurors understand instructions and are capable of distinguishing between instructions in their actual usage than their verbal responses to the questionnaire would lead us to believe.

When we examined the responses of the *uninstructed* jurors on the favorableness to the defendant item, we found that 35 per cent selected the instruction they had heard and 25 per cent saw no difference between the instruction heard and the proposed alternative. Among the jurors who perceived the *uninstructed* version as most favorable to the defendant, 81 per cent recommended it for future usage by the courts.

When verdicts[4] and recommendations for future usage were compared, 41 per cent of the NGI-verdict jurors recommended the version they had heard, 16 per cent saw no difference, and 43 per cent recommended *M'Naghten* or *Durham*. Among the guilty-verdict jurors, 46 per cent recommended the version they had heard, 28 per cent saw no difference, and 26 per cent recommended *M'Naghten* or *Durham*.

In summary, if we take the responses of the *uninstructed* jurors at face value, we find that they were no less willing to recommend the version to which they were exposed than were jurors who had been exposed to *M'Naghten* (37 per cent) or *Durham* (45 per cent). Furthermore, jurors who perceived the *uninstructed* version as favorable to the defendant were no less, indeed they were more, willing to recommend its adoption by the courts. Eighty-one per cent of the *uninstructed* jurors who believed that version was favorable to the defendant recommended it for future usage in contrast to the 69 per cent who recommended *M'Naghten* and the 58 per cent who recommended *Durham*.

Secondary effects of the rules of law

Chapter 3 described how the rules of law affected the most important part of the jury's task — its verdict. In this chapter we evaluated the jurors' reactions to the rules of law by comparing which rule of insanity the jurors thought the courts ought to adopt. We turn now to a final examination of the jurors' responses to legal rules and look at how some peripheral aspects of the jurors' behavior reflect their attitudes toward the rules. Specifically, we report the jurors' relative satisfaction with their deliberations under each of the rules of law and the jurors' preference for a bench or a jury trial after having participated in a deliberation in which the rules of law

---

[4] *Uninstructed* jurors who did not shift their verdicts between the pre-deliberation and post-deliberation assessments distributed their verdicts: 42 per cent NGI and 58 per cent guilty.

were considered. Neither of these factors, jurors' satisfaction or jurors' preference for a bench or jury trial, is as significant a measure of the relative impact of the rules of law as are verdicts and recommendations about future policy. But they are useful in explaining some additional facts about jurors' behavior and for this reason they are of interest to us.

Jurors' satisfaction scores

A measure of juror's satisfaction was obtained by adding individual responses to a series of six items that appeared on the post-deliberation questionnaire. These items were included to determine whether jurors derived greater satisfaction from deliberating under one rule of law as opposed to another, and whether the absence of an instruction on responsibility affected their satisfaction with the deliberation. Each question had six alternatives, from "strongly disagree" to "strongly agree." These were assigned numerical values so that the *greater* the satisfaction the *lower* the score. For each item the scores ranged from 1 to 6 and the over-all scores could range from 6 to 36.

The six items that formed the satisfaction score appear below:[5]

1. Some of the members of our jury did not show enough consideration for the feelings of others.

Strongly Agree	Agree	Slightly Agree	Slightly Disagree	Disagree	Strongly Disagree

2. Our deliberation would have been better if the jurors had given more attention to the judge's instructions.
3. The reasoning in the deliberation was clear and logical.
4. Some of the people in our jury were unfortunately crowded out of the deliberation.
5. As the deliberation proceeded, each person showed a willingness to go along with the majority.
6. Our deliberation would have been improved if everyone had stuck to the facts in the case.

[5] The satisfaction items were included only on the incest experiment.

We anticipated that jurors' scores would be influenced by two factors: verdicts and instructions. Within each instruction, we expected that jurors who served on juries that reached consensus would be more satisfied than would jurors who participated in groups that hung; and between instructions that *instructed* jurors would be more satisfied than *uninstructed* jurors. We reasoned that the absence of instructions would be more troublesome to most jurors than the presence of instructions because instructions should provide some boundaries to the discussion and because the absence of boundaries is anxiety-provoking.

The distribution of scores by verdicts and instructions is described in Table 57.

TABLE 57. JURORS' SATISFACTION SCORES BY RULES OF LAW AND VERDICTS

	Verdict juries	Hung juries	Combined
Uninstructed	26.0 (216)	22.6 (48)	25.4 (264)
M'Naghten	24.6 (228)	22.1 (12)	24.5 (240)
Durham	22.2 (240)	21.6 (72)	22.0 (312)
Combined	24.2 (684)	22.0 (132)	23.5 (816)

Neither instructions nor verdicts contributed significantly toward differentiating jurors' satisfaction scores.

Jurors' choices between a bench and jury trial

What proportion of the jurors would be willing to have a jury determine the fate of a member of their family, or, indeed, of themselves if they were on trial? In the housebreaking case jurors were asked the following question before and after they deliberated: "If a member of your family was on trial, would you prefer that he be tried before a judge or a jury?"

Table 58 describes the proportion of jurors who favored a jury trial before and after they deliberated for each instruction version.

TABLE 58. PER CENT OF JURORS WHO FAVOR JURY TRIAL BY RULES OF LAW

	Uninstructed	M'Naghten	Durham
Before deliberation	85(120)	88(120)	90(120)
After deliberation	84(120)	84(120)	87(120)

The jury system received strong support across the board: support that was not noticeably diminished as a result of having participated in a deliberation.[6]

In the incest trial, the jurors were asked a somewhat different question.

> Do you believe the following types of cases should be tried before a jury or before a judge sitting alone?
> Criminal trials
> Automobile negligence trials
> Contract disputes

Table 59 describes only the proportion of jurors in each instruction version who indicated that they would favor a jury trial. We have omitted, for the moment, the jurors' responses to other kinds of trials.

TABLE 59. PERCENTAGE OF JURORS WHO FAVOR A JURY TRIAL FOR CRIMINAL CASES BY RULES OF LAW

	Uninstructed	M'Naghten	Durham
Before deliberation	91(264)	93(240)	93(312)
After deliberation	90(264)	91(240)	92(312)

Again, the jury system received strong endorsement. We note that neither the presence or absence of instructions nor the

---

[6] Support, we might also add, that was not diminished as a result of participating in a hung jury. Jurors in groups that failed to reach consensus supported the jury system as strongly as jurors who reached a verdict. In hung juries, 84 per cent of the jurors favored trial by jury; in NGI verdict juries, 83 per cent and in guilty verdict juries, 85 per cent. There were no differences by rules of law within homogeneous verdict categories.

content of the instructions altered the jurors' preferences for trial by jury.[7]

But jurors' support for jury trials in criminal cases should not be generalized to all cases, as witness the jurors' responses to auto negligence and contract disputes.

TABLE 60.   PERCENTAGE OF JURORS WHO FAVOR
JURY TRIAL FOR CIVIL ACTIONS BY RULES OF LAW

	Uninstructed	M'Naghten	Durham
Auto negligence actions			
Before the deliberation	59	58	62
After the deliberation	61	57	59
Contract disputes			
Before the deliberation	43	34	40
After the deliberation	39	36	39

In all three instruction versions, about 60 per cent of the jurors favored jury trials for auto negligence actions and about 40 per cent for contract disputes.   Jurors' choices changed hardly at all before and after they deliberated.

The rules of law did not differentiate jurors' preferences for a jury trial over a bench trial.   For criminal cases, over 80 per cent of the jurors in both the housebreaking and the incest trials reported a preference for jury trials over decisions by a judge.   But the jurors were not nearly as unanimous in their reactions to civil actions, especially contract disputes which are likely to involve more technical and complex information than the typical auto negligence or personal injury action. For contract disputes, only about 40 per cent of the jurors in each instruction version preferred trial by jury.

[7] As in the housebreaking case, the jurors' enthusiasm for trial by jury was not diminished by their failure to reach consensus.   In the hung juries, 88 per cent of the jurors favored trial by jury; in the NGI verdict juries, 92 per cent and in the guilty verdict juries, 91 per cent. The rules of law made no difference in the jurors' responses.

Concluding remarks

On the major point in this chapter, the jurors' recommendations to the court, we found that their choices were divided almost evenly between *M'Naghten* and *Durham;* 33 per cent recommended *M'Naghten,* 36 per cent recommended *Durham,* and 31 per cent did not see enough of a difference between the two instructions to make a recommendation.

Three factors that might have influenced the jurors' recommendations were then examined: the jurors' prior exposure to the rule, their perceptions of how favorable to the defendant the rule was likely to be, and their desire for verdict consistency. As expected, the jurors who were exposed to *M'Naghten* were more likely to recommend *M'Naghten* and the jurors who were exposed to *Durham* were more likely to recommend *Durham.* The margin of preference was slightly larger for *Durham* (6 per cent) as opposed to *M'Naghten.* On favorableness to the defendant, independent of recommendations for future usage, 49 per cent of the jurors selected *Durham,* 19 per cent *M'Naghten,* and 32 per cent saw no difference. But 69 per cent of the jurors who believed *M'Naghten* favorable to the defendant recommended it as opposed to 58 per cent of the jurors who believed *Durham* favorable. On verdict consistency 22 per cent of the jurors who voted not guilty by reason of insanity recommended the *M'Naghten* rule, 55 per cent the *Durham* rule, and 23 per cent saw no difference. Among the guilty verdict jurors, 37 per cent recommended *M'Naghten,* 28 per cent *Durham,* and 35 per cent saw no difference. Thus, the jurors who voted for acquittal on grounds of insanity were more favorably disposed to the *Durham* rule than the jurors who found guilty were to the *M'Naghten* rule.

On each of the items, between a third and a quarter of the jurors said that they saw no difference between the instruction they heard and the proposed alternative. We think that it is just as likely that the jurors failed to make a choice because of the form in which the problems were posed than because they could not recognize the differences had they been asked to choose under more realistic circumstances. The practical implications suggested are that differences between *M'Naghten* and *Durham* may be too subtle to be fully grasped by reading a brief paragraph describing the responsibility criterion in each rule.

The responses of the *uninstructed* jurors pose a similar dilemma. How should we interpret the responses of two thirds of the jurors who recommended the *uninstructed* version or who saw no difference between the version they had heard and either of the two formal rules? This finding is surprising. Did the jurors recognize the absence of instructions and were they, by their choices, recommending that courts adopt the practice of omitting a formal criterion of responsibility on the grounds, perhaps, that the jury functions just as well without it? Our data on the behavior of the *uninstructed* jurors compared to the *M'Naghten* or *Durham* jurors lend a certain plausibility to such an interpretation. The verdicts of the *uninstructed* juries follow almost exactly the verdicts of the *Durham* juries, and the proportion of hung juries is no higher among *uninstructed* than among *instructed* juries — to select just two of the important similarities between the behavior of the *instructed* and *uninstructed* juries.

The other interpretation is that the jurors did not perceive or did not understand the difference between the version they were exposed to and either of the two sets of instructions. If readers are inclined to go along with this lack of understanding interpretation they should ask how much of that failure was due to the form in which the problems were posed. It is certainly possible that these kinds of issues do not lend themselves to study by the traditional paper and pencil attitude surveys.

On the less crucial measures of jurors' reactions to the rules of law, those that compared jurors' satisfaction and preferences for a judge or a jury trial, we found that there were no important differences. The jurors preferences for a jury instead of a bench trial were determined primarily by the type and complexity of the case and hardly at all by the rules of law.

CHAPTER 10

Postscript: The *Durham* Rule in the Real World

The *Durham* rule has certainly been one of the most important legal decisions in criminal law in the last hundred years. The author of a recent article in the *Georgetown Law Journal* said this of it: "It is doubtful whether any single case in the criminal law has stirred more comment and controversy than *Durham*." [1] This is a comment about a legal doctrine that is applicable in about 2 per cent of all criminal jury trials.[2]

In trying to explain the impact that *Durham* has had on the legal world, no one claims that it has changed the basic ideology of the criminal law, which says that persons of sound mind convicted of a criminal offense should be punished. *Durham's* importance stems primarily from the fact that it has served as the impetus for a basic re-examination of the criteria for criminal irresponsibility, and for reform of the procedures for dealing with the insanity issue in criminal cases.

In this chapter we leave the jury room and return to the outside world to review reactions to the *Durham* rule. In Chapter 9 we polled the jury for its recommendations. In this chapter we poll, figuratively speaking, the bench. Two kinds of data are available. The first compares decisions in the District of Columbia before and after the adoption of the *Durham* rule. The second reviews appellate decisions in

[1] Halleck, The Insanity Defense in the District of Columbia, 49 Geo. L.J. 296 (1961).

[2] Weihofen's judgment was a little more conservative. He observed: "Probably no criminal case in the past decade has been the subject of such widespread debate." See Weihofen, The "Test" of Criminal Responsibility: Recent Developments, 172 International Record of Medicine 638 (1959).

which the adoption of the *Durham* rule was the critical question.

The Durham rule in the District of Columbia

We compared the percentage of acquittals by reason of insanity in the District of Columbia for three years preceding *Durham* and for seven years following the *Durham* decision with the aim of answering the question: Has the adoption of the *Durham* rule increased the proportion of acquittals on grounds of insanity? Table 61 lists the total number of indictments and compares them by the percentage of cases disposed

TABLE 61. PROPORTION OF CRIMINAL CASES IN THE DISTRICT OF COLUMBIA: PRE- AND POST-DURHAM

	Number of indictments	Per Cent of cases disposed of by pleas of guilty	Per Cent of cases disposed of by verdicts of guilty	Per Cent of cases disposed of by verdicts of not guilty	Per Cent of verdicts of not guilty by reason of insanity
		PRE-DURHAM			
1951	1400	$68_{(956)}$	$23_{(316)}$	$9_{(128)}$	$0_{(0)}$
1952	1314	$70_{(921)}$	$21_{(279)}$	$8_{(111)}$	$.2_{(3)}$
1953*	1446	$48_{(696)}$	$48_{(687)}$	$4_{(60)}$	$.2_{(3)}$
1954†	1345	$64_{(864)}$	$25_{(341)}$	$10_{(133)}$	$.6_{(7)}$
		POST-DURHAM			
1955	1166	$67_{(785)}$	$23_{(265)}$	$9_{(106)}$	$1_{(10)}$
1956	1198	$66_{(790)}$	$26_{(305)}$	$7_{(88)}$	$1_{(15)}$
1957	1048	$65_{(686)}$	$27_{(286)}$	$7_{(69)}$	$1_{(7)}$
1958	1176	$64_{(756)}$	$27_{(321)}$	$7_{(81)}$	$2_{(18)}$
1959	1010	$62_{(628)}$	$28_{(276)}$	$7_{(73)}$	$3_{(33)}$
1960	966	$68_{(657)}$	$24_{(236)}$	$4_{(39)}$	$4_{(34)}$
1961‡	985	$60_{(591)}$	$29_{(286)}$	$5_{(52)}$	$6_{(56)}$
Combined	13,054	64(8330)	28(3598)	7(940)	1(186)

* Anomalous as the figures for 1953 look, they have been checked and found to be correct.

† The year the Durham rule was adopted.

‡ We were unable to locate figures for the years following 1961.

of by pleas of guilty and by verdicts of guilty, not guilty, and not guilty by reason of insanity for each year.

Two facts are apparent from a first inspection of Table 61: the great majority of cases are disposed of before trial by pleas of guilty, and the number of not guilty by reason of insanity verdicts is small. In the three years preceding the adoption of the *Durham* rule, the rate of acquittals on grounds of insanity was .0016 (slightly more than one and one half per thousand).[3] In 1954, the year of the *Durham* decision, the figure rose to .0058 (almost six per thousand). In the post-*Durham* era, between 1955 and 1961, the figure rose again to .025 (twenty-five per thousand).

By absolute standards, the number of cases resulting in acquittals on grounds of insanity compared to other verdicts is not large. But if we focus only on the magnitude of the *differences* between the pre- and post-*Durham* years, rather than on the numbers themselves, it turns out that the differ-ences are significant; they cannot be attributed to chance. There has been a fifteen-fold increase in the proportion of de-fendants who were acquitted on grounds of insanity. The *Dur-ham* rule has made a difference in the percentage of defendants who have gained acquittals on grounds of insanity in the Dis-trict of Columbia. But we note also that the increase in the percentage of NGI verdicts took place at the expense of the acquittals and not at the expense of the guilty verdicts. There was no decrease in the percentage of pleas of guilty or guilty verdicts.

Judge Bazelon believes that much of the increase in the number of acquittals on grounds of insanity comes from di-rected verdicts.[4] Unfortunately, the figures in column 5 do

---

[3] This figure was obtained by substracting the number of not guilty verdicts for the three-year period from the total number of indictments (4160 − 299 = 3861) and taking a percentage of the total number of NGI verdicts over the sum of the indictments.

[4] A directed verdict is one in which the court legally commands the jury to acquit, if the court is of the opinion that the evidence is not sufficient to sustain a guilty verdict. Judge Bazelon expressed this opinion in a discussion with members of the Jury Project Staff at the Law School of the University of Chicago.

not distinguish between acquittals based on "directed verdicts" and acquittals that are the result of the juries' interpretations of the *Durham* rule. A few years ago a note in the *Columbia Law Review* commented on this problem:

> It seems from the trend of the recent cases in the District that when a defendant introduces psychiatric evidence supporting his claim of insanity, the prosecution must present contrary psychiatric evidence to avoid an adversely directed verdict, at least in the absence of favorable testimony by lay witnesses trained in judging sanity or having had prolonged and intimate contact with the accused just prior to the time of the crime.[5]

Also unfortunate is the fact that the figures in Table 61 do not tell us the number of defendants who introduced a plea of insanity and who subsequently were found guilty. In other words a further breakdown of column 3 is needed. But we know that the adoption of the *Durham* rule aroused a good deal of controversy in the District of Columbia, and we would guess that the visibility of the rule probably did serve to increase the number of pleas of insanity. For the nation as a whole, however, the figure is still estimated at about 2 per cent.[6]

Another prediction about the effects of the *Durham* rule which we can test goes to the consequences that *Durham* would have on commitment policy. Persons who opposed *Durham's* adoption claimed that it would increase the number of defendants who would employ the insanity defense successfully. They believed that instead of being found guilty and receiving a long or life term in prison, under the *Durham* rule these men would be released from mental hospitals after only relatively brief commitments. Since a defense of insanity is usually introduced for heinous crimes where there is a strong likelihood of conviction, they argued that the dangers to society were even greater than they would be if ordinary criminals were involved.

---

[5] Note, Implementation and Clarification of the Durham Criterion of Criminal Irresponsibility, 58 Colum. L. Rev. 1260 (1958).

[6] Kalven and Zeisel, in The American Jury, report the number of defense of insanity pleas as 2 in a hundred for criminal jury trials.

The District of Columbia has kept some records on the status of offenders who were found not guilty by reason of insanity since the adoption of the *Durham* rule. The data are presented in Tables 62 and 63.

TABLE 62. STATUS OF OFFENDERS FOUND NOT GUILTY
BY REASON OF INSANITY FROM JULY 1, 1954,
TO DECEMBER 31, 1959 *

Crime	Still in hospital	Con- ditionally released	Per- manently released	Total
Murder	13	2	1	16
Assaults	4	5	—	9
Housebreakings	7	—	6	13
Robbery	9	—	4	13
Thefts	5	1	2	8
Forgery	5	—	5	10
Other felonies	6	1	2	9
Municipal court	10	—	2	12
Total	59	9	22	90

* In Halleck's article in the Georgetown Law Journal, note 1 *supra,* he states that as of April, 1960, 160 persons were found not guilty by reason of insanity and committed to St. Elizabeth's. Of those 160, 24 have been unconditionally released.

Five years later, in 1964, 59 out of 90, or 66 per cent, of the offenders were still confined in mental hospitals. Except for offenders who were committed from municipal court.[7] persons charged with murder had the highest proportion of confinement (84 per cent).

Of the 31 offenders who were conditionally or permanently released:

4 (13 per cent) were later convicted of a minor crime;

3 (10 per cent) were later convicted of a serious crime;

3 (10 per cent) were arrested on release.

The remaining 21 (67 per cent) had no record of further diffi-

[7] These are persons charged with lesser crimes, whose insanity probably stems from alcoholism or senility.

culty with the police. Considering that the rate of recidivism for offenders who are found guilty and are imprisoned is generally estimated at between 45 and 50 per cent, the belief that defendants acquitted on grounds of insanity pose greater dangers to society because of inadequate commitment safeguards does not have empirical support.

Table 63 describes the number and proportion of defendants who were found not guilty by reason of insanity in the United States District Court for the District of Columbia, committed to Saint Elizabeth's Hospital, and as of June 30, 1962, unconditionally or permanently released from custody.

TABLE 63. STATUS OF OFFENDERS FOUND NOT GUILTY BY REASON OF INSANITY FROM 1954 TO JUNE 30, 1962 *

Fiscal year	Total received by Saint Elizabeth's Hospital as not guilty by reason of insanity	Number unconditionally released as of June 30, 1962	Percentage unconditionally released as of June 30, 1962
1954	4	4	100
1955	8	7	87.5
1956	14	12	85.7
1957	8	5	62.5
1958	18	2	11.1
1959	33	13	39.4
1960	35	3	8.6
1961	64	2	3.1
1962	67	2	3.0
Combined	251	50	19.9

* These data were obtained from a Report of the Committee on Problems Connected with Mental Examination of the Accused in Criminal Cases, Before Trial, Judicial Conference of the District of Columbia Circuit, 1964, p. 170.

These data also support the thesis that the great majority of offenders acquitted on grounds of insanity remain in custody for several years. Thus, the fear that verdicts of acquittal on grounds of insanity will enhance the likelihood that persons dangerous to themselves and society will remain at large appears unwarranted.

Apellate decisions on the Durham rule

In the previous chapter we reported that there was little difference in the jurors' preferences between *M'Naghten* and *Durham*. About one third favored each rule and one third saw no difference between them. When we examined the relationship between the jurors' prior exposure to a rule and their recommendations, we found that *Durham* fared slightly better than *M'Naghten:* about 6 per cent better.

In the main, the judges' choices were limited to the same two preferences.[8] They could elect to retain the *M'Naghten* rule or they could adopt *Durham*. One obvious difference between the two polls is that all of the judges had been previously exposed to the *M'Naghten* rule and that one must assume, also, their greater familiarity with the *Durham* rule. In each jurisdiction, the *Durham* rule was the proposed alternative. Let us examine how the judges' preferences compared.

Since 1954, the *Durham* rule has been reviewed by thirty state courts and five federal courts and has been rejected by all.[9] Two states adopted the *Durham* rule by statute: Ver-

[8] Some jurisdictions considered, and New York State adopted, a rule proposed in the Model Penal Code drafted by the American Law Institute. It says a person is not responsible for criminal conduct if at the time of such conduct, as a result of mental disease or defect, he lacks substantial capacity either to appreciate the criminality of his conduct or to conform his conduct to the requirements of law.

[9] Twenty-eight state courts that declined to follow Durham were: Arizona: State v. Crose, 357 P.2d 136 (Ariz. 1960); Arkansas: Downs v. State, 330 S.W.2d 281 (Ark. 1959); California: People v. Ryan, 140 Cal. App. 2d 412, 295 P.2d 496 (Dist. Ct. App. 1956); Colorado: Early v. People, 352 P.2d 112 (Colo. 1960); Connecticut: State v. Devies, 146 Conn. 137, 148 A.2d 251 (1959), *cert. denied*, 360 U.S. 921; Florida: Picott v. State, 116 So.2d 626 (Fla. 1959); Illinois: People v. Carpenter, 11 Ill. 2d 60, 142 N.E.2d 11 (1957); Indiana: Flowers v. State, 236 Ind. 151, 139 N.E.2d 185 (1956); Kansas: State v. Andrews, 357 P.2d 739 (Kan. 1960); Maryland: Cole v. State, 212 Md. 55, 128 A.2d 437 (1957); Bryant v. State, 207 Md. 565, 115 A.2d 502 (1955); Thomas v. State, 206 Md. 575, 112 A.2d 913 (1955); Massachusetts: Commonwealth v. Ches-

mont in 1957 and Maine in 1961.[10]   One state, Minnesota, adopted it for civil actions but retained *M'Naghten* for criminal cases.[11]

Among jurors, the *Durham* rule was at least as popular as *M'Naghten,* and after one exposure it gained a slight edge over *M'Naghten.*   But among judges, the *M'Naghten* rule with one exception was the favorite.

---

ter, 337 Mass. 702, 150 N.E.2d 914 (1958); Minnesota: State v. Finn, 100 N.W.2d 508 (Minn. 1960); Missouri: State v. Goza, 317 S.W.2d 609 (Mo. 1958); Montana: State v. Kitchens, 129 Mont. 331, 286 P.2d 1079 (1955); Nevada: Sollars v. State, 73 Nev. 248, 316 P.2d 917 (1957); New Jersey: State v. Lucas, 30 N.J. 37, 152 A.2d 50 (1959); New York: People v. Johnson, 169 N.Y.S.2d 217 (Westchester Cty. 1957); Ohio: State v. Robinson, 168 N.E.2d 328 (Ohio App. 1958); Pennsylvania: Commonwealth v. Novak, 395 Pa. 199, 150 A.2d 102 (1955); Commonwealth v. Woodhouse, 164 A.2d 98 (Pa. 1960); Utah: State v. Kirkham, 7 Utah 2d 108, 319 P.2d 859 (1958); Washington: State v. Collins, 50 Wash. 2d 740, 314 P.2d 660 (1957); but cf. Anderson v. Grasberg, 247 Minn. 538, 78 N.W.2d 450 (1956) (Durham rule applied in civil case in jurisdiction which follows M'Naghten rule in criminal cases).   Collection of cases is from Krash, The Durham Rule and Judicial Administration in the District of Columbia, 70 Yale L.J. 905 (1961).

Since 1961 the Durham rule was reviewed but rejected in the following state courts: Spurlock v. State, 212 Tenn. 132, 368 S.W.2d 299 (1963); Newsome v. Commonwealth, 366 S.W.2d 174 (Ky. 1962); State v. Esser, 16 Wis. 2d 567, 115 N.W.2d 505 (1962); Chase v. State, 369 P.2d 997 (Alaska, 1962); State v. Gramenz, 256 Iowa 134, 126 N.W.2d 285 (1964); Longoria v. State, 53 Del. 311, 168 A.2d 695 (1961); Dare v. State, 378 P.2d 339 (Okla. 1963).

The federal courts that rejected Durham were: Vosa v. United States, 259 F.2d 699 (8th Cir. 1958); Sauer v. United States, 241 F.2d 640 (9th Cir. 1957), *cert. denied,* 354 U.S. 940; Anderson v. United States, 237 F.2d 118 (9th Cir. 1956); Howard v. United States, 229 F.2d 602 (5th Cir.), *rev'd on rehearing en banc,* 232 F.2d 274 (1956); United States v. Hopkins, 169 F. Supp. 187 (D. Md. 1958).   See also United States v. Kunak, 5 U.S.C.M.A. 346 (1954); United States v. Smith, 5 U.S.C.M.A. 314 (1954).   Krash, id. at 906 n.8.

Since 1961, Durham was rejected in the following federal courts: United States v. Currens, 290 F.2d 751 (3d Cir. 1961); Wion v. United States, 325 F.2d 420 (10th Cir. 1963).

[10] Vt. Stat. Ann. tit. 13 §4801 (1959); Me. Rev. Stat. Ann. tit. 15, §102 (1964).

[11] Anderson v. Grasberg, 247 Minn. 538, 555, 78 N.W.2d 450, 461 (1956).

It would strain both the purposes of this volume and the author's competence to try to review and evaluate in any detail the reasons for the courts' rejection of *Durham*. We offer only a brief summary of the courts' reactions.

In fifteen of the thirty-five jurisdictions, the *Durham* rule was rejected as the less sound rule as a matter of policy. In the remaining jurisdictions, *M'Naghten* was upheld on grounds of precedent. It was argued that the adoption of a different concept of criminal responsibility should come from the legislature.

One of the more colorful endorsements of *M'Naghten* came from the federal bench of the Ninth Circuit. In *Anderson v. United States* the court said:

> This court has no desire to join the courts of New Hampshire and the District of Columbia in the "magnificent isolation" of rebellion against M'Naghten, even though New Hampshire has been traveling down that lonesome road since 1870. See State v. Pike. . . . Rather than stumble along with Pike, we prefer to trudge along the now well-traveled pike blazed more than a century ago by M'Naghten. We are fortified in this choice by the thought that the Supreme Court also has steadfastly journeyed with M'Naghten.[12]

The positions of the courts that have chosen to retain *M'Naghten* are represented by the opinion in *Sauer v. United States* which said:

> But it is not for this court to undertake a drastic revision in the concept of criminal responsibility, a task which would necessitate a searching analysis of philosophies, purposes, and policies of the criminal law, and which might substitute freedom of insane persons for either confinement or commitment. If change there is to be, it must come from a higher judicial authority, or from the Congress.[13]

And in *Commonwealth v. Woodhouse:*

> The protection of society is our paramount concern. The science of psychology and its facets are concerned primarily

[12] 237 F.2d 118, 127 (9th Cir. 1956).
[13] 241 F.2d 640, 652 (9th Cir. 1957).

with diagnosis and therapeutics, not with moral judgments. Ethics is the basic element in the judgments of the law and should always continue to be. Until some rule, other than "M'Naghten," based on a firm foundation in scientific fact for effective operation in the protection and security of society, is forthcoming, we shall adhere to it. We shall not blindly follow the opinion of psychiatric and medical experts and substitute for a legal principle which has proven durable and practicable for decades, vague rules that provide no positive standards.[14]

And in *Downs v. State:* "Without attempting to pass on the merits of these citations and authorities we feel inclined and bound to follow the rule heretofore announced by our own Court. . . . 'These tests [the *M'Naghten* rule used by the trial court] are in accord with the great weight of modern authority.' " [15]

The courts that have rejected *Durham* on its merits have done so primarily because: "The Durham rule leaves the triers with virtually no standard to guide them. . . . The chief criticism directed against the Durham rule is that it leaves the words disease, defect and product, undefined." [16] In *People v. Carpenter,* the Illinois Supreme Court said: "The need in this area is for more clarification and the Durham instruction does not supply it." [17] In *Flowers v. State,* the court said:

How would the jury be instructed on what would be "the product of mental disease?" Would it be the sole cause, or merely a cause, or when would a cause be too remote to be a product of a diseased mind? Should we attempt to adopt the law of torts on proximate cause? The historic function of the jury is to find the facts and apply the law as instructed by the court. . . . Such an indefinite standard as a product of mental disease or mental defect can hardly clarify a juror's mind, or do more than put the matter for his decision according to his personal sense of justice as matter of legal right.[18]

[14] 164 A.2d 98, 107 (Pa. 1960).
[15] 330 S.W.2d 281, 283-284 (Ark. 1960).
[16] Commonwealth v. Chester, 337 Mass. 702, 712-713, 150 N.E.2d 914, 919-920 (1958).
[17] 11 Ill. 2d 60, 68, 142 N.E.2d 11, 15 (1957).
[18] 236 Ind. 151, 165, 139 N.E.2d 185, 194 (1956).

And in *State v. Goza:*

> The Durham instruction fails to give the jury any sufficient guide as to what constitutes mental disease or mental defect. An instruction which submits the defense of insanity to the jury in such general terms is wholly inadequate to guide the jury in choosing between conflicting theories of experts in the psychiatric field as these experts attempt to determine the criminal responsibility of the accused. . . . Such a rule might well fail to provide adequate protection for the public.[19]

As we conclude our study, the situation remains that the *Durham* rule or its equivalent is law in New Hampshire, the District of Columbia, Vermont, and Maine. New York State adopted the rule drafted by the American Law Institute. In all other jurisdictions, the *M'Naghten* "right from wrong" standard prevails.[20] The final determination as to the influence of the *Durham* decision on the law of criminal responsibility must await further decisions by the courts and actions by the legislatures.

---

[19] 317 S.W.2d 609 (Mo. 1958).

[20] Note that in 1956 the Circuit Court in the District of Columbia held that the "right from wrong" and "irresistible impulse" tests could be used along with Durham instructions. But the ultimate issue is: Did the mental defect of disease cause the act? Douglas v. United States, 239 F.2d 52-58 (D.C. Cir. 1956). And in Wright v. United States, 250 F.2d 4 (D.C. Cir. 1957), the court said that while capacity to distinguish right from wrong is no longer *the* earmark of legal sanity, the lack of that capacity is *one* of the earmarks of legal *insanity.*

CHAPTER 11

Summary and Concluding Remarks

Although defense-of-insanity trials represent only about two per cent of all criminal jury trials, such trials are important for at least two reasons. First, there has been a good deal of controversy among judges, lawyers, psychiatrists, and newspapermen about the changes introduced in the legal doctrine defining the criterion for legal insanity. And second, the cases in which the plea is offered usually involve serious offenses.

This study described the reactions of over a thousand jurors to two experimental trials involving a defense of insanity. The experiments were conducted in the courts and the subjects were chosen by lot from the jury pools of three metropolitan areas: Chicago, St. Louis, and Minneapolis. The jurors listened to recorded trials based on cases that had been decided previously. They were told at the outset that their deliberations would be recorded. The use of recorded trials and the jurors' awareness that their deliberations were being recorded might be considered such barriers to realism as to make one seriously question the value of the entire experience. We have no *direct* evidence that contradicts this point should one wish to press it. But our *indirect* evidence is impressive. It is based primarily on the content and quality of the deliberations. We mean such matters as the involvement the jurors showed in the issues raised during the trial, the length of time the jurors deliberated, the tenacity with which they defended a position, yet at the same time the concern they expressed about costs to the county if they were a hung jury and the case would have to be retried.

While we feel that the recorded trials did not seriously diminish the realism of the experience, they had the important advantage of permitting us to systematically vary information on matters concerning important aspects of the trials. The findings reported in the first, substantive section of the book described jurors' reactions to the three experimental variables: rules of law, expert psychiatric testimony, and commitment information. In addition, we compared the verdicts of jurors of different socio-economic backgrounds and personality characteristics. We also gained access to the "inner sanctum" of the jury room and recorded the juries' deliberations on these experimental trials. In the final chapters, we polled the jurors for their recommendations on the future usage of alternative rules of law and reported the decisions reached by state supreme courts and the federal appellate bench on cases in which attorneys urged the adoption of the *Durham* rule in place of *M'Naghten.*

Of the 1176 jurors involved in the study, 360 were exposed to the housebreaking trial and 816 to the incest case. Martin Graham, the defendant in the housebreaking trial, was described by two psychiatrists as a "psychopathic personality with psychosis." He had a long history of mental disturbances, previous commitments to mental hospitals, and attempted suicides. He was unable to hold a job and his testimony during the trial was incoherent. When psychiatrists were asked the crucial question on the matter of responsibility, in the *M'Naghten* version they testified that they were unable to answer. In the *Durham* version they testified that the defendant's actions were "certainly influenced by his behavior."

Jason Lunt, the defendant in the incest case, was described by two psychiatrists as suffering from "paraphiliac neurosis." He was not now, nor had he ever been, psychotic. He had no history of commitment to mental institutions or of anti-social behavior. He received high efficiency ratings for his work as a lieutenant in the fire department and his friends and associates testified that they had no inkling of his bizarre relations with his daughters. When psychiatrists were asked the crucial question on the matter of responsibility, in response to the *M'Naghten* criterion, both doctors answered that in their opinions the defendant could distinguish right from wrong. Under *Durham,* they answered that Lunt's behavior *vis à vis* his daughters was a manifestation of his mental disease.

When deciding individually, two thirds of the jurors in the housebreaking trial believed that Martin Graham was not guilty by reason of insanity and one third that he was guilty. The group verdicts followed the pattern of the individual decisions: 56 per cent found not guilty by reason of insanity, 17 per cent found guilty, and 27 per cent of the juries hung.[1] The jurors who received no instructions as to the criterion of responsibility they were to apply had the highest proportion of not guilty by reason of insanity verdicts. Jurors who were exposed to the *M'Naghten* rule had the lowest and *Durham* jurors were in between. The difference in verdicts between the *M'Naghten* and *uninstructed* jurors was significant. But between *M'Naghten* and *Durham* there was no significant difference.

For reasons explained in Chapter 3, after running only thirty juries, ten under each rule of law, we decided that the housebreaking trial was not as good a vehicle for experimentation as our second case, the incest trial. Therefore, we ran more than twice as many replications of the incest case and spent most of the time discussing the findings from our second experiment.

Concerning the individual verdicts, in the incest trial one third of the jurors believed the defendant not guilty by reason of insanity and two thirds guilty. The proportion of guilty verdicts on the group ballots was even higher: 71 per cent found guilty, 13 per cent found not guilty by reason of insanity, and 16 per cent hung. Unlike the responses to the house-

[1] In both trials, about half the jurors had no conflict because their individual pre-deliberation preferences matched the eventual group decision. About 25 per cent of the jurors found themselves in groups in which the group sentiment opposed their individual opinions. Among those jurors, 60 per cent in the housebreaking trial and 67 per cent in the incest trial were convinced by the group discussion and changed their minds as well as their verdicts.

breaking trial, the variations in the rules of law did produce significant differences. There was a 12 per cent difference between jurors exposed to *M'Naghten* and *Durham* with jurors exposed to *Durham* more likely to vote for acquittal on grounds of insanity. The verdicts of jurors who received no instructions as to the criterion of responsibility they were to apply matched very closely those reported under *Durham*.

Members of the bench and bar who opposed adoption of the *Durham* rule because they believe it would increase greatly the number of defendants acquitted on grounds of insanity will take special note of the 12 per cent. Two points about it should therefore be made. One, while the 12 per cent is significant statistically, it is not a difference we can attribute to chance, it is 12 per cent and not 25 or 50 per cent. Although we also note that when the individual verdicts are translated into group decisions the difference increases from 12 to 19 per cent. (None of the juries instructed under *M'Naghten* found. not guilty by reason of insanity but 19 per cent of the juries instructed under *Durham* did.) Two, the verdicts of the *uninstructed* jurors and of the jurors exposed to the *Durham* rule were almost identical. We conclude from this that the criterion for criminal responsibility as defined under *Durham* is closer to the jury's natural sense of equity than is the *M'Naghten* rule. This finding about the similarity in verdicts between *Durham* and *uninstructed* juries is particularly interesting in light of the fact that in at least half of the juries instructed under the *Durham* and *uninstructed* versions, jurors considered the defendant's ability to distinguish right from wrong in the course of their deliberations. The jurors seemed to be acting as if they had been instructed along the lines proposed by the circuit court in the District of Columbia when it said: "while the capacity to distinguish right from wrong is no longer the earmark of legal sanity, the lack of that capacity is one of the earmarks of legal *insanity*." [2]

Another fear about the effects of the *Durham* rule on the

[2] Wright v. United States, 250 F.2d 4 (D.C. Cir. 1957). See Chapter 10, note 17.

jury that was not borne out by our data concerns the belief that juries instructed under *Durham* would be deprived of their basic responsibility. If length of deliberation is at all a valid index of the difficulty of the jurors' task or of the jurors' involvement with their task, and we believe it is, then the *Durham* rule serves to enhance the jurors' responsibility. We found that juries deliberated significantly longer when instructed under *Durham* than they did under *M'Naghten*. And we also found that they had no more difficulty reaching consensus under *Durham,* as witnessed by the lack of significant differences in the proportion of hung juries between the two rules of law.

One of the most significant findings that emerged from our study was the failure of the "model" and "typical" versions of expert testimony to produce differences in verdicts. The typical testimony was the testimony that was given in the original incest trial. The model testimony was drafted in consultation with psychiatrists who are critical of the existing procedure and who have extensive courtroom experience. Given the opportunity to provide the kind of testimony that would present a comprehensive picture of the defendant's medical history and current symptoms and would still be in keeping with the adversary system, they drafted the "model" version. But jurors were no more likely to find the defendant not guilty by reason of insanity after exposure to the model version than they were after listening to the typical version. Neither did the combination of the "model" version with the *Durham* rule produce higher percentages of not guilty by reason of insanity verdicts than did the "model-*M'Naghten*" version. As we suggested earlier, perhaps had the changes in the expert testimony been made along different lines (for example, emphasis on the defendant's behavior at the time of the crime, as opposed to early childhood experiences and background) it would have made a difference in the juries' verdicts.

On the more general question of the jurors' reactions to the psychiatric testimony, we found that jurors reviewed the testimony during the deliberations and seemed to understand its essence. But they were also very conscious of their responsibilities as jurors and adhered to the division of labor whereby the experts advised and they, the jurors, decided whether the defendant was responsible for his behavior. When jurors were asked directly: Which do you believe is the best way of deciding what should be done with a person who has committed a crime and pleads that he is insane? two thirds of the jurors in the housebreaking case (a relatively mild offense and a patently psychotic defendant) recommended that psychiatrists make the decision, but only one third of the jurors in the incest case (a more heinous offense coupled with a less severe mental condition) were willing to delegate responsibility to psychiatrists.

Another aspect of jury behavior that we examined concerned the important practical question: Which jurors are likely to be more sympathetic to the defendant? We offered two competing hypotheses. One, that the relationship between lower socio-economic status and defendant proneness observed in criminal cases would generalize to criminal cases involving a defense of insanity. The other, that jurors of higher status, and therefore those with more education, would be more sympathetic to defendants who plead "insanity" because they are more sophisticated about mental illness. While our results were not conclusive, we found some confirmation for the first hypothesis and none for the second.

Our attempts at extending the inquiry from demographic characteristics to personality and attitudinal factors were not successful. While we obtained fairly good distributions on responses to many of the personality assessment items, with one exception, there was no relationship between the jurors' attitudes and their verdicts.

Chapter 8, The Sound of the Jury, is probably the most interesting chapter in the book. In part, it is interesting because there is so much lore and almost no "hard data" on how the jury spends its time, what it talks about, and how it goes about its business. Chapter 8 supplies some of the answers.

But mostly it is interesting because what the jurors say is interesting; because they are obviously very involved in what they are supposed to do and are trying to do a good job.

Two characteristics about the deliberations are worth emphasizing because they do not support the lore and because they tell us something basic about human behavior. The first is that the jurors spend most of their time reviewing the record. By the time they have finished deliberating they have usually considered every bit of testimony, expert as well as lay, and every point offered in evidence. The second point is the jurors' willingness to talk about intimate and in some instances painful experiences that they have had with spouses or parents who have become mentally ill. We noted how such accounts had a cathartic effect on the narrator and how it helped the jury reach consensus.

The last section offers a look to the future from two perspectives: from the vantage point of the jury and from that of the court. The first part describes the jurors' recommendations as to the criterion of criminal responsibility that courts should adopt in future cases and also offers some general indicators of the jury's preference for the *M'Naghten* and *Durham* rules.

When jurors were asked explicitly which rule of law they would recommend for future usage, a third recommended *M'Naghten,* 36 per cent *Durham,* and 31 per cent indicated no preference. Jurors were more likely to recommend the rule they "used" than the alternative, and *Durham* received a slight edge over *M'Naghten.* When jurors were asked which rule they would request the judge to read to the jury if they were the defendant's attorney, *Durham* was favored by more than two to one over *M'Naghten.* On more peripheral matters, the jurors' preference for a jury over a bench trial and their satisfaction with their deliberations was no greater for having been exposed to one rule as opposed to another.

Chapter 10 reviews recent decisions in which the defense sought to introduce *Durham* in place of *M'Naghten.* In contrast to the slight preference that jurors have for the *Durham* rule over the *M'Naghten* rule, the appellate bench has been almost unanimous in its rejection of *Durham*.

Finally, in keeping with the general tone of this study we leave the last word to the jury. Appendix A describes a deliberation.

The Deliberation of Jury 57

The most persuasive evidence of the success of this study in simulating the deliberations of real juries is the recordings themselves. We could not distribute a sound recording of a deliberation with each copy of the book. But we did the next best thing, by including a protocol of one of the deliberations.

The jury selected (No. 57 in the incest case) deliberated under the *Uninstructed-model* version and returned a verdict of guilty. We selected Jury 57 because it was one of the most interesting deliberations. We make no claim that it is typical.

The protocol has been edited, primarily by the addition of a brief narrative and the exclusion, for reasons of economy, of repetitious sections (the full protocol runs over a hundred typed pages).

The jury's profile, shown below, adds interest to a study of the deliberation.

The sixty-eight deliberations in the incest experiment lasted from approximately a half hour to over six hours. Jury 57's deliberation lasted four hours and forty-five minutes. On the pre-deliberation questionnaires, seven jurors believed that the defendant was not guilty by reason of insanity; five that he was guilty. Almost five hours later, the jury reported a unanimous verdict: guilty. This concession of the majority to the minority did not occur often,[1] and in Jury 57 it was brought

---

[1] As indicated in Chapter 6, in the incest experiment, of the 57 juries that reported unanimous verdicts 6 represented victories for minority factions. Twice a minority, once of four and once of five jurors, who believed the defendant guilty succeeded in swinging the

JURY 57

Version: Uninstructed on Responsibility
           Model Expert Testimony
City: Chicago
Verdict: Guilty

Jurors	Age	Sex	Occupation	Education	Verdicts Pre-deliberation	Post-	Participation (in per cent)
1	45-54	F	Clerical worker	High school	NGI	G	16.0
2	55-64	M	Skilled laborer	High school	G	G	0.7
3	25-34	F	Housewife (clerical worker*)	High school	NGI	G	2.0
4	55-64	F	Housewife (Proprietor*)	Grade school	NGI	G	22.0
5	35-44	F	Laborer	Grade school	G	G	1.0
6	35-44	F	Clerical worker	Two years high school	NGI	G	11.0
7	35-44	M	Skilled laborer	Two years high school	NGI	G	5.0
8	45-54	F	Clerical worker	Grade school	G	G	0.6
9	45-54	F	Skilled laborer	College	NGI	G	6.0
10	— 25	F	Clerical worker	High school	G	G	1.0
11	45-54	M	Laborer	Grade school	NGI	G	0.0
12	55-64	M	Clerical worker	High school	G	G	35.0

* Husband's occupation.

about largely by the skill and tenacity of the foreman, Juror Twelve. (The other four jurors whose pre-deliberation vote was guilty showed only 3.3 per cent participation.)

In two other respects Jury 57 did not fit the general pattern: there were no businessmen on it,[2] and eight of its members were women.[3]

---

majority to their side; and four times five jurors on each jury who favored a NGI verdict convinced a majority of guilty verdict jurors.

[2] There were 145 proprietors in the total jury population. An equal distribution would have assured at least two businessmen on each of the 68 juries.

[3] Women were a majority on only 11 out of the 68 juries.

Jury 57 conducted its first piece of business, the election of a foreman, with typical dispatch. Juror Twelve, one of the four men in the group (a sixty-year-old white-collar employee), was nominated and elected in less than two minutes. In fact, Juror Twelve engineered his own election. It came about in this way. As soon as the jury convened, Juror Twelve nominated Juror One, a woman in her late forties employed as a clerical worker:

12-1   As long as you're sitting in the head chair, you may as well take it.
1-1   Well, I have never served before on a jury, and they tell me you have. You know a little more about the procedures, supposing you sit up here.
6-6   I don't believe it's really necessary to know anything about it really, it's merely a discussion to find out whether . . .
12-1   No, you're just supposed to run the discussion. See to it that no two people talk at the same time.
1-1   Well.
12-12 The only thing that didn't come out. Oh, first we have to settle that.
1-1   Well, what would be the opinion of the guilt or innocence of the defendant?
12-1   Well, I think you should invite an open discussion.
1-12   Why don't you . . .
12-1   I'm too tired to get up.
9-12   Oh, you can stay right where you are.
1-12   Go on, you act as foreman.
12-12 Well, let's talk it over. See what, what's been bothering me, those two doctors . . .

With the election out of the way Juror Twelve lost no time providing the jury with his opinion of the case:

12-12 The defendant is a sex pervert; but he knew what he was doing. He knew that it was wrong but he did it to satisfy his own desire. Even the psychiatrists could not come right out and say that an oversexed man is insane.

Juror Four objected. Juror Four was a housewife, about the same age as the foreman.

4-12   I'll tell you he may have been emotionally disturbed until he committed that, but when he committed that, he really was insane.

1-1   The very fact that he was cautious enough to use a preventative indicates that he might have been off . . . but, he also was crafty enough and sly enough not to want anybody to know. Or, to have any repercussions as far as that is concerned. Now most insane people are a little on the sly secretive side . . .

4-1   They are.

1-1   But, I think he was sane enough to not want any scandal. Now whether that would be from his own viewpoint or for his daughter's sake we can't tell. But, he couldn't have been thinking very much of his daughter on that score, so it had to be solely on his own, which is selfishness. To some extent selfishness and slyness run in insanity cases, I think, where they are always very crafty and want to outwit somebody else, their associates, or somebody they are connected with. But on the other hand, the very fact that he carried on his job, had friends and still was ashamed to make any effort to seek outside help. What would you call that? [4]

Juror Four answered, "The defendant was only insane on a certain subject. He spoke about it as if it was nothing. That shows he was insane. He didn't understand what it was all about." Juror Six, another woman of about forty, commented: "But remember how long he has been doing this. He started on the younger daughter when she was twelve." [5] Juror Four declared: "The mother was more insane than he was. It is just like murdering her daughter. Even if she were half crazy, she would still fight for her child."

For the next few minutes the discussion drifted off in several directions. Some jurors asked about the sons' roles in the fam-

[4] At this stage in the discussion it seemed that Juror One was not as convinced of the defendant's sanity as Juror Twelve. But as the deliberation proceeded she became the foreman's strongest ally in persuading the majority to accept a verdict of guilty.

[5] It would have been difficult to judge from Juror Six's first comment that she would become Juror Four's strongest ally. Juror Six relinquished her position only after Juror Four admitted that she was ready to concede.

ily. Others considered the relationship between organic disorders and mental illness. A few continued to discuss the mother. Finally, Juror One addressed the group as a whole:

1-1   He is insane. He is absolutely insane. Without question, a normal person would not do anything like that. He was insane and I think this man should be committed.

12-12   Well, let's see what the two psychiatrists said about degrees of insanity. All they kept harping on was emotionally disturbed. See, there is a fine point. How about the judge's instructions? Is there anything in there . . .

9-12   I was just trying to read it over and find it.

12-12   I don't see where the judge said how to determine the degree of insanity. That's what we have to find out.

The foreman read the first few pages of the instructions, up to the part about differentiating lay and expert witnesses, then Juror One interrupted:

1-12   All right now, the prosecution's doctor did not observe the defendant.

12-1   Oh, that one, that's right.

1-12   He made absolutely no personal observations of the defendant.

12-1   No, all he was asked was, is a sex pervert insane. And he said no.

1-12   Okay. Go ahead.

12-1   See. Now these two other fellows didn't say that a sex pervert was insane. They didn't say that.

1-12   He was a psychotic.

12-1   Yes, but what does that mean? In our language. Crazy?

4-12   Psycho, that means he's got a neurosis, that at certain times he's crazy and at certain times he can think straight.

12-4   Most of us would be in the nut house if that were the case.

4-12   Well, this is an emotional disturbance. This is a mental disorder of the brain.

3-12   Well, I think the man, even in going over what he did, he knew what he did, but I think in his mind, I think he thought he was right.

4-3   That's right.

3-12   He told about it so calmly.

12-3   That doesn't mean anything.

4-12   Oh, I think if he thought it was awful, he wouldn't talk that way as though it was nothing. The man doesn't know.

A few minutes later Juror One asked the foreman to continue reading the instructions. Juror Twelve read without interruption to the end. Juror Ten, the youngest member of the jury, observed:

10-10 He did say that he considered the necessity of psychiatric treatment and lacking funds delayed any attempt to obtain such.

7-12 That was during the time of the depression. He mentioned that, and he tried to go and get the treatment, but he had no money at the time. He knew there was something wrong then.

1-7 He said he considered it, he didn't say he tried to go.

4-4 He considered it because he knew there was something wrong with his mind.

1-1 His mind or his lust.

4-4 Lust or mind. It's his mind that makes the lust. It's your mind that works over your body. It's your mind. It's the mind. The mind does everything.

6-1 If it was just lust why didn't he go around doing it to other women instead of his own daughters?

12-6 That didn't come out in the testimony. We don't know whether he did.

The jurors considered the likelihood that the defendant had extra-marital affairs, but the discussion soon dribbled off. The general consensus was that they did not know and that the topic was not really relevant.

Juror Twelve called the group's attention to something that the defendant mentioned in his statement to the police:

12-12 It says something about him noticing something as a three-year-old. Now, that's not possible.

1-12 I don't remember that.

12-12 He was three years old when he noticed the older boys in the candy store or whatever it was.

4-12 Who knows if three years old is too young?

1-1 Is there anything in that record that would indicate whether a three-year-old would get any sexual satisfaction from masturbation?

The question was not answered and the jury returned to the basic issue.

12-12 Can you hide behind the word insane, whenever you are going to commit a crime of violence?

4-12 Well, there are different kinds of insanity. Probably everybody has a different kind of insanity.

12-12 He knew what he was doing. He was, he was just a sex maniac. He knew what he was doing.

1-1 Any rape case that you read about in the paper, are they all insane?

12-12 Seems they can hide behind it. In my opinion they are not insane.

4-4 Well, can I say something?

12-4 Wait till this lady gets through.

1-1 Can the whole business of sex be based on an insane desire?

12-12 I don't think so, no.

4-4 Well, can I say something?

12-4 Yes, go ahead.

4-4 Well, I'll tell you, when you attack somebody else that is different than attacking your own. You have to be insane to do that.

12-4 You have to be insane to do anything wrong.

4-12 Absolutely.

12-4 For that matter. Any crime of violence.

4-12 Well, this man is mentally ill.

1-4 He's unbalanced.

12-4 There is something wrong, he's unbalanced, but he knew what he was doing. He knew what he was doing.

Juror Nine, who said almost nothing in these first twenty minutes of discussion, interrupted:

9-12 I'd like to refer to the judge's instructions here. It says the important point of all this discussion of expert witnesses and opinion testimony is that you are not bound as jurors to accept the testimony of expert witnesses. You should certainly carefully consider the qualifications of the witnesses. Well, why don't we start there? [6]

12-9 Well, they were qualified men, there is no doubt about it. But did they come right out and say the man was insane? They kept harping on emotional instability and a few other big words, but they did not come out and say the man was

---

[6] Juror Nine, a woman, was the only college graduate on the jury. At first, she supported Jurors Four and Six, but about halfway through the discussion she shifted to the guilty side.

insane. And the third doctor, Grant, he didn't say anything about Jason Lunt in particular, but he did say that a
sex pervert is not necessarily insane.

1-12   Yes, but the defense threw that out because he didn't even
examine the defendant. Do you want to throw out the
testimony of the prosecutor's doctor?

Jurors One and Twelve wrangled over whether or not they
ought to "throw out Doctor Grant's testimony." While they
were discussing that, Juror Four remembered that during the
trial something was said "about the defendant doing funny
things on his job such as tampering with an automobile." Another juror commented: "Well, then, all these kids stealing
hub caps ought to be in the nut house."

To make the point that insanity can take many forms, Juror
Four told the following story:

4-4   Well I'll tell you. I heard of a case where this girl always
used to run around, would always come home pregnant to
her mother. Finally they put her out in _____ Hospital
and she is there forever. But, every time she would go out
she would come home pregnant. Well, she's crazy in that
way. What I am trying to say is that there is insanity of
sex, insanity of stealing, insanity of this, all kinds of insanity, but they are insane. You call them insane.

12-4   But what degree of insanity did this man have, that's what
we want to know.

4-12   That I don't know, but he's insane, but I don't know what
degree of insanity . . .

12-4   It may have started out as a lustful act, and then he had to
keep it up and cover it up. He had to cover up his tracks.

6-12   Why did he have to cover up his tracks?

12-6   Well, because the more he did it, the more chance there
was of his being found out.

4-12   Well, why couldn't he go elsewhere, like why did he have
to go to his own home to his daughters? There are plenty
of other dames. He could have gone out. The man is not
normal.

12-4   I don't know.

6-12   I don't think he would be insane if he didn't go to his own
daughters, but when a man does that to his own daughters,
I can't see him being in his right mind.

4-6   Neither do I. I say he's insane. He's insane to a certain extent.

10-4   If your husband died you would be emotionally upset but that wouldn't necessarily mean you were going insane.

4-10   Just a minute. If I was emotionally upset over my husband's death and I started doing funny things it would be insane.

7-12   But they let it go on, so they knew he was sick. They knew he was sick at the time, and so they didn't . . .

10-4   There was something wrong with his wife to let his daughters do that.

4-10   There is something wrong with his daughters because of if anyone tried that on me, I'd stop it right away, they couldn't get me.

Juror Nine shifted the group's attention to another topic:

9-9   We still want to go back to the fact of whether this man should be allowed to go free, isn't that what it amounts to?

12-9   Well, no. There are two alternatives. If he were crazy, pardon me, if he were insane, he would go to an institution.

4-12   That's right.

12-9   And if he was sane, he would go to jail.

3-12   All right. Say he is found guilty and he goes to jail and he gets out, maybe for good behavior.

12-3   He won't get out so fast.

3-12   No, but say he does . . .

4-12   But they can keep him in these mental hospitals for a long time.

3-12   But say he does, and he goes berserk and does the same thing over again.

4-12   That's right.

3-12   Where if he is found not guilty by reason of insanity, he will get treatment. And maybe it will cure him.

4-3   That's right.

12-3   I don't think they ever will cure him, because the older they get the worse they get.

4-12   Well, we have to take that chance.

7-12   You're taking a chance both ways.

4-12   You've got to take that chance. That man needs treatments . . .

10-12 Do you think he might have said that he was insane, and he knew he would be committed to an institution for a short period? If he didn't plead insane, he would be sent to jail and maybe his sentence would be something like ten years.

12-10   Very possible.

10-12   He might get out of the institution in two only.

12-10   Very possible.

4-10   Well, that's taking chances again.

6-10   What makes you think he would be sentenced to a short period? That is up to the doctors in question. He had no idea of how long . . .

10-6   Because he knows that he's sane.

Woman   How does he know that he's sane?

4-10   A crazy person don't know whether he's insane or not. That's why they do crazy things. They don't know if they're coming or going.

At this point the jury had deliberated for a little over an hour. Juror Nine asked for a vote. The jurors decided to use a closed ballot. The vote was seven not guilty by reason of insanity and five guilty. As soon as the vote was announced Juror Twelve commented:

12-12   All right, now the thing is, we have to determine the extent of insanity. There are different degrees of it.

Juror Four responded:

4-12   We don't know. There are all kinds of insanity. There is a lady who told me that she went down to the _____ Hospital and she spoke to a woman, and she didn't know she was insane. And this woman said to her, "Oh, I am just longing for certain foods which I had all the time, and they don't give it to me here, and boy I would really love to have it." And the woman didn't look like she was, what will I say, insane, or emotionally disturbed. So she said, "All right, I will be here next week and I am going to bring you that food." Next week she came in with the food and she gave it to the woman. As soon as she gave it to the woman, this woman turned around, and hit her over the head and split her head. And she seemed so sane to her a week or two before. Now how do you know there are degrees to insanity? Sometimes they act so well and sometimes they are on the rumpus, but they are insane.

12-4   All right, okay. Then in other words, an oversexed person is insane.

4-12   To a certain extent.

12-4   All right. Now wait a minute. Don't give me that. Wait a minute. Now we're starting all over again. You're putting me back where I was yesterday.

4-12   Well, they are not normal.

12-4   I want a yes or no answer. That's what we didn't get from those two doctors.

4-12   Now, wait a minute, that's the thing now. A person that attacks his own, I think is insane. An oversexed person will run around. But he will probably know the difference between attacking someone outside. When you attack your own, now, you're insane.

12-12 Look, this guy was sane enough to take precautions to keep those girls from becoming pregnant and he was sane enough to quit when he saw his friends coming up the stairs.

Juror One: "He was sane enough to know that he didn't want anybody else to know what he was doing." Juror Six: "But, actually those girls could have gone out into the street or gone to the school the next day and talked and he couldn't have stopped them." Juror One suggested that fear might have stopped them from talking about it. She added also:

1-1   Now here's a thought that doesn't even come into it at all. But what would your opinion be on sterilizing these men?

4-1   I believe in that. I believe that oversexed people should be sterilized. It is dangerous to let them run the streets.

12-12 You're getting away from this particular case.

Juror Nine brought the group back to the main theme by commenting on a rather subtle point:

9-9   Didn't the doctors point out the fact that they thought that he reacted in a rather abnormal fashion to the questioning they did of him? It amazed them that he was not embarrassed and that he didn't show any reaction.

4-9   That's right.

1-9   He knew it was wrong.

12-9   He knew it was wrong, and he knew what he was doing. That's the way I feel about it.

9-12   I don't think an insane person can always keep from doing what they are doing. In other words, they may know that they are doing wrong, but they don't know why they are going ahead and doing it anyway.

4-4   There is a force that forces them.

1-9   Oh, hell's bells.

9-12   Don't you believe that?

4-9   I do.

12-9   You're generalizing that if a man has intercourse with his daughter, he is crazy.

4-12   That's right. That's all I say, he's crazy.

4-4   If he went out and done it to someone else, you wouldn't say he's crazy, but to do it to your own daughters then you're really insane.

6-12   You support them, you bring them through health and through illness and through everything and you take care of them and then you do something like that . . .

12-6   How about these fathers that whip their children, I mean whip them until they are bleeding and black and blue. Are they insane?

6-12   I think they're crazy too.

7-12   They're sick too.

6-12   I think they are crazy and they belong in an institution.

4-12   I know fathers that beat their children. I read it in the paper. They're crazy, yes. Or mothers that kill their children. Yes, she's crazy. Yes.

One of the less active participants, Juror Seven, began to read the defendant's statement aloud. Juror Seven was a man about forty, employed as a skilled worker. His reading was interrupted at several points. The first time as he read, "At the time I was three years old, I recall acts of —"

1-7   Now just a minute — right there — how many of you here remember anything when you were three years old?

4-1   That's why he's crazy. What do you remember when you were three years old?

6-6   You made a point there. How many people remember what happened when they were three years old?

4-6   I'm sure I don't know.

7-12   My earliest recollection was when I was five years old. I think that most doctors will agree, that it is on a rare occasion when a child is conscious of anything before they are five years of age. Then they can vividly remember. Well, anyway, getting back to this. At that time I was three years old and vividly recall acts of masturbation . . .

12-4   You see where you are misleading yourself. You are saying that a man who does that is crazy. We all know that he isn't right. The thing is what we have to determine is, when he was doing it, did he know it. He knew what he was doing regardless of the fact of whether an insane person would do it or not. The judge said, the thing that we have to work with is to determine whether he knew what he was doing at the moment. He knew that he had his daughter in that bed. He knew it. That's what we have to determine. I'll go along with you when you tell me that a man who has intercourse with his daughter is a nut. Okay. It may be. But at the time, he knew what he was doing. He knew that he was doing wrong, he said that. That is the point.

6-12   I disagree with you.

12-6   You mean to say that when he was having intercourse with his daughter, he didn't know it was his daughter?

6-12   Any man that tells his daughter to get ready, to use a diaphragm, is crazy.

4-12   Yes, insane.

6-12   Crazy, crazy, crazy.

12-6   That's not the point.

6-12   That is the point, because this is the most important part, is the man sane when he can do that to his daughter? That is the most important aspect of this whole case.

12-6   All right. Now another point.

6-12   Everything leading up to it.

12-6   We are trying to determine, did he know what he was doing, while he was doing it, did he know it was his daughter? He gets up from the lunch table, they are eating, and he turns to his daughter and says get ready.

6-12   There is only one person that can answer that, himself. In his own mind.

12-6   Well then, we're stuck.

4-12   That's why he's sick.

7-12   He's sick. He showed that he is sick. Right there.

12-7   Not necessarily.

7-12   Sure.

12-7   There is something wrong with the man. Any man who commits incest, there is something wrong with him. But we're trying to determine, does he know he's doing it while he's doing it. That's what I, that's what we have to determine.

7-12   We have to determine whether he's guilty of the crime or whether he's insane, that's what the judge said.

12-7 No, the judge said, did he know what he was doing, while he was doing it?

6-12 He probably knew what he was doing, but he had it in his mind with whom he was doing it.

4-12 He didn't. Does that answer your question?

12-4 He must have if he tells his daughter to go get ready.

4-12 Why, he doesn't know. He doesn't know.

5-5 If he just wanted sexual release, he could have gone out any place.[7]

1-12 He could have gone to his wife.

12-1 But she was frigid, he said.

7-12 She offered herself.

4-4 That's right.

12-12 But evidently she wouldn't satisfy him.

4-12 Oh, he was so crazy, he didn't know what he was . . .

1-12 His daughter was young. He's just full of lust, that's all.

12-12 That's all. He's just an oversexed man, that's all there is to it.

Juror One picked up the defendant's statement and read: "During the period over which these acts occurred, I made all effort to avoid pregnancy with my daughter and such never occurred. The following contraceptive methods were used: diaphragm, vaginal douche, suppositories and prophylactics."

2-1 He knew all about that.

12-12 Sure, he knew all about it but what does a twelve-year-old girl know about . . .

4-12 You'd be surprised what some twelve-year-old girls know . . .

12-4 I know they know, you're right.

4-12 Why, they can tell you a few things. You'd be surprised what some twelve-year-old girls know.

7-12 Here the thing is, you either want to convict the man to prison or you want to send him to a mental institution for this.

12-7 I think he should go to prison because he will stay in prison longer.

7-12 You can't tell either way, what's going to happen.

12-7 If he goes to the nut house, in a couple of years they will

---

[7] Juror Five had not said anything until this time. She was a woman about forty and she worked as a laborer.

give him another examination and they will say, you are all right.

Woman   How do you know? How do you know?

7-12   All right, he can get out of prison on good behavior.

4-12   Yes, that's right.

12-4   You people are making me feel that I condone incest. There has to be something wrong with a person who commits incest. But we're trying to determine, at the moment, when he was doing it, did he know that that was his daughter. I say he knew it after, and he knew it while he was doing it, that it was his daughter who was in the bed with him, not a stranger. What we have to determine is whether the man knew right from wrong. We know that his actions were wrong, we know that incest is no good.

Speaking in a more conciliatory tone, Juror Nine asked:

9-9   Could we approach this from another angle? We have a man who we realize should not be left in society. Something has to be done to the man. Will prison bars improve him more than medical care? I may not be putting this question the way I want to, but I'm doing the best I can. But anyway do you think that we should put him in prison with the hope that he will get medical care, or should we put him in a mental institution where doctors are in control and where we feel that he will be kept until he is all right?

12-9   I don't think that is any of our business.

1-9   No, you can't gauge it that way because you've got to determine that he will not go to a mental institution unless we term him insane . . .

4-9   Otherwise he goes to prison. Just as a healthy person and they treat him the same way . . .

12-4   Oh no, no. They will give him treatment. You know you are getting away from the whole story of what we're supposed to do. Here's the thing you are confusing the severity of the act. Which we know. Which everybody admits that was a terrible thing for a man to do, but he knew what he was doing when he was doing it. He knew it was his daughter. He invited her. He took her . . . or whatever it was. He knew what he was doing and he knew he was doing wrong and that's the point that we have to consider.

5-4   He knew what he was doing, but what we have to consider too is, is that man sick? He knew what he was doing, but you can't condemn a man . . .

12-5   No, we have to determine, whether, at the time, did he know what he was doing.

12-7   It was established that he was emotionally upset.

7-12   All right, say he knew at the time that he was doing it. Right? All right, now you want to condemn a man to be sent to prison on that, or would you rather have a man sent to a hospital, and cured of that?

12-7   That's not the point. This man is accused of, and he admitted incest.

7-12   Yes.

12-7   Now, what we have to determine is, was he out of his mind at the moment or was he just oversexed and he knew what he was doing? The man was oversexed, he was a pervert. And he knew that he had his daughters. He knew they were his daughters. He knew what he was doing, because when he got through he felt pretty, whatever the words he uses there . . .

4-7   He felt guilty.

The jurors continued this discussion for several more minutes. Finally Juror Twelve offered a "rational" explanation for the defendant's behavior. He suggested:

12-12 It could be, for financial reasons, you know. And another thing, he can't go out on the street and consort with women on the street and have the neighbors in this small town or wherever it is, see him with other women. He had got to do it where he wasn't seen. And if he should go to a professional, then that amounts to a lot of money for a man.

4-12   Sometimes yes and sometimes no.

12-4   Why?

4-12   Professional, I say sometimes it would be some money and sometimes they can get it without money.

12-4   Oh, no.

4-12   It all depends. Yes, sir.

12-4   Oh, no. No ma'am.

1-12   Go to a bar and pick up a dame I guess.

4-12   Yes, sir.

12-4   He has to go to a bar and get a drink . . .

4-12   Now listen, there are some professionals that will pay the man just as well as the man pays the woman. I know.

12-4   When we get to the moon we will find that.

4-12   Yes. Well, don't talk. Don't talk. I talk from experience and I heard cases like that. I know.

12-4   I'm an old man and I've never heard of that.

4-12   Yes. Yes. I've heard of some . . .

Finally, Juror One intervened to end the conversation, and the jury returned to more familiar themes. Did the defendant know what he was doing? Did he know that it was wrong? Juror Twelve complained:

12-4   Well, these doctors didn't say he was insane.

7-12   They didn't say he was sane, either.

12-7   That's why the doctors aren't helping us at all. They left us out on a limb.

7-12   They didn't say he was sane, they didn't say he wasn't. That one doctor said he could be insane.

12-7   That third doctor said that a sex pervert is not necessarily insane.

6-12   The doctor said it was not mental disease, that's what they did say. But it could be a mental disorder.

12-6   That third doctor didn't examine him. He was just called up there to say is a sex pervert necessarily insane. And he said no.

6-12   Not necessarily.

4-12   Not all the time they're not insane.

12-6   That don't mean because he's a sex pervert that he's crazy.

6-12   No, I'll admit that much, but when he does it with his own daughters that is just crazy.

12-6   Not necessarily. Maybe he's a beast. Just because he's a beast doesn't mean he's crazy.

4-12   He can't be that much of a beast.

12-4   What? Why not? To commit incest and not be a beast?

4-12   He can be a beast outside but not to his own. He has to be crazy.

12-4   He couldn't, because he couldn't go outside, maybe for financial reasons or for social reasons.

4-12   Ohhh. Those financial reasons are not there . . .

12-4   Oh, yes, they are.

4-12   If he molested his daughters that way, I can't see no other way.

12-4   He was on safe ground with his daughters. He had them intimidated and they wouldn't talk, until that last one got hysterical because the man came up and rang the doorbell, or came up the stairs and then something snapped in her. Why didn't she scream before? A while ago you just said that a twelve-year-old girl knows a whole lot. Why didn't she say something . . .

10-7   Would you say then that a murderer is not insane?

7-10   Which one?

10-7   Any murderer. Something must be wrong with someone who commits a murder. Are you going to put all murderers in institutions?

7-10   No, not all of them.

10-7   It's a crime against nature to kill somebody.

3-10   But that's a different case again.

7-10   You can't judge everyone like that.

10-7   You're going to end up by saying something must be wrong with him because he committed a murder.

9-12   Well, a person that attempts to commit suicide is usually considered sane, but they are treated at a mental hospital. I mean, they know what they are doing at the time. They deliberately plan every step of it.

4-9   That's right.

9-12   Sometimes they plan it over a period of weeks and weeks. But still there is something mentally wrong.

1-9   But that is self-destruction.

12-9   That's the point that we're bringing out. When they were doing it, they knew they were doing it. That person that jumps out the window knows he is going to jump out the window.

9-12   But do you consider him sane?

12-9   You never can tell. I know a man who had cancer, they had to strap him in bed because he was going to jump out the window. And he wasn't crazy.

3-12   I knew a man very well who had been home sick for quite some time. I think it was a slight stroke. The woman worked and there was no one at home with him, and he laid there. He asked to be put in a hospital, and it wasn't taken care of. They moved in the meantime and someone was going home at noon time to give him his lunch and found him with his wrist slashed. They took him, they bound him to save his life, and then they took him to the psychopathic ward down at _____ Hospital. They asked him why he did it. He said he was in a despondent mood, that's why he did it.

12-3   Yes?

3-12   But now it's a crime to try to take your life. But he was taken to _____ [a mental hospital] and they don't know when he will get out. He's being treated. They are trying to cure the man. But to try and take your life is a crime. Yet, he wasn't sent to jail. He was sent to _____ Hospital to be treated.

12-3   I know. But I can't understand . . .

9-12   But he knew what he was doing. This man knew what he was doing.

6-12   Whether he knew it, in my opinion, or whether he didn't know it, doesn't make any difference. I feel that any man, even if he knows he's taking his own daughter, must be out of his mind to do a thing like that.

12-6   Then you're not following the testimony or the judge's instructions.

6-12   I'm sorry. I think I am.

12-6   You're following your own feelings, and I can understand . . .

6-12   I don't think I am. I find this young lady agrees with me.

12-6   I can understand your feelings.

6-12   I haven't got any feelings. I don't even know the people. I'm trying to use logic and common sense.

12-6   But we have to use the testimony and the judge's instructions, with logic.

6-12   I'm using the judge's instructions.

9-12   The testimony of the witnesses.

12-6   The defense attorney did not say that the man was insane at the time of the action. And that is what we are concerned with. Was he insane at the time of the action?

6-12   You say the action. There were several . . .

12-6   I mean all the actions.

Most of the jurors were curious about why the wife and daughters remained silent for as long as they did, and most of them concluded that their silence must have been motivated by fear. A few suggested other explanations. Concerning the younger daughter, Juror Three asked:

3-6   Why didn't she try to get away from him?

6-3   Well, what could she do? Maybe he was her only means of support. What could a girl fifteen years old do? And she is still subject to him under the law.

3-6   I understand that, but why didn't she try to get away from him?

6-3   She can't get away from him because she is subject to him under law.   She is a minor.

10-6   She is not.   What he is doing is wrong.

6-3   Unless she proves that.   Maybe she was too embarrassed to go in front of everybody and tell them that.

4-6   That could be, she was so embarrassed.

12-6   Well, she wasn't embarrassed at the time that Franklin came up.

The jurors were also puzzled about the defendant's relations with the men on the job.   They were surprised that Franklin, his friend for twenty years, and others in the fire department had no idea of the activities that were going on in the defendant's home.   Juror Twelve explained:

12-9   You take a man, in most cases, their private life comes out with the men they work with, somewhere down the line, you can get a hint from the men working with you.   I know I can.   In my work, we have some men who are always talking about their sex life at home, and out of home. Others keep quiet, they don't say anything.   But if a man is so, if he had something like that on his mind, some hint would come out with his fellow workers, and this Franklin did not say one word against this man's character.

1-12   And his chief didn't.

12-12   All they said was that he got drunk once in a while.   If a man had such a terrible thing on his mind somewhere down the line, he would have given himself away, maybe just one little word.

1-12   There was only one thing, as I recall the testimony, that was brought out by the defense and that was tampering with the car.

Juror One, who had been reading the instructions in a whisper for the past few minutes, remarked to the group:

1-1   The fact that the defendant was off his rocker as far as his sex life was concerned doesn't judge him insane in my estimation.

She referred again to the defendant's statement and read the part that described the use of contraceptives:

1-1 If he was out of his mind he wouldn't give a tinker's damn who it was that got pregnant.

Juror Twelve pointed out:

12-1 And the girl had to go out and be fitted for that diaphragm. Heavens, they all knew what they were doing. She couldn't walk into a dime store and buy it off the counter.

8-1 She had to get it at a pharmacy . . .

1-12 In other words, the diaphragm she had to be fitted for, the vaginal douche her mother could buy, and the suppositories her mother could buy, and he might even buy the prophylactics. But nonetheless, if it's the diaphragm, she would have to be fitted. And over a period of five years, she had to have more than one.

The jury continued discussing the intricacies of diaphragms for some minutes more. Finally, Juror Six suggested that they take another vote. They had deliberated for about three and a half hours. Juror Twelve told the following story while the jurors filled in their ballots:

12-12 I don't know if you people read about the old west. But there was a character in the old west named Belle Starr. Belle Starr and her son were committing incest. I read about it. This fellow Rascoe, Burton Rascoe, wrote a story about Belle Starr, one of the old Calamity Jane gals. Now just because a person commits incest doesn't mean he is crazy.

The ballots were collected and the foreman counted ten guilty verdicts and two not guilty by reason of insanity verdicts. In the two and a half hours between the first and second ballots the group which favored the guilty verdict gained five votes. Juror Seven admitted that he switched his vote because he was convinced that the defendant knew what he was doing. And Juror Nine confessed:

9-9 The defendant's deliberate planning is the thing that changed my mind.

Even Juror Four sounded as if she might be weakening when she agreed:

4-6   He knew wrong from right.

1-4   Sure he did.

12-4 He knew wrong from right. Absolutely. And he's hiding behind an insanity plea.

4-12 He says he knew wrong from right but I wonder if he knew what he was talking about when he said it.

7-7   He knew what he was doing and he took all those safety precautions.

Juror Four remarked with some sadness in her voice:

4-7   Oh, you went over on his side too?

Juror Six explained:

6-4   They all did. There is only you and I left.

4-6   What will we do?

Loyal to the end, Juror Six answered:

6-4   It's up to you. I don't know.

4-6   Well, we all have to sing the same tune or we are going to be locked in.

Whereupon Juror Twelve began to discuss the accommodations and the dinner they would probably receive if they could not agree and had to be locked up:[8]

12-4 They will put us up at the _____ Hotel and then they will give us supper. I've never stayed at the _____ Hotel. But I hear that it is one of the best hotels in town. Friday night they served us a perch dinner that was pretty good. And they gave us a nice piece of pie. I had a hunk of cherry pie that was delicious.

7-12 That's getting off the subject.

12-12 And they had nice apple pie and they had a nice piece of cake with a lot of goo on it. A lot of whipped cream. Oh, it was delicious looking.

4-6   Now, what are we going to do? I think the way you do, and I don't know what to do.

12-7 This lady [points to Juror Four] and I were on the same

[8] This excerpt is included primarily to demonstrate the realism of the experience for the participants. Most of the jurors knew from prior experience that a jury is "locked up" if it fails to reach a verdict by the end of the day. The jurors assumed the same procedure would prevail in this case.

jury. And they served us. They came and said there is fish, being Friday. I played safe and ordered fish . . . Those who ordered meat got some sort of meat balls with tomato sauce. And the coffee, gee, they brought it in a container. It was like a thermos jug. A tall jug about that big around and there were three cups of coffee for everybody. I mean, we sent coffee back. I had two and almost everybody had two cups of coffee. And we sent coffee back.

While the foreman was engrossed in recounting the events of the past Friday, Juror Four asked for the defendant's statement. Someone suggested another vote.

6-6   There is only two of us, why take another vote? We have to decide whether we want to submit to the rest of you.

Juror Twelve replied hurriedly:

12-6   Oh no, no. You don't have to; you are not submitting to us. I don't blame you, you have a terrible aversion to the crime. And that is natural. We all do. It was a terrible thing. But the testimony shows that he knew what was going on. He knew what he was doing.

Juror One added, supportingly:

1-6   And the testimony of all the witnesses indicated that he was perfectly normal in his everyday functioning.

6-4   I am just trying to think it out in my own mind without reading his statement because I don't believe his statement. A man of that kind, I don't put much faith in his statement.

1-6   But you heard the testimony of the outside witnesses.

6-1   The one, Mr. Franklin.

1-6   And there was the fire department chief.

12-6   The fire department chief said he was responsible.

1-6   And the only thing the daughters testified to was the actual act.

12-6   They didn't testify to his actions at home. They didn't say whether he was mean or tough, or what he was. And his wife didn't testify, at all. See if for a moment you can forget the actual crime and how terrible the crime is, then I think you will be able to decide.

9-12   It isn't as if it was one instance. He had been doing it for years, and preparing, and so on, and to me, as I say, that makes a difference.

Juror Six conceded:

6-6   Okay, I will vote guilty.

Juror Four quickly agreed:

4-6   I guess that is what we will have to do.
12-12   Okay, then, it's unanimous.

As the foreman was filling out the verdict form, Juror Four acknowledged:

4-12   You should be proud of yourself. You really swayed us on this.
12-4   Who swayed you? I did not even open my mouth.

Note

Contrary to the foreman's impression that "he did not even open his mouth," he accounted for 35 per cent of the group's total participation. He and Juror One, his main supporter in the guilty faction, contributed 51 per cent of the total acts in the group. Their participation was greater than the participation of the four jurors (Jurors Four, Six, Seven, and Nine) who were most active among the NGI faction. One juror, Number Eleven, did not participate at all except for his votes.[9] Jurors Two, Three, Five, Eight, and Ten said very little; altogether they accounted for only about 5 per cent of the total acts.

As for the content of the discussion, all of the jurors agreed that there was something wrong with the defendant; there must have been, or he could not have done what he did. To this extent, they gave credence to the popular belief that anyone who commits incest must be crazy. In the end, however, all of them, even Jurors Four and Six,[10] agreed that whatever

[9] The failure of one of the jurors to participate at all is unusual. In most deliberations each juror contributes at least one comment.

[10] Note that in response to the item on the post-deliberation questionnaire which asks: "If you were a one-man jury, how would you

the "something" was, it was not enough to exempt the defendant from responsibility.

All of the jurors accepted the criterion of responsibility formulated by the foreman, which was: Did the defendant know what he was doing at the time he committed the acts and did he know that it was wrong? In other words, the jury used *M'Naghten,* even though the only instructions they received from the court as to criteria of responsibility were:

> If you believe that the defendant did not have the mental capacity to commit the crime for which he was charged because he was for legal purposes insane at the time, you may find him not guilty by reason of insanity.

At no time did any of the jurors indicate that they missed a more definitive statement from the court as to the criterion of responsibility they were to apply. The validity of the criterion suggested by the foreman was not challenged even though the jury read the instructions aloud at least twice and several jurors studied them privately.

The only aspect of the proceedings which caught the jurors' ire was the testimony of the medical experts. The failure of the psychiatrists to state explicitly whether the defendant was insane annoyed all of the jurors, even those who were initially sympathetic to the defense's plea. Perhaps a more definitive statement by the psychiatrists would have provided Jurors Four and Six (perhaps even Nine) with enough support to withstand the arguments of Jurors Twelve and One.

The jurors were concerned about how their decision would affect the defendant's family and the defendant. They did not spend much time considering the possibilities of rehabilitation for the mother, but they were concerned about the younger daughter. They believed that through a combination of fear and shame she had gone along with the situation until it became unbearable. Now that she was (or would soon be) free of her father, perhaps she was still young enough to escape without permanent psychic or social scars.

---

find the defendant, Jason Lunt?" both Jurors Four and Six checked the "Guilty" alternative.

As for the defendant, a few of the jurors talked about "curing" him, but most of them wanted only to be assured that he would be put away for as long a time as the law would allow. There was little discussion of the rehabilitory or therapeutic effects of imprisonment.

We think that the content and the tone of this deliberation speak for the realism of the experience. The jurors' involvement with the implications of their verdict, their willingness to continue deliberating until Jurors Four and Six agreed with the majority rather than declare themselves a hung jury, and the formality that surrounded the voting demonstrated the impact of the experience on the jurors and the seriousness with which they fulfilled their responsibilities.

Bibliography

BOOKS

American Bar Foundation, *The Mentally Ill and the Law,* Chicago, University of Chicago Press (1961).

Biggs, *The Guilty Mind,* New York, Harcourt, Brace (1955).

Cassity, *The Quality of Murder,* New York, Julian Press (1958).

Glueck, *Law and Psychiatry,* Baltimore, Johns Hopkins Press (1962).

Guttmacher, *The Mind of the Murderer,* New York, Farrar, Straus, and Cudahy (1960).

—— and Weihofen, *Psychiatry and the Law,* New York, Norton (1952).

Hall, *Studies in Jurisprudence and Criminal Theory,* Dobbs Ferry, N. Y., Oceana (1958).

Isaac, *A Treatise on the Medical Jurisprudence of Insanity,* Cambridge, Belknap Press of Harvard University Press (1962).

Joint Committee on Continuing Legal Education of the American Law Institute and the American Bar Association, *The Problem of Responsibility,* Philadelphia, American Law Institute (1962).

Keeton, *Guilty but Insane,* London, MacDonald (1961).

Nice, *Crime and Insanity,* New York, Philosophical Library, Inc. (1958).

——, *Criminal Psychology,* New York, Philosophical Library Inc. (1962).

Roche, *The Criminal Mind; a Study of Communication Between the Criminal Law and Psychiatry,* New York, Farrar, Straus, and Cudahy (1958).

Weihofen, *The Urge to Punish,* New York, Farrar, Straus, and Cudahy (1956).

Western Reserve University, *The Mind: A Law-Medicine Problem,* Cincinnati, W. H. Anderson Co. (1962).

Zilboorg, *The Psychology of the Criminal Act and Punishment,* New York, Harcourt, Brace (1954).

ARTICLES

Acheson, "McDonald v. United States: The Durham Rule Redefined," 51 *Geo. L.J.* 580 (1963).

Bazelon, "Criminal Responsibility," and Discussion, Gray, Smout, Bull, 3 *Crim. L.Q.* 359 (1960).

Bazinet, "Mental Disease and Criminal Responsibility," 11 *Themis* 162 (1961).

Bennett, "Insanity Defense — A Perplexing Problem of Criminal Justice," 16 *La. L. Rev.* 484 (1956).

Bernstein, "Criminal Responsibility: The Bar Must Lead in Law Reform," 50 *ABAJ* 341 (1964).

Blackman, "Criminal Responsibility and the Community," 4 *J. For. Sci.* 403 (1959).

Cavanagh, "Problems of a Psychiatrist in Operating Under the McNaghten, Durham and Model Penal Code Rules," 45 *Marq. L. Rev.* 478 (1962).

———, "A Psychiatrist Looks at the Durham Decision," 5 *Catholic U.L.R. Rev.* 25 (1955).

Clayton, "Courts Taking New Look at Crime and Sanity," *Washington Post*, (Feb. 23, 1958), E H (reprinted, *Cong. Rec.* (Feb. 25, 1958) A 1762-64).

———, "Durham Rule Weighed After Five Years in Use," *Washington Post* (Aug. 9, 1959).

———, "Six Years After Durham," 44 *J. Am. Jud. Soc.* 18 (1960).

Clemmer, "Hopeful Elements in the Correctional Process," 22 *Fed. Prob.* 16 (June, 1958).

Cohen, "The Durham Decision; Editorial Notes," 18 *Psychiatry* 93 (Feb. 1955).

———, "Insanity and the Law: Toward a Rational Development of Criminal Responsibility," 39 *Dicta* 325 (1962).

———, "McNaghten v. Durham: A Discussion of the Legal Test for Insanity as Adopted by the Federal Courts," 3 *J.A.G.J.* 12 (1961).

Currie, "McNaghten: Yes or No?" 34 *Wis. B. Bull.* 36 (1961).

Danziger, "Psychiatrist's View of Insanity as a Defense in Criminal Cases," 40 *Marq. L. Rev.* 406 (1957).

Dearman, "Criminal Responsibility and Insanity Tests: A Psychiatrist Looks at Three Cases," 47 *Va. L. Rev.* 1388 (1961).

De Grazia, "The Distinction of Being Mad," 22 *U. of Chi. L. Rev.* 339 (1955).

Diamond, "Criminal Responsibility of the Mentally Ill," 14 *Stan. L. Rev.* 59 (1961).

———, "Current Conflicts in the Legal Definitions of Insanity," 1 *J. of Correctional Psy.* 39 (Dec. 1954).

———, "From McNaghten to Currens, and Beyond," 50 *Calif. L. Rev.* 189 (1962).

Donnelly, "Establishment of Criminal Responsibility," 33 *Conn. B.J.* 137 (1959).

Douglas, "The Durham Rule: A Meeting Ground for Lawyers and Psychiatrists," 41 *Iowa. L. Rev.* 485 (1956).

Duty, "Criteria of Insanity," 30 *Ohio Bar J.* 176 (1957).

Ehrenzweig, "Psychoanalysis of the Insanity Plea — Clues to the Problems of Criminal Responsibility and Insanity in the Death Cell," 73 *Yale L.J.* 425 (1964).

Erickson, "Psychiatry and the Law: An Attempt at Synthesis," 1961 *Duke L.J.* 30.

Freedman, Guttmacher, and Overholser, "Mental Disease or Defect Excluding Responsibility," 1961 *Wash. U.L.Q.* 250.

Gershman, "Search for a Legal Standard of Criminal Responsibility: An Exercise in Medieval Scholasticism," 21 *U. Toronto Fac. L. Rev.* 45 (1963).

Goldstein and Fine, "Indigent Accused, the Psychiatrist, and the Insanity Defense," 110 *U. of Pa. L. Rev.* 1061 (1962).

Goldstein and Katz, "Abolish the 'Insanity Defense' — Why Not?" 72 *Yale L.J.* 853 (1963).

Guttmacher, "Implications of the Durham Case Decision," 3 *J. For. Sci.* 135 (1958).

———, "The Psychiatrist as an Expert Witness," 22 *U. of Chi. L. Rev.* 325 (1955).

Hall, "McNaghten Rules: A Plea for Their Revision," 31 *N.Z.L.J.* 140 (1955).

———, "McNaghten Rules and Proposed Alternatives," 49 *A.B.A.J.* 960 (1963).

———, "Mental Disease and Criminal Responsibility — McNaghten v. Durham and the American Law Institute's Tentative Draft," 33 *Ind. L.J.* 212 (1958).

———, "Psychiatry and Criminal Responsibility," 65 *Yale L.J.* 761 (1956), reprinted in Hall, *Studies in Jurisprudence and Criminal Theory*, Dobbs Ferry, N.Y., Oceana (1958).

———, "Psychiatry and the Law," 38 *Iowa L. Rev.* 687 (1953).

———, "Responsibility and Law: In Defense of the McNaghten Rules," 42 *A.B.A.J.* 917 (1956).

———, "Science, Common Sense, and Criminal Law Reform," 40 *Iowa L. Rev.* 1044 (1964).

Halleck, "Insanity Defense in the District of Columbia — A Legal Lorelei," 49 *Geo. L.J.* 294 (1960).

Hallows, "Recent Developments on Criminal Responsibility," 34 *Wis. B. Bull.* 7 (1961).

Hinkle, "Alternatives to Tests of Criminal Responsibility," 10 *Crime and Delin.* 110 (1964).

Hittrie, "Justice for the Mentally Ill," 41 *J. Am. Jud. Soc.* 46 (1957).

Hofstadter and Levitan, "McNaghten Preferred," 18 *Record of N.Y.C.B.A.* 716 (1963).

Ibanez, "Bridging the Gap on Concepts on Mental Illness," 1 *Crim. L.Q.* 23 (1963).

James, "Juror's Evaluation of Expert Psychiatric Testimony," 21 *Ohio S.L.J.* 75-95 (1960).

Karpman, "On Reducing Tensions and Bridging Gaps Between Psychiatry and the Law," 48 *J. Crim. L.* 164 (1957).

Kenny, "Insanity in Uniform: Responsibility Test Unchanged as Durham Rule Comes and Goes," 17 *J.A.G.J.* 155 (1963).

Krash, "The Durham Rule and the Judicial Administration in the District of Columbia," 70 *Yale L.J.* 6 (1961).

———, "Durham Rule and Judicial Administration of the Insanity Defense in the District of Columbia, 70 *Yale L.J.* 905 (1961).

Kuh, "Insanity Defense — An Effort to Combine Law and Reason," 110 *U. of Pa. L. Rev.* 771 (1962).

Lasswell, "The Impact of Psychiatry Upon Jurisprudence," 21 *Ohio S.L.J.* 17-27 (1960).

Lynch, "Insanity as a Defense to Crime: The McNaghten Rules: A Plea for Their Retention," 31 *N.Z.L.J.* 216 (1955).

MacCaulay, "Insanity and the Prosecution," 1963 *Crim. L.R.* 817.

McDonnell, "The Right-Wrong Test," 21 *J.B.A. of D.C.* 389 (1954).

Morris, "Criminal Insanity: The Abyss Between Law and Psychiatry," 12 *Record of N.Y.C.B.A.* 471 (1957).

Morris, Taft and Angus, "Criminal Responsibility and Insanity; The Significance of Durham v. United States for Australian Courts," 3 *U. Austl. Ann. L. Rev.* 309 (1955).

Nutter, "Change in the Rules of Criminal Responsibility," 39 *Calif. S.B.J.* 101 (1964).

Opack, "Insanity Defense in the District of Columbia," 9 *Am. U.L. Rev.* 45 (1960).

Ostby, "Mental Disorders, Specific Intent and Knowledge in Military Law," 17 *J.A.G.J.* 171 (1963).

Overholser, "Criminal Responsibility: A Psychiatrist's Viewpoint," 48 *A.B.A.J.* 527 (1962).

————, "Psychiatry's Contribution to Criminal Law and Procedure," 12 *Okla. L. Rev.* 13 (1959).

Raub, "Moralist Looks at the Durham and McNaghten Rules," 46 *Minn. L. Rev.* 327 (1961).

Roche, "Durham and the Problem of Communication," 29 *Temp. L.Q.* 264 (1956).

Rome, "McNaghten, Durham, and Psychiatry," 34 *F.R.D.* 93 (1964).

Rubin, "New Approach to McNaghten v. Durham," 45 *J. Am. Jud. Soc.* 133 (1961).

Schiele and Paulson, "The Minnesota Supreme Court Employs the Durham Test," 113 *Am. J. Psychiatry* 559 (1956).

Schreiber, "The Durham Decision — A Beacon in the Dark," *Mental Hygiene* 295 (1956).

Silving, "Mental Incapacity in Criminal Law," 2 *Current Law* 3 (1961).

Skeel, "McNaghten v. Durham," 12 *Clev.-Mar. L. Rev.* 330 (1963).

Slovenko, "Mentally Disabled, the Law, and the Report of the American Bar Foundation," 47 *Va. L. Rev.* 1366 (1961).

————, "Psychiatry, Criminal Law, and the Role of the Psychiatrist," 1963 *Duke L.J.* 395.

Soboloff, "Insanity and the Criminal Law: From McNaghten to Durham and Beyond," 41 *A.B.A.J.* 793 (1955), 15 *Md. L. Rev.* 93 (1955).

Sullivan and Winger, "Insanity Defense: Psychological and Psychiatric Testimony," 7 *Trial Law. Guide* 53 (1963).

Swartz, " 'Mental Disease': The Groundwork for Legal Analysis and Legislative Action," 111 *U. of Pa. L. Rev.* 389 (1963).

Szasz, "Psychiatry, Ethics and the Criminal Law," 58 *Colum. L. Rev.* 183 (1958).

Thomsen, "Insanity as a Defense to Crime," 19 *Md. L. Rev.* 271 (1959).

Tuchler, "Century of Progress: The Durham Case," 1 *J. For. Sci.* 41 (1956).

Wechsler, "The Criteria of Criminal Responsibility," 22 *U. of Chi. L. Rev.* 367 (1955).

Weihofen, "Crime Law and Psychiatry," 25 *New Mexico Quarterly* 196 (1955).

————, "The Definition of Mental Illness," 21 *Ohio S.L.J.* 1-16 (1960).

————, "The 'Test' of Criminal Responsibility: Recent Developments," 172 *International Record of Medicine* 638 (1959).

Weintraub, "Criminal Responsibility: Psychiatry Alone Cannot Determine It," 49 *A.B.A.J.* 1075 (1963).

Wingersky, "Insanity Defense," 4 *Trial Law. Guide* 97 (1960).
Woodley, "Insanity as a Bar to Criminal Prosecution," 3 *So. Texas L.J.* 204 (1958).
Younger, "McNaghten Must Go!" 31 *Calif. S.B.J.* 37 (1956).

PANELS AND SYMPOSIA

Panel, "Criminal Responsibility and Mental Disease: A Panel," 26 *Tenn. L. Rev.* 221 (1959).
Panel, "Psychiatry and the Law," 32 F.R.D. 547 (1963) (panel members: Murrah, Biggs, Settle, Burger, Menninger, Rubin, Satten).
Symposium, "Forensic Psychiatry: Uses and Limitations — A Symposium," 57 *N.U.L. Rev.* 1 (1962).
Symposium, "Insanity and the Criminal Law — A Critique of Durham v. U.S. — A Symposium," 22 *U. of Chi. L. Rev.* 317 (1955).
Symposium, "Law and the Mentally Ill: A Symposium," 21 *Ohio S.L.J.* 1 (1960).
Symposium, "Mental Disease and Criminal Responsibility: A Symposium," 4 *Catholic Law.* 294 (1958), 5 *id.* 3 (1959).
Symposium, "Mental Disorders and the Court — Ontario Magistrates' Conference," 6 *Crim. L.Q.* 86 (1963).
Symposium, "Symposium of Criminal Responsibility," 4 *Kan. L. Rev.* 349 (1956).
Symposium, "Symposium on Insanity as a Defense in Criminal Law," 45 *Marq. L. Rev.* 477 (1962).
Symposium, "Symposium on Mental Responsibility and the Law," 45 *Ky. L.J.* 215 (1956-1957).
Symposium, "Symposium on the Mentally Ill Offender," State Hospital, Atascadero, Calif. (1960).
Symposium, Washington Criminal Justice Association, "Crime in the Nation's Capital, 1959; Twenty-fourth Annual Report," Washington, D.C. (1960) (includes recommendation for revision of Durham rule).

NOTES AND COMMENTS

Note, "The Durham Case — 'Mental Cause' as a Criminal Defense," 43 *Geo. L.J.* 58 (1954).
Note, "Criminal Law — Criminal Responsibility — The Defense of Insanity," 31 *N.D.L. Rev.* 170 (1955).
Note, "Criminal Law — A Significant Development in the Law Relating to Insanity as a Defense to Crime," 1955 *Wis. L. Rev.* 506.

Note, "Insanity and the Criminal Law in the Distict of Columbia," 44 *Geo. L.J.* 489 (1956).

Note, "Insanity Defense: The Need for Articulate Goals at the Acquittal, Commitment and Release Stages," 112 *U. of Pa. L. Rev.* 733 (1964).

Note, "Implementation and Clarification of the Durham Criterion of Criminal Irresponsibility," 58 *Colum. L. Rev.* 1253 (1958).

Note, "Mental Disease as a Justification for Relief from the Consequences of an Act: Some Comments on the Legal Criteria," 41 *Minn. L. Rev.* 334 (1957).

Comment, "Change in the Law Governing the Criminal Responsibility of the Insane," 27 *Rocky Mt. L. Rev.* (1955).

Comment, "Criminal Insanity — A Study of Legal Inertia," 10 *W. Res. L. Rev.* 597 (1959).

Comment, "Criminal Law: Defense of Insanity: Partial Responsibility: Adequacy of Present Law," 43 *Cornell L.Q.* 283 (1958).

Comment, "Criminal Law — Insanity as a Defense — New Test for Determining," 33 *N.C.L. Rev.* 656 (1955).

Comment, "Criminal Law — McNaghten Test — Proposed Revision of Section 1120 of the New York Penal Law," 9 *N.Y.L.F.* 220 (1963).

Comment, "Criminal Law — Re-examination of Tests for Criminal Responsibility," 53 *Mich. L. Rev.* 963 (1955).

Comment "Criminal Law and Procedure — Partial Insanity Affecting the Degree of a Crime," 22 *La. L. Rev.* 664 (1962).

Comment, "Criminal Responsibility — The Durham Rule in Maine," 15 *Maine L. Rev.* 107 (1963).

Comment, "Criminal Responsibility and Insanity: Past — Present — Future," 27 *Tenn. L. Rev.* 389 (1960).

Comment, "Criminal Responsibility at Random," 14 *Baylor L. Rev.* 285 (1962).

Comment, "Criminally Insane — An Appeal to the Sane," 17 *Sw. L.J.* 112 (1963).

Comment, "Defense of Insanity — A Sword and a Shield," 10 *Am. U.L. Rev.* 201 (1961).

Comment, "The Durham Decision — A Recognition of Medical Concepts in the Determination of Criminal Responsibility," 4 *Buffalo L. Rev.* 318 (1955).

Comment, "Legal Insanity and the Law of Crimes," 29 *Tul. L. Rev.* 576 (1955).

Comment, "A Modern Test for Criminal Responsibility of the Mentally Afflicted," 9 *Sw. L.J.* 110 (1955).

CASE NOTES

Case note, "Causal Element in the Durham Test of Criminal Responsibility" (Carter v. United States, 252 F.2d 608 (D.C. Cir. 1957)), 7 *Buffalo L. Rev.* 303 (1958).

Case note, "Court of Military Appeals Refuses to Accept Lead of District of Columbia Court of Appeals in Liberalizing Traditional Tests of Criminal Insanity for Military Offenses" (United States v. Smith, 17 C.M.R. 314 (1954)), 4 *Utah L. Rev.* 419 (1955).

Case note, "Criminal Law: Commitment of the Criminally Insane: The Insanity Defense in the District of Columbia" (Lynch v. Overholser, 369 U.S. 705 (1962)), 10 *U.C.L.A.L. Rev.* 408 (1963).

Case note, "Criminal Law — Defense of Insanity — Mental 'Disease and Defect' in Durham Rule Defined" (McDonald v. United States, 312 F.2d 847 (D.C. Cir. 1962)), 12 *Am. U.L. Rev.* 219 (1963).

Case note, "Criminal Law — Defenses — Insanity — 'New Test' " (Durham v. United States, 214 F.2d 862 (D.C. Cir. 1954)), 1 *How. L.J.* 106 (1955).

Case note, "Criminal Law — Defenses — Insanity — 'New Test' " (Durham v. United States, 214 F.2d 862 (D.C. Cir. 1954)), 57 *W. Va. L. Rev.* 99 (1955).

Case note, "Criminal Law — Defenses — New Legal Tests of Insanity" (Durham v. United States, 214 F.2d 862 (D.C. Cir. 1954)), 39 *Minn. L. Rev.* 573 (1955).

Case note, "Criminal Law — Defenses — Rejection of the Durham Rule as the Test of Insanity" (Sauer v. United States, 241 F.2d 640 (9th Cir. 1957)), 11 *Vand. L. Rev.* 218 (1957).

Case note, "Criminal Law — Durham Sanity Test Rejected" (State v. Lucas, 30 N.J. 37 (1959)), 19 *Md. L. Rev.* 344 (1959).

Case note, "Criminal Law — Durham Rule — Dissatisfaction with the Operation of the Durham Rule Expressed by Three Judges of the Court of Appeals for the District of Columbia" (Blocker v. United States, 288 F.2d 853 (D.C. Cir. 1961)), 36 *Notre Dame Law.* 581 (1961).

Case note, "Criminal Law — Insanity — Burden of Proof — Durham Rule" (Wright v. United States, 250 F.2d 4 (D.C. Cir. 1957)), 7 *Am. U.L. Rev.* 110 (June 1958).

Case note, "Criminal Law — Insanity — 'But for' in the Test of Causation to Be Used Under the Durham 'Product' Test of Insanity" (Carter v. United States, 252 F.2d 608 (D.C. Cir. 1958)), 19 *U. of Pitt. L. Rev.* 671 (1958).

Case note, "Criminal Law — Insanity Defense — The Durham Rule"

(Durham v. United States, 214 F.2d 862 (D.C. Cir. 1954)), 40 *Iowa L. Rev.* 652 (1955).

Case note, "Criminal Law: Insanity as a Defense and the Problem of Definition" (State v. Esser, 16 Wis. 2d 567 (1962)), 56 *Marq. L. Rev.* 542 (1963).

Case note, "Criminal Law — Insanity: McNaghten-Durham Conflict, a Recent Approach" (United States v. Currens, 290 F.2d 751 (3d Cir. 1961)), 22 *Md. L. Rev.* 74 (1962).

Case note, "Criminal Law — Insanity — The McNaghten and Irresistible Impulse Tests Held Inadequate" (Durham v. United States, 214 F.2d 862 (D.C. Cir. 1954)), 40 *Va. L. Rev.* 799 (1954).

Case note, "Criminal Law — Insanity — McNaghten v. Durham" (State v. White, 60 Wash. 2d 551 (1962)), 35 *U. Colo. L. Rev.* 274 (1963).

Case note, "Criminal Law — Insanity — Product of Mental Disease Test — Degree of Causality Necessary to Acquit" (Douglas v. United States, 239 F.2d 52 (D.C. Cir. 1956)), 2 *Vill. L. Rev.* 263 (1957).

Case note, "Criminal Law — Utility of Durham Rule Attacked" (Blocker v. United States, 288 F.2d 853 (D.C. Cir. 1961)), 13 *Syracuse L. Rev.* 152 (1961).

Case note, "Insanity — It Is Not Error for a Federal District Court to Refuse to Instruct a Jury, Subsequent to the Durham Decision, That an Accused Should Be Acquitted by Reason of Insanity if His Act Was the 'Product' of a Mental Defect or Disease" (Anderson v. United States, 237 F.2d 118 (9th Cir. 1956)), 45 *Geo. L.J.* 516 (1957).

Case note, "Insanity — Minnesota Supreme Court Applies Durham Doctrine in Civil Suit" (Anderson v. Grasberg, 247 Minn. 538 (1956)), 45 *Geo. L.J.* 520 (1957).

Case note, "The Insanity Defense and the Durham Rule" (State v. Davis, 146 Conn. 137 (1959), and Commonwealth v. Chester, 337 Mass. 702 (1958)), 50 *J. Crim. L.* 47 (May-June, 1959).

Case note, "Mental Disorder Causing Prohibited Acts as Exempting from Criminal Responsibility" (Durham v. United States, 214 F.2d 862 (D.C. Cir. 1954), 54 *Colum. L. Rev.* 1153 (1954).

Case note, "A New Test of Criminal Responsibility in Cases of Insanity" (Durham v. United States, 214 F.2d 862 (D.C. Cir. 1954)), 18 *Mod. L. Rev.* 391 (1955).

Case note, "The Parsons Criminal Insanity Test in the Light of the Durham Rule" (Parsons v. Alabama, 81 Ala. 577 (1886)), 10 *Ala. L. Rev.* 118 (1957).

LIST OF TABLES

Index

I N D E X